THE CINCINNATI REDS

WRITING SPORTS SERIES
Richard "Pete" Peterson, Editor

The Cleveland Indians
Franklin Lewis

The Cincinnati Reds
Lee Allen

THE CINCINNATI REDS

☻

By LEE ALLEN

The Kent State University Press

KENT, OHIO

© 2006 by The Kent State University Press, Kent, Ohio 44242

All rights reserved.

Library of Congress Catalog Card Number 2006002385

ISBN-13: 978-0-87338-886-3

ISBN-10: 0-87338-886-0

Manufactured in the United States of America

10 09 08 07 06   5 4 3 2 1

Library of Congress Cataloging-in-Publication Data

Allen, Lee, 1915–

The Cincinnati Reds / Lee Allen.

p.   cm. — (Writing sports series)

Originally published: New York: G. P. Putnam's Sons, 1948, with a new foreword by Greg Rhodes.

Includes index.

ISBN-13: 978-0-87338-886-3 (pbk. : alk. paper) ∞

ISBN-10: 0-87338-886-0 (pbk. : alk. paper) ∞

1. Cincinnati Reds (Baseball team)—History.   2. Baseball—History.

I. Title.   II. Series.

GV875.C65A55   2006

796.357′640977178—dc22   2006002385

British Library Cataloging-in-Publication data are available.

To WAITE HOYT,

NOT ALONE BECAUSE HE UNDERSTANDS
BUT BECAUSE HE LOVES THE GAME OF BASEBALL

CONTENTS

FOREWORD

In his photographs, he bears a slight resemblance to the comedian Don Rickles, with a friendly, perhaps mischievous, look on a large round face ready to break into a smile. And like any good comedian, Lee Allen was quick witted and a born storyteller, and his vast knowledge of his beloved National Pastime earned him the accolade "Baseball's Walking Encyclopedia."

He was in great demand as a speaker. There is a flyer in his file at Cooperstown that heralds Lee as "Lecturer, Raconteur, Author, Sportsworld Figure." His remarks often touched on amusing moments and coincidences of fact that kept his audiences enthralled. And after those speeches, Lee was the master of "Q-and-A," his rapid-fire responses peppering the crowd with concise answers and entertaining embellishments to seemingly any question.

During his all-too-short lifetime, Lee Allen served as the historian of the National Baseball Hall of Fame and was one of the driving forces behind the publication of the first Macmillan *Baseball Encyclopedia*s, published just after his death, in 1969. Lee wrote ten baseball books, including the one you hold in your hands, *The Cincinnati Reds,* originally published in 1948. Perhaps his best-known work was a collection of stories and profiles, *The Hot Stove League,* published in 1955. He also wrote a weekly column for *The Sporting News* called "Cooperstown Corner"; the Society for American Baseball Research (SABR) collected the best of these in *Cooperstown Corner: Columns from the Sporting News,* published in 1990.

Allen grew up in Cincinnati and quickly became immersed in the fortunes and history of the club that traced its roots to the first professional team, the 1869 Red Stockings. In 1931, at the age of sixteen, the familiar kid who always seemed to be hanging around the ballpark was noticed by someone in the Reds organization who gave Lee a job telephoning the scores of other games from the press box to the scoreboard operator. The pay was 75 cents. Allen later said he lost money on the deal, for he spent more than that on "ice cream, pop and peanuts," a generous food allowance in the Depression years. Allen was the son of Alfred Allen, a noted Cincinnati lawyer and congressman.

In 1938, fresh out of Columbia's journalism school, Lee joined the Reds full time in their publicity department, where he served until the mid-1940s. According to John Murdough, who worked in the Reds' front office at the time, Lee was a character who could sometimes let a situation get out of hand. One day a prospective player showed up unannounced at the Reds' offices asking for a tryout. It was clear that this gentleman, something of a "hayseed," had no idea how scouting was done. He simply thought he was good enough to play for the Reds, and so here he was at the Reds' doorstep. Lee decided to have a little fun with him and pretended to conduct a tryout right in the office. At one point he sent the man sprinting down the hall and yelled at him to slide. The "prospect" badly wrenched his ankle, and Allen had a problem on his hands. Lee took him to a hospital, had the ankle treated, paid for it out of his own pocket, and bought the man a bus ticket back home. It was, according to Murdough, "the first and last tryout Lee Allen ever conducted."

For baseball history, this was the right career move. Allen proved far more adept at researching past players than scouting future ones. "My concern is the players," he once said. "Who are these men? What are they? What problems have they faced? Where are they now?" His insatiable curiosity and determined detective work led him to big cities and small towns, visiting libraries, historical societies, and newspaper offices. He corresponded with hundreds of relatives and associates of deceased players, tracking down essential biographical information. Nearly every newspaper story about Lee Allen included some reference to his graveyard sleuthing.

Many of Lee's investigations provided fodder for the banquet circuit, where he told stories of a chance encounter or dogged search that finally ended in the confirmation of the birth or death date of some long-forgotten player. Once when searching the whereabouts of a member of the Reds from the 1880s, he secured the name of a widow of a former catcher who just might know what happened to the missing Red. "I received a letter from the old lady," recalled Allen. "It was a 16-page effort that was an attack on Franklin D. Roosevelt. She never got around to the baseball matter."

When he became the historian of the Baseball Hall of Fame in 1959, he made completing the biographical record of every player a project for the Hall. Of course, he wasn't starting from scratch. When he moved to Cooperstown, he brought his files with him— all fifty-five cartons of books and papers weighing some 5,000 pounds. It was the largest private baseball library at the time. His reference material and correspondence remain in the library to this day, a gift from Lee to all future historians.

He produced millions of words on baseball, and it wasn't all biographical minutia. Allen could write. He once described Babe Ruth as "a large man in a camel's hair coat and a camel's hair cap standing in front of a hotel, his broad nostrils sniffing at the promise of the night." In Chapter 18 of this Reds history, Allen reports that when pitcher Rube Benton, who played for the Reds in the 1910s and 1920s, was asked by the National League to prove a gambling charge he had leveled against his former manager, Buck Herzog, Benton said the deal was struck in a Chicago saloon, and NL president John Heydler accompanied Benton as he visited several drinking establishments. Allen writes, "Rube was unable to locate the bartender who could verify his story, one of the few occasions in his life when he was unable to find a bartender."

The Cincinnati Reds is full of such anecdotes and wry observations. Lee's obvious interest in the players and their lives off the field shows up on page after page of this narrative history. Its value for today's readers and fans resides in the personal details that convince you that Lee Allen must have known each and every one of these players.

Lee's last appearance in Cincinnati came on May 18, 1969, fittingly at a ceremony at Crosley Field, where he began his baseball career as the press box boy some thirty-eight years before. The ceremony, on the occasion of baseball's centennial tribute to the first professional Red Stockings of 1869, honored the greatest players in Reds history. Lee presented one of the awards to Edd Roush, and after sharing stories with players and friends at a reception, he headed back home to Cooperstown. Driving through Syracuse, he suffered chest pains. He managed to reach a hospital, but there he died of a heart attack. He was fifty-four.

Lee Allen's spirit lives on in the books he wrote and the contributions he made to the biographical record of major league baseball players. He is also recalled annually at the National History Day competition, which brings together middle school and high school students from around the country who present research papers and projects. Those with baseball topics compete for the Lee Allen Award, offered by SABR to the outstanding baseball presentation. I suspect Lee would be pleased.

GREG RHODES

Executive Director, Cincinnati Reds

Hall of Fame and Museum

ILLUSTRATIONS

Cincinnati Reds

CLUBHOUSE SCENE WHEN PENNANT WAS CLINCHED
IN 1939

PREFACE

Considering the fact that the Cincinnati Reds have attracted national attention to the city that they represent for more than three quarters of a century, it is remarkable that so little has been published concerning their early days. Organized as an amateur team in 1866, the Reds shattered precedent by forming a professional club in 1869 and then embarked on a grand tour of the nation that was completed without a single defeat.

When the National League was founded in 1876, an event that was made possible because the Cincinnati Red Stockings of 1869 had so stimulated interest in the game, Cincinnati was chosen as a charter member. Only once since that time, in 1881, has the city been without major-league baseball.

Throughout the years the city of Cincinnati has had no better advertisement than its Reds. The admission that one is from Cincinnati invariably brings from an alien the query, "How are the Reds doing?" or "What's the matter with the Reds?" Among Cincinnatians, it is a better opening wedge for conversation than banalities about the weather.

In Cincinnati's early days most of the interest in the baseball club centered around the "Over the Rhine" section of the downtown district among the beer gardens and music halls. The entertainers, sports, and idlers of that area loved the Reds with a fervor that approached mania.

Baseball is a great social leveler, and in Cincinnati today followers of the club are to be found in every stratum of the city's structure. The coming of radio has created hordes of new fans, many of them women, and has also ended the practice of men milling about on the sidewalks in front of cafés, watching the inning-by-inning scores painted at painfully long intervals on a board. And radio has put an end to the electric scoreboards that used to be hung out in front of the city's newspaper buildings at World Series time, so that an awed populace could follow every play.

When the Reds won a pennant in 1939 and another, with a world's championship added, in 1940, the game of baseball even became popular with the rotogravure set, and Crosley Field became a mecca as desirable as the Zoo Opera or a horse show. The Reds are now as fit a subject for discussion among the suburbanites of Clifton and Hyde Park—the sort of people who put paper panties on highball glasses at garden parties and rave over Ewell Blackwell under the Japanese lanterns—as they are among the canned-heat drinkers who swelter in the flea-by-night hotels of upper Vine Street.

If there is a hero of this book, it is the fan. Invariably optimistic in April, frequently disappointed in September, he has unfailingly supported the club, come what may. He has found himself seated in the bleachers when economy dictated such a choice, and until 1935, when Cincinnati introduced night baseball to the majors, he had to steal time from his employer, if any, to attend games. In spite of these and other handicaps, he has consistently found himself at the corner of Findlay and Western Avenues whenever his beloved Reds were scheduled to play.

Because the fan is the hero, little attention is paid in these pages to the inner workings of the front office or the business aspects of the sport. Baseball is any number of things, but it is primarily a game. Of course, the players are heroes too, many of them, but they are also fans or they wouldn't be engaged in playing baseball for a living.

It would be impossible to thank all the people who have helped in the task of putting this story together. Warren Giles, president of the Reds, and his assistant, Gabriel Paul, have been most helpful and co-operative. J. G. Taylor Spink, editor and publisher of baseball's bible, *The Sporting News*, is due a great debt because of the valuable clippings and pictures he has made available.

The man to whom the author is most indebted is Harry Pence, librarian of the *Cincinnati Enquirer*, and his fine staff, along with

Morris Turner of the same publication. Pence not only permitted the examination of every one of the ten thousand box scores of the Reds' games that the Enquirer printed, but also was extremely gracious in remaining silent about lights that were left on and ash trays unemptied while the research was being done.

This book makes no attempt to predict what the future holds for the Reds, although the immediate future appears to be encouragingly safe in the hands of Powel Crosby, Jr., Warren Giles, and Johnny Neun. The story may serve, however, as a guide to what has happened on the club in the past.

LEE ALLEN

St. Louis, Mo.
November 1947

THE CINCINNATI REDS

1

THE IMMORTAL RED STOCKINGS

1

Among the least known facts in Cincinnati's long and glowing history as a baseball town is the rather startling one that the late William Howard Taft was one of the city's first and finest players. It is difficult to imagine President Taft lugging his 354 pounds of jovial corpulence around the bases, but in the days when he was a ballplayer, he hadn't achieved the avoirdupois we associate with him.

As originally played in Cincinnati, baseball was an amateur endeavor engaged in by the elite. Numerous teams played the game, probably with more enthusiasm than ability, and their rosters, which have fortunately been preserved, bear a striking resemblance to the society pages of today's Cincinnati newspapers. William Howard Taft, in his youth, was a member of the Mt. Auburn nine, one of many teams that took the field shortly after the Civil War.

But as frequently happens in America, the game improved as it became more democratic. Teams from the bottom areas of the city soon outdistanced the nines of bluer blood, and a really capable team was not formed until those hardy athletes of the lower social strata had thoroughly permeated the ranks.

The date usually given for the founding of the Cincinnati Baseball Club is July 23, 1866, when lovers of the pastime gathered in the law offices of Tilden, Sherman & Moulton to adopt a suitable constitution and elect officers. The club at this time was composed mostly of members of the bar, many of whom were graduates of Yale and Harvard

3

in the latter fifties and early sixties. The team made an alliance with the Union Cricket Club and obtained the use of that organization's grounds. This merger enabled many members of the cricket club to take up baseball, and by this means the new game received a great impetus locally.

Prior to 1868 every baseball team in the country had been an amateur one. But as interest in the game increased, the demand for skilled players led prominent citizens to import them, and what started out to be purely a civic pastime soon developed into a professional one. The Red Stockings of 1868 had four paid players in their ranks, including Harry Wright, a veteran cricketer, who gave up his job as a jeweler to accept $1,200 a year to play baseball for the Red Stockings.

During the winter of 1868–69 the Red Stockings decided that they could not really establish themselves unless the amateur element were completely liquidated. This was a courageous step because other teams throughout the nation attempted to hide behind the mask of amateurism. The Red Stockings, unwilling to be bound by rules that were not respected, flatly announced their intention of forming a professional team, the first professional team in America. Cincinnati, then, is justifiably known as the cradle of professional baseball.

Aaron B. Champion, a well-known attorney, was elected president of the Red Stockings, with Harry Wright as manager. Players were imported from all sections of the country, and the following roster was the result:

PLAYER	AGE	OCCUPATION	POSITION	SALARY
Harry Wright	35	Jeweler	Center field	$1,200
Asa Brainard	25	Insurance	Pitcher	1,100
Douglas Allison	22	Marble cutter	Catcher	800
Charles H. Gould	21	Bookkeeper	First base	800
Charles J. Sweasy	21	Hatter	Second base	800
Fred A. Waterman	23	Insurance	Third base	1,000
George Wright	22	Engraver	Shortstop	1,400
Andrew J. Leonard	23	Hatter	Left field	800
Calvin A. McVey	20	Piano maker	Right field	800
Richard Hurley	20	. . . .	Substitute	600

The extent to which foreign talent had been brought in is demonstrated by the fact that Charlie Gould, the first base-

4

man, was the only resident of Cincinnati on the club. Allison and Leonard were from New Jersey; Sweasy from New Hampshire; Waterman had played with the Mutuals of New York; and George Wright, the younger brother of manager Harry, although only twenty-two, had long played the game as an amateur in the East and was perhaps the greatest player in the country at the time.

The immortal Red Stockings of 1869 went through their entire season without losing a game. They outclassed all other teams in the country, and more important, they attracted so much attention to baseball on their swing around the nation that the game was given a terrific uplift. The Red Stockings were responsible in many ways for the founding, seven years later, of the National League.

Early in the season of 1869, after several practice games that were handily won, the Reds inaugurated their eastern tour, rolling through New York and Massachusetts, taking on all comers and defeating them with ridiculous ease. Their first really important contest took place in New York City, where they played the celebrated Mutuals and trounced them, 4 to 2. This was an unprecedented score, since most contests in those days reached double figures. The extraordinary result of the battle, played amid much excitement, caused an equal tumult in Cincinnati, where two thousand fans milled around the Gibson Hotel, firing salutes, burning red flares, and cheering themselves hoarse.

After that victory, the Reds journeyed to Philadelphia, Washington, Baltimore, and Wheeling, finally returning home to be greeted by a brass band and wined and dined by the grateful populace.

It was at a banquet on the club's return that Aaron Champion, the team's president, rose to his feet and said:

"Someone asked me today whom I would rather be, President Ulysses S. Grant or President Champion of the Cincinnati Baseball Club. I immediately answered him that I would by far rather be the president of the baseball club."

In the light of what the future held for President Grant, Champion's choice seems to have been a happy one.

Apparently the entertainment to which they were subjected had little effect on their play, for the Red Stockings almost immediately started off again to resume their winning ways. The one blotch on their otherwise perfect escutcheon occurred in a game with the Haymakers of Troy, New York, and it happened under circumstances picturesque enough to record. After five innings, the score was a tie, 17 to 17. In the first half of the sixth, Cal McVey, the Redleg outfielder, hit a foul tip that the Haymakers contended was a third strike. Using this slight pretext to halt play, Cherokee Fisher, pitcher and captain of the lads from Troy, ordered his team from the field, and a near riot ensued. It developed later that a group of New York gamblers had placed a large bet on the Haymakers, and fearing defeat, had entered into collusion with the team from Troy to stop the contest. Months later, perhaps because their share of the gate receipts had been withheld, the Haymakers offered a written apology. But the game went into the records as a tie, the only occasion in sixty-five that year that the Reds did not emerge victorious. Under present rules, the game would have been declared a Cincinnati victory by forfeit.

In September the Reds visited the Pacific Coast and humiliated the leading teams of that region with the same casualness they had displayed in their eastern contests. The final game of the season was played in Cincinnati in November with the hated Mutuals, and although the latter tried their best to send the Reds to ruin, the final score was 17 to 8 in favor of the unbeaten Red Stockings.

2

A gentleman bearing the rather stately name of Edward P. Atwater joined the Reds as a substitute the next season, displacing Richard Hurley, the first professional player to draw a release, but otherwise the team was composed of the same men who had breezed through all their games in 1869.

The club started off in the same spectacular fashion, disposing of all local opposition readily, and then made a journey through the South, winning games at such points as New Orleans, Louisville, and Memphis by such exotic scores as 79 to 6, 94 to 7, and 100 to 2.

But this couldn't go on forever. All balloons must eventually burst, and the Red Stockings had theirs explode with a robust bang on the afternoon of June 14, 1870, when they were finally defeated by the Atlantics of Brooklyn, 8 to 7, in eleven innings.

This historic game took place on the third swing the Reds made through the East and happened only after the Red Stockings had played through 130 contests in two seasons without tasting defeat.

A crowd estimated at nine thousand milled around the Capitoline grounds in Brooklyn that day to see the most exciting game in baseball's brief history. Betting was lively with the unparalleled Red Stockings established as four-to-one favorites.

At the end of nine innings the score stood 5 to 5, and many of the spectators left the park as Ferguson, captain of the Atlantics, proposed to Harry Wright that the game be declared a draw. But the Reds insisted on finishing, and when they scored two runs in the first portion of the eleventh, they seemed certain to win again.

It was perhaps at this point in history that Brooklyn's reputation for baseball daffiness was born. For in the last half of the eleventh, a Brooklyn spectator jumped on the back of Redleg outfielder Cal McVey as he was in the act of picking up a fairly hit ball. When order had been restored, one Atlantic run had crossed the plate and the tying marker was resting on third. The crowd, of course, went promptly wild, and the spectator responsible for this turn of events was ceremoniously led from the scene by police, the first in a long line of proud Brooklyn fanatics to be escorted from the premises.

The Reds were so demoralized by the proceedings that two more base hits and an error by Charlie Sweasy at second base settled the issue in favor of the home club.

Undismayed, and bowing to the inevitable, President

7

Champion dispatched the following wire to the fans of Cincinnati:

NEW YORK, JUNE 14, 1870—ATLANTICS 8; CINCINNATI
7. THE FINEST GAME EVER PLAYED. OUR BOYS DID
NOBLY, BUT FORTUNE WAS AGAINST THEM. ELEVEN
INNINGS PLAYED. THOUGH BEATEN, NOT DISGRACED.

AARON B. CHAMPION,

CINCINNATI BASEBALL CLUB

Two more games were staged between the Red Stockings and Atlantics that season, and they were split. On the basis of the three-game series, the Atlantics were declared national champions, although the Reds finished the year with a much higher percentage of games won.

Even so, there were indications that an era was about to end, and in spite of their fine work, the Red Stockings were beginning to disintegrate. Public interest had somewhat slackened, the players had become dissatisfied, and other strong professional clubs were now entering the field.

When several of these clubs made handsome offers to certain members of the Red Stockings, the local club was unable to match them. A public meeting of the team's members was then held, and it was voted to disband.

But the success of the Red Stockings had so stimulated interest in baseball in the East that the clubs became numerous enough and strong enough to form a professional league. So it was that on March 17, 1871, the first convention of delegates from professional teams met in the friendly shadows of Collier's Café, at Broadway and Thirteenth Street, New York, to consider the matter of forming a compact league. What emerged from that meeting was the National Association of Professional Base Ball Clubs, the forerunner of the National League, and the first major league in all history. But Cincinnati, which had helped make such an organization possible, was not represented in the circuit.

All nine of the regular Red Stockings made good in the National Association. Harry Wright went to Boston to man-

8

age that city's club, and took with him his brother George and Charlie Gould. Allison, Leonard, Waterman, Brainard, and Sweasy all joined the Olympics of Washington. Cal McVey cast his fortunes with Chicago.

⊗ 2 ⊗

DISORDER AND EARLY CHAOS

1

Irked by five seasons of inactivity and determined that Cincinnati should again take a leading part in baseball affairs, lovers of the pastime raised enough money to obtain a franchise in the National League when it was organized in 1876.

Cincinnati, then, was granted a team and took its place as a charter member of the National, along with nines from Chicago, St. Louis, Louisville, Boston, Hartford, Philadelphia, and New York. The last-named club played its games in Brooklyn and was known as the Mutuals, and is not to be confused with either the Giants or the Dodgers of today.

It was thought that Cincinnati, having given birth to the Red Stockings, would immediately become one of the strongest teams in the organization. Stockholders in the club chose as president Josiah L. Keck, a meat packer of note, and because of his occupation, his team came to be known as the Porkopolitans in addition to the more common designation, Reds. Charlie Gould and Charlie Sweasy, members of the old Red Stockings, were secured, with Gould chosen as manager of the club. Gould, of course, stationed himself at first base with Sweasy at second. The infield was rounded out with Henry Kessler at shortstop and Will Foley at third.

9

Kessler was from Franklin, Pennsylvania, and Foley from Chicago.

The outfield consisted of Emanuel Snyder from Camden, New Jersey, in left; Charlie Jones from Alamance County, North Carolina, in center, and Dave Pierson from Newark, New Jersey, in right. Pierson also was a catcher, and Amos Booth, a local lad, also caught and filled in at infield chores. Cherokee Fisher, who had pitched for the Haymakers of Troy in the disputed game with the Red Stockings in 1869, was obtained to do the hurling. Bobby Clack, an outfielder from Brooklyn, and Sam Field, of Sinking Spring, Pennsylvania, were the utility men. Those eleven men were the only ones on the team as the season started.

There was tremendous excitement when the Reds opened their first National League season at home on April 25, 1876, by nosing out the St. Louis Browns, 2 to 1, beating George Washington Bradley, a pitcher destined to roll up sixteen shutouts before the campaign was over. And when the Reds trounced Bradley again the next day, all Cincinnati fandom was certain that Mr. Keck's Porkopolitans were about to bring new grandeur to the city.

But those two victories just about constituted the extent of the team's winning for the season. A schedule of seventy games had been arranged, less than half of today's total, but in spite of the brevity of the season, the Reds found time to manufacture losing streaks of eleven, thirteen, and eighteen in a row, ending the year with a mark of nine victories and fifty-six defeats. This unprecedented incompetence guaranteed a finish in the league basement, far below the other seven clubs.

Oddly enough, the team was supported by the fans of the city and by the newspapers, which were the club's greatest apologists. The games were played at a park far from the business district of town on the site of what was later Chester Park, a location reached only by special train and carriage. Admission to the grounds was priced at fifty cents, and crowds of about three thousand frequently turned out.

Gambling on the games in those days was a common

occurrence, and the daily papers even quoted odds on the contests. Unquestionably, a large portion of the people in attendance was of the rougher element of the city's populace. But even at that early date the club and the National League attempted to give the game greater dignity. An interesting sidelight of this attempt is shown by the following dispatch from the *Cincinnati Enquirer:*

"We wish to call gentlemen's attention to the fact that the whole of the grandstand is reserved for ladies and their escorts, and holders of season tickets. It is so enclosed that a lady is as free from insult there as at a theater. No smoking is allowed in the grandstand."

After the two wins against the Browns, the Reds dropped a pair to Chicago, split two with Louisville, and then started their first road trip. They were gone for more than a month, visited every city in the league, and won exactly one game out of eighteen.

In Boston on May 23 the Reds ran into the first no-hit game ever pitched in the National League. The hurler who accomplished the feat was Joseph Borden, who pitched under the name of Josephs. He had previously pitched a no-hitter in the National Association in 1875, the first major-league no-hitter of all time.

Borden's feat is not listed in the record books because O. P. Caylor, who sent the Cincinnati scores into the league office, counted bases on balls as hits. All the other scorers in the league counted them as times at bat without hits. Borden walked two men during the game, which Caylor listed as hits. But a thorough check of the box score proves that Borden authored the circuit's first no-hit job. Before the season was finished, Borden's arm went lame, and he finished the year as the club's groundkeeper and never pitched again, thus becoming the first and greatest flash in the pan of all time.

When the Reds finally returned home on June 20, it was obvious that Cherokee Fisher was no longer capable of pitching in fast company so he was let go and replaced with a young Cincinnatian named Henry Dean.

11

The name of Dean is a famous one in baseball, thanks to the accomplishments of Jay Hanna (Dizzy) Dean, but the first of the pitching Deans, Henry, was something else again. He lost his first four games for the Reds, then won two in a row over Philadelphia. But on July 11 he started a losing streak that extended to thirteen. Finally a third pitcher was signed, Elisha (Dale) Williams, of Ludlow, Kentucky. He lost his first five starts, won one from Louisville, and then started losing again. No matter who pitched that year, Fisher, Dean, or Williams, the result of the game was almost a foregone conclusion.

When the Reds visited Hartford on September 9, they became the first team to play two games in a single day. Double-headers are common practice today, but in those days they were most unusual. Dean lost to Hartford that morning, 14 to 4, and in the afternoon Williams absorbed an 8-to-4 drubbing. William (Candy) Cummings worked both contests for Hartford to become the game's first iron man.

The Reds closed their first National League season on October 9, as a crowd of about two hundred watched the lugubrious proceedings, with Hartford winning, 11 to 0.

2

President Keck, dissatisfied with Gould as manager, replaced him for the league's second season with Lipman E. Pike, an outfielder and the first Jewish player in major-league history. Gould, however, was retained as the club's first baseman. The only other holdovers were Charlie Jones, who moved from center to left field as Pike stationed himself in the middle pasture, and Will Foley, who remained to play third base. Bobby Matthews, well known in the East, was hired to pitch, and he brought with him a catcher named Winfield Scott Hastings. Bob Addy, credited with being the first player to steal a base by sliding, came to the club to play right field, and other newcomers were second baseman Jimmy Hallinan and shortstop John Manning, both of whom had played National League ball the season before.

The season opened ominously when the Reds were rained out three successive days and finally had to abandon the plan of opening at home at all. They took a boat for Louisville, first team to use that mode of transportation, and inaugurated hostilities at the Falls City, winning a 15-to-10 slug fest.

Back in Cincinnati following the Louisville series, the boys proceeded to resume their losing ways of the year before. Finally after the record showed three wins and fourteen defeats, President Keck decided to call it quits.

"The dog is dead," he announced tersely at a clubhouse meeting. "If this club goes on its eastern trip, it goes on its own responsibility. I lost money last year on the trip, and I can't afford to run such risks again this season."

That statement posed quite a problem for the league, which could do little with a team that chose to secede, and also posed a problem, mostly financial in nature, for the players who had signed contracts to play out the full schedule.

One of the players, infielder Jimmy Hallinan, apparently considered the team's situation more tragic than did his mates, or at least he devised a more picturesque way of reacting to it. To put the matter as briefly as possible, Jimmy Hallinan got drunk. That might appear to be the normal reaction to such a state of affairs, but Hallinan didn't stop there. Somewhere during the course of a confusing evening he encountered one Abe Wald, a printer on the *Enquirer*, and they engaged in a street fight with such raucous overtones that the police were called and Hallinan's bibulous night evolved into a bilious dawn at the city's celebrated hoosegow. While resting in that estimable establishment, he was suddenly confronted by a visitor, Louis Meacham, a Chicago sports writer who offered to pay his bail. Hallinan cheerfully accepted and accompanied his newly found benefactor to the street.

Meacham took Hallinan to a saloon, bought him enough drinks to assure amiable compliance, and signed him to a contract with the Chicago White Stockings, explained that he might as well sign, as the Reds were no longer in the

National League. This was not actually the case, for at that moment eight prominent Cincinnatians were organizing a stock company to assume Keck's obligations and have the team finish the schedule. But Hallinan fell for the bait and was off for Chicago.

The situation was further complicated by the fact that William A. Hulbert, the league president, was also president of the Chicago White Stockings. He took advantage of the crisis in the affairs of the Cincinnati club to sign Hallinan, and through Meacham he put Charlie Jones, the Red outfielder, in a compromising position.

For Jones also agreed to join the White Stockings, but only with the understanding that the Reds would no longer operate. He accepted an advance in salary from the Chicago club and promised to join the Sox as soon as the Cincinnati affair was straightened out.

By this time the stock company had raised enough money to operate the club, but when they applied to Hulbert for readmission to the league, they were told that such reinstatement would require the unanimous consent of the other clubs, because the Reds had failed to pay their June dues to the league, a matter of $100.

Meanwhile, Jones and Hallinan were playing in Chicago uniforms in a series at St. Louis, and the Reds couldn't get any satisfaction from the league office. But eventually the other club owners prevailed upon Hulbert to act with decency. Jones rejoined the Reds, Hallinan remained with the White Stockings, and the Reds, after an interval of three weeks, resumed their place in the circuit.

J. Wayne Neff, a prominent business executive, was elected president by the stockholders, and Bob Addy took over as manager.

The revamping of the Reds served only to confuse the newspapers of the country, some of which printed the league standings including the Reds' record, others dropping the Reds from the league entirely, and still others printing two sets of standings, as if asking the reader to take his pick. As a matter of fact, the entire business is still something in the nature of a minor mystery, although at the league meeting following the 1877 season all Cincinnati games were declared null and void.

The revamped Reds, though, carried through their schedule, or more accurately, staggered through it. But the gentlemen charged with the team's affairs certainly acted in good faith, paid all of Keck's outstanding bills, and paid the contract of each player in full.

After Hallinan's departure, Lip Pike, the deposed manager, took over at second base, with Manning moving from shortstop to the outfield, and Levi Meyerle, a veteran who had played in the National Association as early as 1871, signing to play short.

Bobby Matthews' pitching left much to be desired, and the team acquired William Arthur Cummings, whose name is today inscribed in the game's Hall of Fame at Cooperstown, New York, for the very good reason that he was the first pitcher to throw a curve. As a young boy in Ware, Massachusetts, Cummings got the idea for the curve from watching the peculiar flight of clam shells that he threw. Cummings practiced his curve with a baseball in the face of all sorts of skepticism, and although he weighed only 120 pounds when he was pitching in the National League, he proved to be one of the most capable hurlers in the game. Throughout the years ballplayers, college professors, and mathematicians have all argued as to whether an athlete can actually make a ball curve in flight; and although all players know that there is such a thing as a curve, the silly business has raged to this day.

Curve or no curve, though, Cummings had definitely lost the touch by the time he joined the Reds. His pitching became so shockingly bad that one newspaper was moved to observe:

"This thing of examining scores of the games in which the Cincinnati Reds play, and seeing from 18 to 25 hits each game piled up against Cummings' record, is getting sickening. His presence on the team is demoralizing. Unless the

15

evil be remedied, the club on its return will not attract 100 people to the games. No change could be for the worse."

Not dreaming that he would one day be enshrined in the great game's national museum, Cummings apparently brooded over the dispatch, for the next day he quit the team. Learning of his departure, this journal charitably printed this obituary:

"Private advices received here state that Cummings has left the Cincinnati team. Whether he left voluntarily or was urged to do so by the directors was not stated. No one who has pride in the game will mourn this loss (?) to the club. True, the team is now without a pitcher, for although Booth is doing well in the position, he never made any pretense of being a pitcher. It is safe to say that he is better in the position than Cummings was."

Such outspoken criticism of players was typical of the journalism of the day. As a matter of fact, the turmoil that existed in baseball during the years 1876 and 1877 existed almost everywhere in our national life. Although the country was celebrating the centennial of its independence, the mood of the nation was more or less nasty. The election of Rutherford Birchard Hayes over Samuel Tilden, an election so close it had to be decided by Congress and an election more disputed than any decision ever made by an umpire, started a terrific fight between Republican and Democratic newspapers, and the tone of most news writing was definitely vitriolic. That some of the venom should drip through to the sporting page is understandable.

3

Today the baseball fan takes for granted the fact that the same eight teams will be battling each other year after year. In the National League, for instance, the same eight clubs have been at it hammer and tongs since 1900. But in the early days of the game the clubs had difficult going and quite frequently were able to finish the season only after surviving great hardship. The Mutuals and Athletics had dropped out

Cincinnati Reds

THE REDS OF 1869

CHARLES A. COMISKEY

The Sporting News

WILLIAM (BUCK) EWING

The Sporting News

of the league after 1876, leaving just six clubs to engage in the 1877 flag race.

Hartford, Louisville, and St. Louis decided to abandon their franchises prior to the 1878 campaign, and they were supplanted by teams from Providence, Indianapolis, and Milwaukee. Boston, Chicago, and Cincinnati stayed on to form the six-club circuit.

J. Wayne Neff, who had guided the Reds with great skill in the face of all the trouble that 1877 had produced, recognized that many changes had to be made if the Reds were to be a factor in the pennant chase. His first move was to dismiss Bob Addy as manager and replace him with Cal McVey, a grand favorite in Cincinnati from his Red Stocking days and a man with a wide acquaintance throughout baseball.

The entire infield was made over. Charlie Gould had come to the end of his string, and he was reluctantly let out. John Manning and Will Foley also departed. McVey installed himself at third base, putting John (Chub) Sullivan, a recruit from Boston, on first; Joe Gerhardt, a veteran from New York, on second; and Willie Geer, a rookie from Buffalo, at short.

Lip Pike and Charlie Jones remained to roam the outfield, and they were joined by Michael Joseph (King) Kelly, who was to add his colorful page to league history before much time had passed.

But the biggest change was made in the pitching and catching departments. The poor pitching that had plagued the Reds for two years was ended with pleasant alacrity by the signing of Will White, a young hurler who had appeared briefly for Boston the year before. Will's older brother, Jim, also joined the team as a catcher, and they formed the first brother battery in the game.

Will was the first player to wear glasses on the field, but despite this handicap, he almost immediately became one of the game's really outstanding hurlers. Jim, called the Deacon because he eschewed tobacco and alcohol, was one of the game's oldest players.

17

Milwaukee came to Cincinnati to open the season, boasting a terror of a pitcher in Sam Weaver. White defeated him in the opener, 6 to 4, beat him the following day, 6 to 2, then, after a day's rest, triumphed over him again, 4 to 1. It was clear that the Reds were definitely on the upswing.

Chicago next paid the Reds a visit, and they suffered the same fate as Will White outpitched Frank Larkin three straight times, 4 to 3, 9 to 1, and 4 to 1.

The Reds then took to the road and ran into a snag in Milwaukee, where Weaver gained a measure of revenge by stopping the Reds twice. Will salvaged the last game of the series, and then picked up three more victories in Chicago. That left the team with ten victories in its first twelve games, and though the Reds weren't able to continue such a stunning pace as all that, they were making it evident that the door-mat days were done.

But there were two pitchers in the league that year who could beat the Reds, and their presence kept Cincinnati from attaining its first pennant. The first of these was Edward (The Only) Nolan, who hurled for Indianapolis, and the second was Boston's Tommy Bond.

Indianapolis trounced the Reds six times in seven meetings during the month of June. When the clubs met in a gala holiday game at Cincinnati on July 4, a crowd of 5,194 filled the grandstand and 600 carriages lined the outfield, and watched the Reds win a 5-to-3 victory.

It was in late July at Boston that Bond came in to assert his mastery, trimming the Reds and White four in a row. The Boston club, which was managed by Harry Wright of the old Red Stockings, had a collection of veteran players who were simply too much for the league. The Reds spurted in late August, winning nine in a row, but it was too late. Boston finished out in front with Cincinnati a strong second.

The Reds ended with a record of 37 victories, 23 defeats, and a tie. White won 30 and lost 21, with Bobby Mitchell, the club's alternate pitcher and the first southpaw in National League annals, taking 7 out of 9.

It was a happy season all around; for the owners, who saw

their patience at last rewarded; for the players, who reached a lofty perch in the league race; and most of all for the joyous denizens of Cincinnati, who loved to go out to the park and root for their favorites and quaff the best products of the town's innumerable breweries.

4

A decline set in in 1879, but at first it was not visible. Ross Barnes, who had led the league in batting in 1876, was obtained to play shortstop, and Pete Hotaling, an outfield aspirant from Ilion, New York, was added to the squad. McVey moved to first base from third, and Mike Kelly was brought in from the outfield to the hot corner. It was thought that the Reds were stronger than the year before, and for the first time Cincinnati fandom had good reason to hope for a pennant.

Another switch in managers was made, with Deacon White taking over the club, but after the team had split its first eighteen games, White yielded the reins to McVey, who became the club's pilot for the second time.

The league had gone back to eight clubs, in spite of the fact that Indianapolis and Milwaukee dropped out. Buffalo, Troy, Cleveland, and Syracuse fielded teams for the first time, and the league seemed on solid footing.

Inability to beat Providence and Buffalo spelled the Reds' doom. John Montgomery Ward, a pitcher from Penn State who had joined the Rhode Island team the season before, proved a hoodoo for Cincinnati, and eight times they submitted to his spell. Gentle Jim Galvin, who pitched for Buffalo, proved equally tough and mastered them on seven occasions.

The managerial switch from White to McVey failed to produce the desired results. The Reds played in-and-out ball against all opponents, and finished the year with 43 wins and 37 defeats, ending up in fifth place.

One pleasant aspect of the season was the continued excellence of Will White's pitching. He set records that year that never will be surpassed. Of the 80 games played by the club,

White pitched 74 complete games and part of another contest, winning 43 and losing 32. In those days it was customary for a pitcher to appear in almost all his club's games. Pitching wasn't the highly developed skill it is today. But nevertheless, none of the other top pitchers of the era—George Washington Bradley, Al Spalding, Old Hoss Radbourne, Gentle Jim Galvin, or any of them—could come close to the record set by the Cincinnati flinger. Will White was one of the game's greats who never received his just deserts.

After the disappointing 1879 season, President Neff resigned, and his loss was keenly felt. His place was taken by Justus Thorner, a gentleman who spent most of his time fighting with his stockholders. In midseason he gave way to one of his directors, Nathan Menderson, and he in turn was succeeded by W. H. Kennett. You won't find any reference to Kennett in any of the record books, nor can you locate him in the Cincinnati city directory for 1880 on the spotty information available. But he was frequently mentioned as the club's president in the daily press.

Whatever the club needed, it was not three presidents.

Baseball historians have long insisted that the manager of the 1880 Reds was Oliver Perry Caylor. Although Caylor did manage the Reds later, in their American Association days, he was in 1880 the baseball editor of the *Cincinnati Enquirer*. The actual pilot of the team was John E. Clapp, a famous catcher of his day, but a man who was able to do little to boost the team.

Two rookies who were to experience long careers in Cincinnati, Long John Reilly at first base and Warren (Hick) Carpenter at third, made their debuts that year. But they were able to do nothing about bolstering the club, which sagged into a pattern of daily losses, and finally fell through to the league basement, where it settled with a record of 21 triumphs and 60 setbacks. So, at the end of five National League seasons, the Reds were back in the abyss.

But the crowning blow was yet to fall. At the league meeting at Buffalo on October 6, the Cincinnati Reds were unceremoniously thrown out of the league, bag and baggage.

And the reason for their eviction was bizarre, to say the least.

At that time, one of the cities in the infant circuit was the decorous community of Worcester, in Massachusetts, a state which then considered itself the guardian of the nation's morals. During the 1880 season, a Worcester newspaper, appropriately named the *Spy*, started a tirade against the Reds because beer was sold at the Cincinnati park and because the club was accustomed to rent its grounds to amateur teams for Sunday baseball.

The Reds, having survived enough trouble of their own making, were bravely trying to put the team on a solid financial footing. Toward that end they counted heavily on the beer concession and the revenue accruing from rental of the park. They quite justifiably didn't consider that the business of anyone in Worcester. In fact, one Cincinnati paper made the issue plain when it said:

"Puritanical Worcester is not liberal Cincinnati by a jugful, and what is sauce for Worcester is wind for the Queen City. Beer and Sunday amusements have become a popular necessity in Cincinnati."

There is, however, something to be said for the point of view of the league, which picked up Worcester's suggestions and started agitation for the removal of the Reds from the circuit. In its early days baseball was associated with gambling, and there were considerable drinking and general rowdiness. The National League had been formed to put an end to those very things, and it did stamp out many of the evils. In viewing the sale of beer in Cincinnati's park as an evil, league officials were guilty only of too much strictness.

But the Reds were stubborn. At the league meeting President Kennett informed the other club owners that beer would be sold at the Cincinnati grounds in 1881, and that the park would be rented again for Sunday play. He was then told that Cincinnati was expelled then and there.

Today Cincinnati *is* in the National League, has been continuously since 1890, and has provided more than its share of thrills and glory for the annals of the game. Today in Cincinnati you can see a National League game on Sunday (usually a double-header), you can drink a bottle of beer at the park, and you can go home without the necessity of any feeling of guilt. What you can do today on a Sunday afternoon in Worcester is something else again. But you can't see a major-league ball game. Worcester has disappeared from the baseball map.

During that first five-year tenure in the National League, Cincinnati employed a total of fifty-three players, not one of whom is still alive. Not many of them were outstanding athletes, and most of them have long since departed from the memories of even the oldest fans.

Deacon White lived until 1939, and at the time of his death at Aurora, Illinois, he was ninety-two, the oldest professional player still extant. Disappointment over failure to have his name included in the Hall of Fame at Cooperstown is said to have contributed to his passing. Younger brother Will had long left the scene. He drowned in Lake Mushoka, near Fort Collier, Ontario, in an ill-fated boating expedition back in 1911.

About half of the others can be traced. One who cannot be and whose eventual fate is still a mystery is Charlie Jones, the outfielder who, with James Hallinan, figured in the 1877 mix-up over joining the White Stockings. Jones was born in Alamance County, North Carolina, and his real name was Benjamin Rippay. He moved to Princeton, Indiana, at an early age and was adopted by an uncle named Jones, whose name he took.

In the late seventies around Cincinnati Charlie was the first grandstand idol. A handsome fellow, he was paid by a clothing concern to walk about town garbed in the firm's latest creations. On one of these strolls he was accompanied by a woman not his wife, and his irate spouse, upon meeting the pair, greeted him by throwing cayenne pepper into his eyes. This unusual injury affected his play, and though he remained to appear for the American Association Reds, he was never again the same player.

⊖ **3** ⊖

ASSOCIATION DAYS

1

Cincinnati, through the years, has had teams that have been good, bad, and indifferent. But only once since the founding of the National League has the city had to submit to the indignity of having no team at all, and that once occurred in 1881, after Worcester, by its moral messing, had forced the Reds from the National and left them with no other league to turn to.

Prior to 1882 no league had ever succeeded in competition with the National. But in that year the American Association, designed as a major circuit, not only finished out its schedule, but also achieved the neat trick of making money. Cincinnati, seeing a chance to join a loop in which beer and Sunday baseball were not anathema, delightedly became a charter member of the infant entente.

It might be more accurate to say that Cincinnati started the league, for the Association was organized at the Rhineland's Hotel Gibson on November 2, 1881, and the perpetrators of the organization were Justus Thorner, who had made an abortive attempt to head the Reds in 1880, and Oliver Perry Caylor, the game's Boswell in the Midwest. Thorner was a man of wealth and distinction, and he was adamant in his ambition to restore the city to major-league ranks. The opportunity became ideal when the National League in 1881 failed to include teams from New York, Philadelphia, Brooklyn, Baltimore, and St. Louis.

The Association's first campaign was entered into by the

Athletic (Philadelphia), Baltimore, and Alleghany (Pittsburgh) teams of the East, and the Cincinnati, St. Louis, and Eclipse (Louisville) clubs of the West.

Only two players remained from the sad outfit that had finished in the National League cellar in 1880, Will White, still a winning pitcher, and Hick Carpenter, the third baseman.

Charles J. Fulmer served as playing manager of the 1882 Reds, his position being shortstop, with Charles N. Snyder acting as field captain and catcher. Other new men included first baseman Dan Stearns, second baseman John (Bid) McPhee, and outfielders John Macullar, Harry Wheeler, and Joe Sommer.

McPhee had previously played only with Akron in a minor setting, but he soon became famous. He is in many ways one of the most remarkable players in Cincinnati annals. Bid performed for the Reds all through their Association days, then played a decade for them in the National, finally retiring in 1899. Few are the players who have remained in one town eighteen years, as did McPhee. He played more than two thousand games for the Reds, and year after year the various executives charged with running the team's affairs refused to sell his contract to envious moguls of other cities. Bid played his position without a glove long after other infielders had adopted the protection, and he refused to wear one until the autumn of his career.

Carpenter, the third sacker, gave an odd touch to the infield because he threw with his left hand. Only two other guardians of the hot corner in all history threw in this manner: Willie Keeler, of the New York Giants and Baltimore Orioles, and the man who made "hit 'em where they ain't" a baseball axiom, was one, and Charles Marr, of the 1890 Reds, the other. But Keeler was more at home in the outfield than at third, and did most of his stellar playing at Baltimore while roving the gardens.

Carpenter, though, was a third baseman all through his career, and didn't seem particularly handicapped by his unorthodox throwing. He was also a dangerous batsman, and his 1882 mark of .354 was robust enough to make him the hitting leader of the club.

Will White had pitching help in the person of Henry McCormick, a native of Syracuse, New York, who had started in the National in 1879, but Will was still called upon to do his stuff almost every day.

The Reds' first Association team was perhaps the most colorful ever assembled as far as uniforms were concerned. Each player wore a suit of a different color. Captain Snyder, behind the dish, was a handsome figure in scarlet, as he received the slants of Will White, who was garbed in blue. Dan Stearns, at first base, was dolled up in red and white; McPhee, at second, was orange and black; Fulmer, at short, was brown; and Carpenter, at third, was black and white. In the outfield Sommer was dressed in white, Macullar in tan, and Wheeler in a lighter shade of blue than Will White.

The Reds started slowly, playing slightly better than .500 ball until June, and then began to click. After losing on June 1, they won ten in a row, four against the Athletics, four more against Baltimore, and twice in opposition to the Alleghanies. The pitching of White, the hitting of Carpenter, and the gymnastics of McPhee around second were beginning to pay off.

White pitched nine of the ten straight victories, and when he won the sixth of the Reds' string of ten over the Athletics on June 13, 4 to 3 in a duel with Frank Mountain, Cincinnati passed Philadelphia and went into first place.

After taking the top spot, the Reds continued to batter down all opposition. Going on an eastern trip in July, they emerged victorious from every series. The only pitcher in the league who had their number was George McGinnis, of St. Louis, who beat them six times in eleven tries.

During the last half of the season the Reds customarily won two games of every three, and finished the year way out in front, winning their last five games for a final mark of 55 wins and 25 defeats. Will White accounted for 40 of the wins and lost 12. McCormick won 14 and lost 12, and outfielder

Harry Wheeler pitched the other 2 games, winning one and dropping the other.

The Reds that year won eleven out of sixteen games with Louisville, ten out of sixteen each from St. Louis, Philadelphia, and Pittsburgh, and fourteen out of sixteen from Baltimore, finishing eleven and a half games in front of the second-place Athletics. The lowly Baltimore Orioles, not yet ready for their days of grandeur, were at the bottom of the nest, thirty-five games off the pace.

One might assume that a team that won as frequently as the 1882 Reds would finish out the schedule without any disturbances in their own ranks. Yet they did have one episode of dissension with rather absurd overtones.

Harry Luff, a substitute first baseman, quit the club in a huff over a matter of five dollars, and probably became the only player in history to jump a first-place team over such a trifle. He was fined the five by Manager Fulmer "for making a one-handed catch."

After the schedule had been completed, the Reds arranged to play two games in Cincinnati with Cap Anson's Chicago White Stockings, who had won the National League pennant, as was their annual custom. Some historians have implied that this meeting constituted the first World Series, but such a conclusion is not justified by the facts.

The games between the Reds and White Stockings were mere exhibitions, played without hoop-la and attended by no excitement whatever and very few spectators. On the day of the first of these games one Cincinnati morning paper said, "This afternoon the champions of the League and the American Association will meet for the first time. This contest will undoubtedly be an excellent one, as White always was a terror for the Windy City team."

White did prove to be a terror and shut out the clan of Anson, 4 to 0, but on the next day the Reds were themselves whitewashed, 2 to 0. That ended the series, and such an inconclusive finish is proof in itself that nothing was at stake and that the atmosphere of a World Series was totally lacking. It was, however, the first postseason meeting of two major-league champions.

The series might have gone further, at that, had it not been for action by the American Association. So much did the Association despise the National League that an ironclad rule was made, forbidding any Association club from participating in an exhibition game against a National League team during the regular season. In order to meet Chicago legally after the campaign was over, it was necessary for the Reds to resort to a technicality, releasing every player after the final championship game, and then forming another club, using the same players, of course, to oppose the White Stockings. But after the two games had been played, Association officials fined the Reds $100 and forbade any further play. Thus, it can be said that the first postseason meeting of major-league champions ended with one of the contending teams fined for participating in the series.

2

When President Thorner went about his work of lining up players for 1883, he met among other things a request by Captain Charlie Snyder that was perhaps the most unusual supplication ever made by a professional athlete. Snyder had received $1,100 for his work in 1882, and the officials were so pleased with his play that they presented him with a gold watch and diamond-studded locket and offered to raise his pay to $1,800. Snyder replied that he would prefer to receive $1,700 and add the other $100 to the salary of another player on the club. This unprecedented solicitation was complied with.

Snyder was one of the best receivers of his day, and a worthy addition to the ranks of the Redlegs. He had previously caught for Louisville, and was said to have been the only catcher capable of handling Jim Devlin, the misguided and unfortunate pitcher tossed out of baseball in 1877 for throwing games.

When the 1883 season opened on May 1, the Reds took the field as champions for the first time in their history. Will

White, once more at his familiar pitching position, thrilled an opening-day crowd of 3,500 when he won a duel with George McGinnis of St. Louis, 6 to 5, in eleven innings.

As champions, the Reds relied on the same players who had won the pennant for them. Only additions to the club were John (Pop) Corkhill, an outfielder, and Lorenzo (Ren) Deagle, a pitcher, although later in the year outfielder John (Podge) Weihe, a native of Cincinnati, and Billy Mountjoy, a pitcher from Port Huron, Michigan, appeared in a few contests.

Pleased with its success in 1882, the American Association added two clubs in 1883, expanding to an eight-team circuit. The new teams were Columbus, Ohio, and the Metropolitans of New York. The schedule was also increased from eighty to ninety-eight games, the Reds meeting each of seven opponents fourteen times instead of contesting against each of five clubs on sixteen occasions.

Inability to defeat one of the new clubs, New York's Metropolitans, prevented the Reds from repeating as champions. The Mets weren't the strongest club in the league by any means, and they eventually finished fourth. But they had a pitcher named Tim Keefe who could knock off Cincinnati just about any time he wanted to. The Reds first ran into him on May 30, and he beat Henry McCormick, 1 to 0, in a morning game at New York witnessed by only five hundred fans. When the game was over the Reds moved on to Philadelphia and in the late afternoon engaged in an eleven-inning slug fest with the Athletics, winning 10 to 9. This was the first time that a major-league club had taken the field against two opponents in two cities in a single day. A week later Keefe beat the Reds again, 3 to 1, winning a duel with Will White. And almost every time thereafter the announcement of Keefe as the Metropolitan pitcher was enough to assure the downfall of the Reds.

Keefe pitched eleven games against the Reds that year, winning nine of them. The Reds were able to trounce John Lynch, the other Metropolitan hurler, twice in three attempts, so they finished with four victories and ten setbacks against the New Yorkers.

Against the other clubs the Reds still had easy sledding. They won eleven brawls from Baltimore and Columbus, ten from Louisville, nine from Philadelphia, and eight each from St. Louis and Pittsburgh, for a total of sixty-one triumphs and thirty-seven reverses. The Athletics finished first, five games ahead of the Reds, with St. Louis in second place.

A decline in hitting was responsible for part of the Red slump. Hick Carpenter, who finished with a .308 mark, was the only player on the club to hit better than .300. Long John Reilly pulled up with .289, and none of the others was even close to that figure.

It was at this point that organized baseball engaged in the first of numerous wars. With two major leagues prospering, a third tried to enter the field in 1884. This third league was called the Union Association, and its players were culled from the ranks of the dissatisfied athletes in the other two. The Union Association was an attempt to found a league to fight the reserve rule, an important part of baseball law that binds a player to his club. Without the reserve clause a player would be free to go to the highest bidder, which would obviously be the club with the most money. This would lead to a monopoly of talent that would destroy the game, and in the long run the player would be impoverished rather than enriched. The reserve rule is absolutely necessary for sound baseball operation.

Guiding spirit behind the Unions, or Onions as they came to be called, was Henry V. Lucas, of St. Louis, who termed the reserve clause "an outrageous and unjustifiable chain on the freedom of the player."

The attempt to form a new league was disastrous. Although Lucas persuaded many players with National and American Association clubs to jump their contracts, many failed him, and the season witnessed many changes of franchises.

Justus Thorner, who had served as president of the Reds in 1880 in the National League, and who had helped organize the American Association club in 1882, became interested in the Union movement, left the Reds in 1883, and made plans for a club in the new league. Thorner's first move was to obtain use of the Reds' park on Bank Street for Union Association games.

That left the American Association Reds without a place to play, and their new president, Aaron Stern, began looking about for one. He found a site a few blocks away, a brickyard on the corner of Findlay and Western Avenues, which he began to convert into a playing field. The Reds opened the American Association season on that site on May 1, 1884, and have been playing there ever since.

A few blocks to the south on the Bank Street grounds the Union Association began its campaign two weeks earlier, meeting Altoona, Pennsylvania, the most obscure city in major-league history. Thorner had brought Dan O'Leary to Cincinnati to manage the Unions, and also to play left field. He was one of those picturesque characters of early baseball who eschewed discipline, drank beer with his players, and gambled heavily on the team's games.

Playing within a half mile of each other all season long, the American Association and Union Reds contended for patronage noisily. Fans headed for one park were apt to find themselves accosted by ruffians and forced to go to the other game. It was a noisy, beery, brawling summer, as the city that failed to have a single team in the majors three years before now found itself with two.

The American Association tried to put the Unions out of business by hiring enough players for four more clubs, Toledo, Brooklyn, Indianapolis, and Washington. This produced an awkward twelve-team league. The Washington club ran into all sorts of difficulty, and moved to Richmond, Virginia, in midseason. But all clubs finished the season.

Will White was made manager of the American Association Reds for 1884, taking the place of Charlie Fulmer, who moved on to St. Louis. Fulmer was replaced at shortstop by Frank Fennelly, a rookie from Fall River, Massachusetts, who was an instant success. Another addition to the club in

30

1884 was Gus Shallix, a local pitcher who took the place of Henry McCormick, who was let out.

In August, after the club had won 48 games and lost 30, White decided he was of too easy a disposition to act as manager, and he induced his battery mate, Charlie Snyder, to take over. Under Snyder the Reds won 20 and lost 11, finishing in fifth place with 68 games won and 41 lost. The Metropolitans, with Keefe again their prize pitcher, easily won the pennant. Columbus, Louisville, and St. Louis also were ahead of the Reds.

Meanwhile, the Cincinnati Unions had a strong nine. George Washington Bradley was their first pitcher, and in midseason they acquired Jim McCormick, a National League veteran who was even better. McCormick jumped to Cincinnati with shortstop Jack Glassock, and that pair made the team extremely formidable.

Only the presence in the league of the St. Louis Maroons kept the Cincinnati Unions from the top. If the Unions were good, the Maroons were simply terrific. They won 91 games and lost 16, 5 of their defeats coming at the hands of Cincinnati. O'Leary's lads finished in second place with a record of 63 won and 35 lost.

The Union Association lasted only one year. It lost money heavily and caused the National League and American Association also to finish in the red. It was with relief that the American Association Reds watched the Union boys disband.

With competition from the Union eliminated, the American Association in 1885 reduced to eight clubs again, dropping Washington, Indianapolis, Toledo, and Columbus. League membership for 1885 was the same as 1883, except that Brooklyn had replaced Columbus.

Once more the Reds had a strong club in 1885, made even stronger by the addition of catchers Clarence (Kid) Baldwin and Jim Keenan and pitcher George Pechiney. But 1885 was the year that the St. Louis Browns won the first of four successive pennants under their fabulous owner, Chris von der Ahe, and the Reds had to be contented with second position.

President Aaron Stern, tiring of Charlie Snyder as manager, decided to take a bold step in 1886. He offered the managership to Oliver Perry Caylor, or O. P. Caylor as he was generally known. This was unusual because Caylor, a sports writer and authority on rules of the game, was not an athlete himself. He was a man of extremely small stature and weighed about 130 pounds. He was also possessed of a sharp tongue and a great vanity.

When Caylor wrote baseball in Cincinnati, he was not one to spare a player's feelings. For instance, he once described a Louisville catcher under a headline that read, "A Keg of Beer Will Catch for Louisville Today."

When the player in question, a huge hulk of a man, read the article, he stormed into Caylor's newspaper office, demanding to see the writer at once. An office boy asked the visitor what he wanted.

"I've been insulted," said the Louisville player. "I want to get my hands on the man who wrote that story."

"I wouldn't do that if I were you," replied the office boy. "You ought to see the man. He's even bigger than you are."

Not the least bit disturbed by that prospect, the player brushed his way into the office, took one disgusted look at Caylor, and snorted, "Are you the man who writes baseball here? Why, you look as if a strong breath would knock you over."

Later, one of the Louisville players asked the catcher if he had avenged his honor. "Why, I wouldn't hit Caylor," the player replied. "You ought to see him. He looks like a pimple on a stick."

With Caylor as manager, the Reds slumped from second to fifth, winning 65 and losing 73 in 1886. But the season was notable because the Reds once more came up with an outstanding pitcher, this one named Antoine J. Mullane. A product of county Cork, Ireland, Mullane soon became affectionately known as Tony throughout the Rhineland. He was a right-handed hurler, although legend has it that he was ambidextrous. This was said to have been the result of injuring his arm in a long-distance throwing contest. After the injury had healed, he is supposed to have resumed throwing with his right arm. Tony didn't wear a glove, and it is said that he frequently trapped men off bases, throwing them out with either arm. This he may have done, but his ambidexterity is a rather hollow claim inasmuch as the game has produced several legitimate bothpaws, the most famous of whom was Lawrence J. Corcoran of the old White Stockings.

Mullane was an illustrious right-hander, though, winning a total of 282 games in 14 major-league seasons, which is no petty achievement. And he was also a good hitter, which brought about his extensive use in the outfield and at other positions. Tony was the successor to Will White as the Reds' ace pitcher, a department of play in which Cincinnati has always excelled.

Stern's experiment with Caylor lasted just that one season, and in 1887 Gustavus Heinrich Schmelz became manager of the club. It is doubtful if anyone could think of a name that would please the German residents of Cincinnati more than Gustavus Heinrich Schmelz. Schmelz was from Columbus, and he wore a fiery-red beard, the only major-league manager in history to possess such foliage.

Schmelz put a strong Cincinnati club on the field in 1887, a team that was able to master all opponents except Chris von der Ahe's Browns. It was the year that the rule makers decided a base on balls should be credited as a base hit, with the result that batting averages were greatly inflated. What effect this had on the averages of the Reds can best be shown by the following table:

The robust batting averages of the 1887 Reds, due almost entirely to the new rule, may have given manager Gustavus Heinrich Schmelz occasion to stroke his red beard with pride, but of course the other clubs increased their percentages too. And von der Ahe's Browns were the same formidable Browns. Possessed of two great pitchers, Silver King and Parisian

PLAYER	1886 AVERAGE	1887 AVERAGE
Long John Reilly, 1b	.270	.334
Bid McPhee, 2b	.272	.354
Frank Fennelly, ss	.258	.368
Hick Carpenter, 3b	.221	.269
Pop Corkhill, of	.283	.330
Charlie Jones, of	.274	.374
Fred Lewis, of	.325	
Hugh Nicol, of		.334
Kid Baldwin, c	.238	.262
Tony Mullane, of, p	.228	.284
George Pechiney, p	.221	
Elmer Smith, p		.288

Bob Caruthers, the St. Louis club rode roughshod over the league, winning 95 and losing 40. The Reds were 14 games off the pace, with 81 victories and 54 defeats.

Schmelz stood pat in 1888, the Reds adding only three players, fewer than in any other year in the club's history. Two of the newcomers, catcher Edwin Bligh and pitcher John Weyhing, appeared in only eleven games between them. The only addition of consequence was pitcher Leon Viau, a graduate of Dartmouth.

A base on balls no longer counted as a hit in 1888, and the players' batting averages declined again, in some cases frighteningly. Shortstop Frank Fennelly fell from .368 to .191, Bid McPhee from .354 to .230.

The Reds of 1888 showed hope only once—early in the season. Starting in May they pieced together a winning streak of ten straight, Mullane, Elmer Smith, and the new man Viau alternating on the mound. Viau, in fact, was a sensation at the season's start, winning his first eight games, not running into defeat until he bowed to Brooklyn, 3 to 1, on June 1. Viau finished with 27 victories against 14 defeats, slightly ahead of Mullane, who had a 27–16 mark, and Smith, who finished with 22–17.

But the club was getting old. Reilly, at first, had a good

year, hitting .324, but some of the other veterans, Carpenter, Fennelly, and Corkhill, for instance, were fading.

Not only the Browns, but Brooklyn and the Athletics finished ahead of the Reds, who wound up in fourth place in 1888, winning 80 and dropping 54.

A winning club is often more disappointing than a daily loser. Fans can become inured to defeat. But a club that shows promise and then just fails to accomplish what it should is the one that creates sadness in the hearts of its followers. Such a club was the 1888 Reds.

Losing ball games is a serious business in Cincinnati. Even in 1888. But there was always the hope of tomorrow, the dawn of another day. If the Reds could just win!

One follower of the team wrote the following jingle in 1888 to show just how important baseball was to him and what a serious matter winning was:

> Thrones may tumble, earthquakes crumble
> Cities in chaotic heap.
> Banks be failing, loss entailing
> On depositors who weep.
> Strikes that threaten commerce deaden
> May envelop all the land.
> Soldiers fighting—some wrong righting—
> With the sabers and the brand.
> In conventions fierce contentions
> Men be struggling for their fame.
> Trifling matters—let our batters
> But win tomorrow's baseball game.

Gus Schmelz managed the Reds for the third and final time in 1889. Mullane and Elmer Smith temporarily lost their pitching magic, and Jesse Duryea, a new man from Osage, Illinois, was added to the hill corps. Shortstop Fennelly was let out, and he was replaced by Ollie Beard, not much of a shortstop but a man who at least had one minor claim to fame. Beard came from a distinguished Kentucky family that invented the famous Kentucky dish that pleases epicurians, burgoo. Another recruit, catcher Billy Earle, was a student of mesmerism. His mates were so certain that he could hypnotize them that he struck terror into their hearts.

But culinary skill and a knowledge of hypnosis do not win ball games. The Reds finished fourth again, winning 76 and losing 63, a pace less successful than that of the year before.

⊖ **4** ⊖

THE KELLY WHO WAS KING

1

Another disturbance in the ranks of organized baseball was the Brotherhood War, which, like the Union Association movement, created a third major league, the Brotherhood or Players' League. Like the Union Association, the Players' League lasted just one season—1890. And again, like the Union Association, it caused all leagues to lose money.

The Brotherhood was the outgrowth of dissatisfied league players' forming a circuit of their own, receiving the backing of various capitalists.

The formation of the Players' League offered an opportunity to Aaron Stern, president of the Reds. He could withdraw his team from the American Association and place it in the Brotherhood, or, better still, he could get the franchise back in the National League. It was the latter course he chose.

Taking with him ten of the players who had been with the American Association Reds of 1889, Stern purchased the contracts of eight additional men and moved back into the National, where the Reds joined teams from Boston, Chicago, Cleveland, Pittsburgh, New York, Brooklyn, and Philadelphia. Substitute St. Louis for Cleveland, and that would be the National League of today.

Catchers Kid Baldwin and Jim Keenan, pitchers Tony Mullane, Jesse Duryea, and Leon Viau, infielders John Reilly, Bid McPhee, and Ollie Beard, and outfielders Bug Holliday and Hugh Nicol were the ten Reds who jumped with Stern to the National.

The eight new men purchased were catcher Jerry Harrington, pitchers Billy Rhines, Frank Foreman, and John Dolan, infielders Billy Clingman, Arlie Latham, and Charlie Marr, and outfielder Jonas Knight.

Stern had purchased Rhines and Harrington, as a battery, from Davenport. They were unheard of at the time, and are remembered by few today. Yet William Pearl Rhines and his battery mate, Jeremiah Peter Harrington, were sensational during the summer of 1890.

Billy Rhines, taking his place on a staff that had such accredited hurlers as Jesse Duryea, Tony Mullane, and Leon Viau, established himself almost immediately. He won his first six starts, dropped one, then added seven more victories. By this time he was a drawing card all over the circuit. Rhines was the original submariner, author of a style of pitching later made famous by Carl Mays. Most underhanders get that way as a result of an accident that precludes their pitching in the normal overhanded fashion. But with Rhines it was his natural style, and one that proved perplexing to the batters. Harrington had no trouble in handling these underhanded shoots, and also proved to be able to throw to the bases from a squatting position, a novelty at the time but now the established position from which to toss out runners.

Stern selected as manager of the 1890 club Tom Loftus, a veteran campaigner whose active days were over. A native of Dubuque, Iowa, he started his career back in 1877 when he came up with St. Louis of the National League as an outfielder.

It was Loftus who saw the promise of Rhines and Harrington as a battery and gave them a place on the squad. It

37

was also Loftus who was instrumental in bringing Arlie Latham to Cincinnati, installing him at third base.

Latham, the son of a Civil War bugler, was born at West Lebanon, New Hampshire, on March 15, 1860. His first connection with baseball was at the age of twelve, and he was still at it in 1947, at the age of eighty-seven, being a park attendant at Yankee Stadium, New York.

At the time he came to the Reds in 1890, Arlie was known as the greatest comedian in the game. He had played with von der Ahe's four-straight world champions from 1885 to 1888, and his aggressive play made him the darling of the galleries. He was called the Duke, was a song-and-dance man, the first player to go on the stage, a man of many scrapes and many marriages, and one whale of a ballplayer!

It is often said that those who are happiest in life are the people who are at ease in any company. By this definition Arlie Latham qualified as a happy man. Not only did he enjoy the company of the flotsam that infested the Over the Rhine saloons in Cincinnati, but he later became a friend of George V, King of England. Arlie lived in the British Isles for sixteen years after leaving baseball. The monarch had seen him play during one of those world tours that players of the era were apt to make, and became fascinated by the game. Latham tried to teach the King to throw, but frequently became discouraged.

"King George had only a fair arm," Arlie later told friends.

Coaches on baseball clubs today can thank Arlie Latham for their jobs. In the game's early days players were employed to coach on the base paths. No man was ever hired solely for coaching until John McGraw hired Latham as a coach on the Giants of 1907. Ball clubs have hired coaches ever since. Arlie also served as a court jester for McGraw, a role that established a custom.

The battery of Rhines and Harrington and the third-base work of Arlie Latham gave Cincinnati fans many hours of pleasure during the summer of 1890, but the club was not particularly distinguished otherwise. It was one of those run-of-the-mine teams that had its moments but was unable to piece together enough successive victories to be a pennant threat. With Rhines setting the pace by winning 28 games while losing 17, the club managed to emerge victorious in 77 contests while losing 55, and finished fourth.

When the season had been completed, Aaron Stern, after almost a decade of running Redleg baseball affairs, decided to sell out. The team had played to 131,980 admissions during 1890, not a bad record for those days, but Stern was tiring of the game. So he sold the franchise for practically nothing to John Talleyrand Brush, a clothing merchant from Indianapolis.

In preparing for the season of 1891, Brush decided to go along with Tom Loftus as manager for another year, and he made the mistake of also going along with the same players.

Early in the season it was evident that Loftus had lost control over his players, and problems of discipline developed. Rhines and Harrington, sensations in 1890 and now heroes to the populace, made a discovery that was quite common at the time. They found that Cincinnati offered as many possibilities for amusement at night as it did for recreation on the ball field in the afternoon. As a consequence, they repeatedly had to be fined or suspended or both. The morale of the club was impaired, and the season wasn't very old before it became apparent that the team was on the downgrade again.

In an attempt to bolster it, Brush and Loftus brought in two fading stars, pitcher Charles (Old Hoss) Radbourne and outfielder Louis (Pete) Browning. Radbourne, considered a phenomenal hurler at Providence in the eighties, reached the Reds far too late to be of much use. He did win 12 games while losing 13, but that rate of achieving victory was far lower than he had been accustomed to.

Browning had also seen better days by the time he reached the Rhine. A native of Louisville, he had starred for years for that city's clubs, being one of baseball's really great hitters. Browning was base-hit crazy. For hours he would sit and compute his batting average. He was a crank about bats, and would carefully examine the timber used by every player in the league. Pete was also one of those picturesque, Waddellesque characters that the game produced in profusion in those years, a man who was just as apt not to show up at the park as to be there.

Baseball has produced many strange personalities, but it is doubtful if any player ever equaled Browning in naïve simplicity and peculiar speech. He always referred to himself in the third person, saying such things as "Old Pete made three hits today."

If Browning had done his dissipating in the winter and remained sober in the summer, he might have prolonged his career. But his method of training was unique. All winter he would work out and watch his habits, and report in the finest possible condition. Then he would proceed to carouse all summer. He made an amiable companion for Billy Rhines and Jerry Harrington.

He did pay some attention to baseball in 1891. At least he purchased over one hundred bats, which brought his collection to over seven hundred. But much as he loved baseball, his passion for the pastimes of the night were too engrossing to pass up.

This inseparable, ill-behaved trio of Browning, Harrington, and Rhines caused many a sleepless night for Loftus and John Brush. It was the only year they were together, and the three of them made the most of it. In the light of their habits, it is interesting to observe what became of them.

Rhines, all credit to him, suffered a complete reformation. He was sold by the Reds to Pittsburgh, but later returned to Cincinnati and was a winning pitcher. When his career was completed at the turn of the century, he went home to Ridgway, Pennsylvania, to tramp the hills he loved, and became a crack hunter of deer, bear, and other game. For years he operated a taxi in Ridgway, and it is pleasant to picture him, sitting in his cab on the public square of that community, dreaming his dreams of the good old days, thinking of the adulation of the mob and the big steins of beer rushed out by mustached waiters in the numerous gardens that made night life famous in the Queen City of the West.

And perhaps wondering whatever became of his battery mate, Jerry Harrington.

Harrington played a few years for Louisville, then quit the game and went to Keokuk, Iowa, where he eventually became an assistant chief of police. He met his end in 1913 when he was struck over the head with a can of beer wielded by a thug named Tom Merritt. He is still recalled by veteran Keokuk police officials, and his name occasionally bobs up in hot stove league sessions there.

Browning returned to his native Louisville, and went to an early death.

The Reds of 1891 played out their schedule, disappointing their new president, losing a job for their manager, Tom Loftus, and winding up in seventh place, with a record of 56 wins and 81 defeats. That winter the club was completely torn apart.

2

Another team also represented Cincinnati in 1891, one of the strangest aggregations of players in the city's history, a club known as Kelly's Killers.

When the Reds returned to the National League in 1890, there were some magnates who thought the city could support two teams, and so a group was formed to secure a franchise in the American Association, which, though on its last legs, was still in operation. Brush's club had possession of the grounds at Findlay and Western Avenues, and the new team constructed a park in a suburb called Pendleton, in the east end of the city, on the site of what is now the Cincinnati Gym Grounds.

President of the team, which entered the American Association in 1891, was a man named Ed Renau, but he was in reality only a figurehead for Chris von der Ahe, owner of the St. Louis Browns.

Renau and von der Ahe selected as manager of the team Michael Joseph (King) Kelly, and it was he who provided the team with its nickname—Kelly's Killers.

King Kelly is one of the Cooperstown immortals. It will

be recalled that he played with the Reds of the National League in 1878 and 1879. But at that time he was just starting out. Originally a catcher, Kelly could play all positions, and with the Chicago club from 1880 to 1887 he was the most famous player in the country. As a batter he was unsurpassed, but he was best loved for his colorful style of play and for his off-the-field antics. In some ways he resembled Latham, in other ways Browning, but he was a far greater player than either. It was he who inspired the cry "Slide, Kelly, slide!"

When Kelly's contract was sold by Chicago to Boston for $10,000 on February 14, 1887, the Chicago fans were stunned. The price paid by Boston for Kelly was unprecedented, and to fans of the Windy City the act of selling him was criminal. When Boston visited Chicago for the first time in 1887, the park was jammed with fanatics who cheered for their hero, Kelly, and who hissed the Chicago team unmercifully. Kelly that day won the game for Boston almost singlehanded.

Off the field, Kelly's exploits as a lover of fun were legendary. Cap Anson, manager of the Chicago White Stockings, was quoted as saying, "No man has ever lived who could drink King Kelly under the table."

The King was a natty dresser, a cane-carrier, a ring-wearer, a spender, a sport. His appetites were Gargantuan, his laughter was hearty, his hand was extended to an acclaiming world.

The idea that men could be paid for playing baseball must have seemed fantastic to such persons as King Kelly. There aren't any King Kellys in the game today, which may be just as well. Today's professional player is a student of physical condition, a man who saves his money, takes his share of the headlines without undue concern, and then retires to the community that spawned him. Today a Kelly coming up would not be called a king. A Kelly coming up today would just be called a fool.

But in the hot summer of 1891 King Kelly and his Killers put on a show at Pendleton the like of which was never seen on land or sea.

First of all, it was a terrible ball club. On any given day

42

it was by no means certain that nine players would show up. After each game the King would hold court, sitting with his players at a long, white table that groaned with food and drink. Far into the night the players would remain to talk over each game with their admirers.

This bacchanal took place on every day but Sunday, for after the Sabbath games, the Killers would all submit to arrest, departing for the police station as a unit to be fined two dollars each for "playing baseball on Sunday," a violation of a newly created city ordinance. Then they would be released for another week, whereupon the whole business would be repeated.

The chief pitcher on the club was Ed Crane, a veteran of service with the Metropolitans who was known as Cannonball. He was one of the fastest pitchers of his time, and he also held the record for long-distance throwing. Cannonball Crane could really pitch, and he also met with the King's requirements for off-the-field endeavor. He was a prodigious eater, his favorite snack consisting of an order of a dozen soft-boiled eggs served in a soup bowl, which he liked to top off with an order of two dozen clams.

The Cannonball wasn't the only pitcher, however. Though it was customary at the time for two or three men to pitch all the club's games, any player on Kelly's Killers could pitch if he so desired. Frequently during the course of a game an outfielder would decide he'd like to pitch, and would trot in from his position to take the mound. King Kelly would always oblige, and welcome the new hurler to the box. A study of the box scores shows that eleven different players acted as pitchers for the Killers, including the King himself.

The informality about pitching extended to the other positions. Every man on the club played wherever he felt like playing. Or if he didn't feel like playing at all, he didn't play. During the course of the season seven men appeared in only one game each and were never heard from afterward. It is quite possible that one game with the Killers was more than enough.

Naturally, such a team was unable to win with any degree

43

of frequency. But there was never a team on earth to whom winning was less important.

Appropriately enough, the first game of the season, played on April 8 between the Killers and the St. Louis Browns, ended in a fist fight and a forfeit, the umpires awarding the game to the Browns. That preview of things to come steamed up the populace, and a conference between Kelly and the Browns the next day resulted in the game's being thrown out of the records entirely.

The season was opened all over again on April 10 with the Killers winning, 11 to 9. Such a score was typical. During the course of the year the Killers defeated Philadelphia, 21 to 16, lost to the Browns, 20 to 12, to Boston, 20 to 5, and triumphed over Washington, 17 to 2. Such were the scores of the games of the Killers.

But by August it was apparent that the Killers, with all their antics, could not compete with the National League club. In the first place, the location of the park was poor, preventing the fans from gaining easy access to their favorites. Anyone traveling to Pendleton was apt not to return until the following day, and even by 1891 business had exerted enough pressure upon most to preclude such excursions as a steady diet. For another thing, the regular Sunday ritual of submitting to arrest became tiresome to many of the players, and they began to yearn to play elsewhere. And finally, the stock setup was a bad one, with Ed Renau being just a front for St. Louis interests.

In the middle of August, almost without warning, the American Association transferred the franchise to Milwaukee, where the players finished the year. That winter the American Association expired after ten years of operation.

King Kelly himself did not have much longer to go. He moved to Boston of the National League in 1892 and played with New York in 1893. After that he went into vaudeville, for Kelly was still King. Visiting players used to see him in the East in the summer of 1894. He was still a gay figure in the cafés, but his health was failing and the strain was beginning to tell. Fortunately he died before he was to know complete poverty and oblivion, succumbing to pneumonia in November 1894. A plaque to his prowess is at the Cooperstown museum. His body lies in a little plot at the Elks Lot, Mount Hope Cemetery, Forest Hills, Massachusetts.

☸ 5 ☸

THE YOUNG ROMAN

1

When the American Association dissolved after ten years of existence following the season of 1891, the National League, once more having survived competitive difficulties, and with the field to itself, decided to expand to twelve clubs. Teams from St. Louis, Washington, Baltimore, and Louisville joined the eight clubs that had composed the circuit in 1891. The league also increased its schedule from 140 to 154 games, the number that still constitutes the season's total. And, for the first and only time in its history, the league voted to have a split season, the first half to end on July 15, the second half to terminate in late October.

John T. Brush, after a year of watching Tom Loftus struggle to maintain order among his players, fired the manager and brought to Cincinnati Charlie Comiskey, the famous first baseman of Chris von der Ahe's Browns. He also added to the front office Frank Carter Bancroft, a veteran showman and practical baseball man who had managed Providence in the National League, and who had come to Cincinnati originally the year before to handle the perplexing business affairs of Kelly's Killers. Bancroft, who was to devote the remainder of his life to the Reds, a span of activity that covered three decades, was one of the game's first great promoters. He is supposed to have arranged the first wedding at home plate, and he devised numerous ways and means of enticing customers with cash through the turnstiles. He was largely responsible for building up Cincinnati's great opening-day tradition, with a packed grandstand being a certainty at each year's inaugural, regardless of the team's finish the season before.

By hiring Bancroft to handle the business details and luring Comiskey to the city as manager, Brush was able to spend most of his time at Indianapolis, worrying about his clothing business.

Comiskey, the first major-league player to become a major-league magnate, was one of the game's great builders. To him is credited the revolutionary idea of having the first baseman play away from the bag, the invention of the coaching box, and the double umpire system.

When the modern fan looks at the playing field, he may well wonder why the coaches are restricted to small spaces marked by chalk lines on either side of first and third bases. The reason is that prior to Comiskey's intervention, coaches used to plant themselves on either side of the visiting catcher, commenting audibly on his ancestry, personal habits, and various other aspects of his character. Comiskey himself was one of the best hecklers in the business, rising to heights of imaginative abuse that were picturesque even in that picturesque era. But he abandoned it for the good of the game, and then brought about introduction of the rule that now requires the coaches to spew their venom from afar.

Opinion is divided on the subject of what sort of club official John T. Brush was. Although he spent a good deal of his time devoting himself to business affairs outside of baseball, he was by no means a novice at the game. He had fostered the salary rule that led to the Brotherhood War of 1890, when he was the controlling head of the Indianapolis team, and he was supreme as a politician. He had a tendency to lop off players' salaries to an extreme degree, thereby setting a pattern for many who followed him in the profes-

46

sion. Brush never won the sympathy of the public, but Comiskey found him an amiable employer.

For the 1892 season, Comiskey installed himself at first base, supplanting the veteran Long John Reilly. McPhee and Latham remained as infield holdovers, as did Shortstop George (Germany) Smith, who had taken Ollie Beard's job in 1891 and who was the only prominent player in the league from the old Altoona, Union Association, club.

The outfield was manned by Curt Welch, Bug Holliday, and Tip O'Neill, the last-named having the reputation of being something of a wit. It was O'Neill who was supposed to have been the hero of this little conversation with a clergyman he encountered on a stroll one Sunday morning:

"Are you goin' to the game today, Reverend?" asked O'Neill.

"No," replied the minister. "I don't go to baseball games on Sunday. Sunday is my busiest day."

"I know," said Tip. "It's my busiest day too."

"Yes," said the pastor. "But I'm in the right field."

"So am I," said Tip. "Ain't that sun terrible?"

Comiskey tried out an even fifteen pitchers during his first summer at the Rhine, or an odd fifteen, if you will. Three of them—Tony Mullane, Frank Dwyer, and Elton (Icebox) Chamberlain—had conspicuous success. Chamberlain's nickname was derived from his austere calm in the face of all hostility on the part of the enemy. Sports writers of that era seem to have bestowed on the athletes a happier nomenclature than is used at present. At least, there is no major-league player of the present called anything half so interesting as an icebox. The other dozen pitchers were of little moment, though one of them, George Earl Hemming, had perhaps the strangest winter occupation of any player who ever lived. He was a cook at an insane asylum.

Like the girl in the nursery rhyme, when the Reds of 1892 were good, they were very, very good, and when they were bad, they were horrid. Their play from the outset was streaky. But on April 24, a Sunday game with St. Louis drew 15,948 fans, a Cincinnati attendance record up to the

47

time. The patrons enjoyed that Sabbath afternoon, too, as Tony Mullane poured it on the Browns, winning 10 to 2.

A few weeks later, on May 6, to be exact, one of the strangest games in history came up. During the course of years ball games have been interfered with by all sorts of freakish activity on the part of the elements. Wind, rain, snow, darkness, fire, and various other vagaries of nature have played their part in halting the national game. But on the afternoon of May 6, 1892, a National League game between the Reds and Boston was called because of the sun. What's more, players and fans alike were unanimous in praising the umpire for his decision.

Jack Sheridan of California was the umpire in question. The game was a spine-tingling one, with both Boston and the Reds being mowed down in order by the respective pitchers, Icebox Chamberlain of the Reds and the veteran John Clarkson of the Beantowners. In the fourteenth inning the game was still scoreless, and interest was at a fever pitch.

At this point the sun assumed an angle that blinded pitcher and hitter alike. In those days home plate was located in the extreme right-field corner of what is now called Crosley Field. The umpire, sizing up the situation, called the whole thing off.

"Mr. Sheridan has distinguished himself," commented the *Enquirer* the next day. "His decision, while it may appear ridiculous on the face of it, was, strange to relate, a just and sensible one."

But an even more remarkable game occurred in the month to follow. At this time the longest contest in league history had been a 1-to-0 affair between Providence and Detroit back in 1882. It had gone eighteen innings, the length of two ordinary games, and the general feeling was that never again would two clubs battle for so long a time.

But on June 20, Tony Mullane and Addison Gumbert of Anson's Chicago club, a great-uncle of Harry Gumbert who pitched for the Reds in the 1940's, hooked up in a pitching duel that extended twenty frames before the umpires called it a tie, 7 to 7, to allow Chicago to catch a

48

train. Since that time, of course, several games of longer duration have been run off, with the prize being the famed twenty-six-inning tie between Brooklyn and Boston in 1920, with two pitchers, Leon Cadore and Joe Oeschger, going all the way, and then amounting to little thereafter.

At the Cincinnati-Chicago tilt, business manager Frank Bancroft brooded as the nineteenth inning of play began. He had been involved in the Providence-Detroit brawl when the record for longevity had been set at eighteen rounds, and he was anxious for the mark to stand.

"What are you worried about, Banny?" asked President Brush, who was sitting in the same box. "Now you will exceed your old record. You will have had a part in both games."

"By gosh, that's right," Bancroft replied, and thereafter he was happy.

When the first half of the season ended, the Reds found themselves fourth among the twelve clubs in the awkward, unwieldy loop, with 44 wins and 31 defeats. Boston and Brooklyn had fought it out for the lead, the Massachusetts club finishing a game ahead of the Flatbushers, with Philadelphia third.

But as the second half got under way, the team began to lose with more frequency. A horrible rout in late July in which Philadelphia trimmed the Reds, 26 to 6, drove away the customers, and after that the club barely played .500 ball. In the last half they won 38 and lost 37, finishing eighth, and when the standings for the two halves were merged, the Reds had a full-season record that placed them fifth, with 82 won and 68 lost.

On the last day of the season, October 15, the Reds were scheduled to meet Pittsburgh. Absolutely nothing was at stake, the Pirates being behind the Reds in the standings, though having a good team with such players as George Van Haltren, Jake Beckley, Foghorn Miller, and a young catcher by the name of Connie Mack in their line-up.

Into the Cincinnati clubhouse before the game strolled a country bumpkin by the name of Charles L. (Bumpus)

Jones, a youth from Xenia, Ohio, who announced that he was a pitcher.

"All right," said Charlie Comiskey. "If you're a pitcher, we'll find it out this afternoon. I'm letting you start against Pittsburgh."

Baseball at the time was leisurely conducted, and Bumpus was sent to the slab without the formality of a contract. In fact, he wasn't even paid for his services.

Making his first start in the majors under such circumstances might seem to be a handicap, but all Bumpus Jones did was let the Pittsburgh club down without a single hit.

Throughout the years, the Reds have produced their share of no-hit pitchers. Ted Breitenstein, Noodles Hahn, Fred Toney, Hod Eller, Johnny Vander Meer, Clyde Shoun, and Ewell Blackwell all have hit the pitching jackpot. But Bumpus was the first.

Sad to relate, when the 1893 season began, Jones failed to exert such talent. To pitch a no-hit game takes a great deal of luck in addition to skill, and Bumpus had his share of both on that chill October afternoon in 1892. But he never won another game in the major leagues. Batted out in five straight engagements in the early part of the 1893 season, Jones drifted off and was never seen again in Redleg livery.

2

Tacky Tom Parrott, a young pitcher who disturbed the slumber of contemporaries at his boardinghouse by playing the cornet and whose greatest delight was to ride to the park on his bicycle, was the only noteworthy addition to the Reds in 1893. The club unfortunately continued its policy of signing players who had seen their greatest glory elsewhere. Possibly believing that they still possessed their cunning, Comiskey in 1893 added such once fine athletes as pitchers Charles (Silver) King and Parisian Bob Caruthers and outfielder Frank (Piggy) Ward. None of these players produced, and the Reds slumped to sixth; still in the first division, to be sure, but definitely border line.

Again in 1894 the decline continued, with William

(Dummy) Hoy, a deaf outfielder who was to have a remarkable career in four major leagues before he finally cast his glove aside, the only addition worth mentioning. The 1894 club slumped into a tie for ninth place with St. Louis, each team winning 56 and losing 76, although the record books, which are not always to be relied on, show the Reds tenth, with 54 wins and 75 reverses.

It can be seen that Comiskey's last two years in Cincinnati, 1893 and 1894, were not particularly distinguished. Important things were happening in the Queen City, but instead of occurring on the playing field, they were going on behind the scenes.

Comiskey had met a young sports writer of the *Cincinnati Commercial-Gazette*, a man named Byron Bancroft Johnson, a fellow with huge ambitions and a thorough knowledge of baseball. Comiskey and Johnson had formed a mutual-admiration society that grew despite Johnson's hatred of Comiskey's employer, John T. Brush. Johnson did a thorough job of sniping at Brush in his column, referring to the Redleg official as a past master of parsimony and a representative of interests best divorced from baseball. The antipathy of Johnson and Brush for each other was as strong as the friendship between Johnson and Comiskey, so they made a strange trio.

At about this time there was founded the Western League, soon to become one of the finest minor circuits in the country. The Western League was in need of a president. Comiskey, always in touch with the baseball situation on a national basis, suggested to the influential Brush that Ban Johnson might be just the man for the job.

This placed Brush in a peculiar position. He saw that if he obtained the presidency of the Western for Johnson, he would be rid of the pest once and for all. But he also saw that by helping Johnson to a position of such esteem, he would be lending a helping hand to a mortal enemy. What he decided in the matter will never be known, as he missed the train that was to take him to the meeting at which the decision was made. But the other delegates, assuming that

51

Brush echoed Comiskey's sentiments, elected Johnson president and thus inaugurated the career of one of the most forceful personalities to appear on the baseball scene.

Comiskey was directly involved in the launching of the Western League. Prior to this time, club owners in southern cities had complained to Charlie about the difficulties encountered in their own territory, and Comiskey pointed out that cities in the northwest were hungry for baseball. The southern owners then moved their franchises northward and formed the circuit that Johnson was to pilot.

Through 1894, Comiskey waited patiently for his contract with Brush as manager of the Reds to expire. As soon as the season was over, he purchased a franchise that he moved to St. Paul, and he and Ban Johnson began collaborating on an expansion program for the Western League that eventually brought about the birth of the American League as a major circuit. It is noteworthy that the idea for the American League was actually conceived in Cincinnati, and that a Cincinnati man was to become its most dynamic leader.

The infant baseball, which grew to have adolescent mishaps at the time of the Union Association squabble and later of the Brotherhood War, finally achieved manhood at the time of the American League's founding at the turn of the century. Since that time, major-league baseball has been conducted on a sound, adult basis, with two eight-club circuits battling each other for attendance with all the prowess of titans in their prime.

⊗ **6** ⊗

BUCK EWING AND THE
YEARS OF ALMOST

1

The passing of Charlie Comiskey and Ban Johnson from the Cincinnati scene following the season of 1894 meant that John T. Brush had lost a manager and a critic. The manager had to be replaced. The departure of the two great personalities also meant that Brush would have to devote his full time to the affairs of the Cincinnati baseball club, aided by his faithful business manager, Frank Bancroft.

First order of business was the naming of a new manager, Buck Ewing. It was an excellent selection for various reasons. First of all, Ewing was the most famous catcher of his day and a native of Cincinnati, the greatest player the city had ever produced. But oddly enough, Cincinnatians had rarely seen him play until recent years. All the time that the Reds were in the American Association, Buck was in the National League. From 1883 to 1889 he had been captain and catcher of the New York club, and in 1890 he managed the New York team in the Players' League. He spent 1891 and 1892 with New York of the National League, then passed the next two campaigns with Cleveland.

Though known best for his work as a catcher, Ewing could also play first base, another reason why his selection as manager was good, as it enabled him to take over the first-base position abandoned by Charlie Comiskey.

The average fan of today, if asked to select the greatest

53

catcher of all time, would probably select Bill Dickey or Gabby Hartnett or Mickey Cochrane. A few generations ago the answer would have been Johnny Kling or Roger Bresnahan. But fifty years ago there was only one answer, Buck Ewing.

The chief reason why Ewing's work was so unanimously admired was his remarkable throwing arm, which was well-nigh perfect. Seldom did runners try to steal on him, and more rarely did they succeed. He was the first receiver to crouch. As a batsman, Buck was outstanding, and he left an all-time major-league average of .311 for eighteen years in the big show. Connie Mack, when asked to name the greatest catcher he has ever seen, unhesitatingly selects Ewing.

Buck was a jollier of umpires. He never complained about a decision, feeling that he could obtain his share of the breaks by being nice to the arbiters. This was a policy unheard of at the time, and it paid off.

"You're right on that one," Buck would say to the umpire, as a ball was called. "You saw that one right. It was just off the plate." Being human, the umpire would appreciate this example of Buck's wisdom, and chances are the next close one would be called in Ewing's favor.

The full name of the Redleg manager was William Ewing, and his nickname of Buck was a relic of childhood. Sports writers have sometimes listed him as William Buckingham Ewing, but though the middle name sounds elegant, it was merely a fertile stroke of a writer's pen and had no basis in fact. Buck had no middle name. Sports writers of that era frequently coined middle names for the athletes out of the thin air, a practice that makes it extremely difficult for present-day delvers who want to know the correct nomenclature.

It is also commonly believed that Ewing was born at Cincinnati, but actually he first opened his eyes in a little hamlet called Hoaglands, Ohio, a few miles from Hillsboro. At an early age, though, the Ewing family moved to Cincinnati, and Buck played his first baseball on the Queen City's sand lots. He caught for the Mohawk Browns, a well-known

54

amateur team, in 1879, and launched his major-league career with Troy of the National League in 1880, before moving on to New York.

In preparing for the 1895 season, Ewing convinced John Brush that it would be wise to take the club on a spring training trip. This was an idea that seemed to be growing. Cap Anson, as manager of the old Chicago White Stockings, was the first manager to take his club south prior to the start of the season. In order to boil out the athletes after a winter of elbow-bending and very little other muscular activity, Anson took his nine to Hot Springs.

By 1895 other clubs had seen the beneficial results of such preseason excursions, and spring training was becoming an established part of the game. Comiskey's Reds had prepared for each season by a week or so of ball-tossing at the home park. But in 1895, under Buck Ewing, the club went south for the first time, training at Mobile, Alabama.

Ewing supplanted Comiskey at first base, and the rest of the infield—Bid McPhee, Germany Smith, and Arlie Latham —remained the same. It was the fifth consecutive year that McPhee, Smith, and Latham had manned the Red infield. Dummy Hoy and Bug Holliday also remained to play the outfield, but the third outfielder of 1894, Jimmy Canavan, was replaced by Charles (Dusty) Miller, a newcomer from Oil City, Pennsylvania.

Hoy, a mute, was a native Ohioan, having been born near Findlay in 1865. He started his professional career twenty-one years later at Oshkosh, Wisconsin, where he swears he once made a catch in the outfield by jumping on the back of a horse and chasing down the ball with the aid of his steed. He also once threw out three runners at home plate in a single game. Hoy played in four major leagues, the National and Players' Leagues, the American Association, and finally the American League, where he ended his career with the Chicago White Sox in 1901. He was a left-handed hitter and a little fellow, standing only five feet six. After his career had been completed he made his home in Cincinnati, and in 1947, at the age of eighty-two, he was still active in the organization of Ball Players of Yesterday, the city's club of former major-leaguers.

It was thought that the trio of Hoy, Holliday, and Miller would assure the Reds of having a capable outer works, but Ewing had to revise his plans early in the year when Holliday, who was expected to be the leading hitter on the team, suffered an attack of appendicitis, which put him out for the year.

Holliday's appendicitis, which, according to the superstition of the era, was attributed to the eating of fruit seeds, caused a mounting wave of rumor to the effect that Bug had died. This is a phenomenon that continues to this day. Periodically, like the visitation of a swarm of locusts, an unfounded rumor will spread that a certain player has died, tying up telephone communications at the ball-club office and at the city's newspaper switchboards for hours. In the case of Holliday, however, there was some basis for fear, for Bug very nearly passed out of the picture.

Holliday was replaced by Eddie Burke of Northumberland, Pennsylvania, and although the latter was not the hitter Holliday was, he did an adequte job as a fill-in.

The pitchers Ewing relied on chiefly in his first season were Frank Dwyer and Tom Parrott, holdovers from the Comiskey administration, Billy Rhines, who returned to the team from exile in Pittsburgh and soon regained his winning form, and Frank Foreman, who had appeared briefly for the Reds under Tom Loftus in 1890. It was an experienced staff quite capable of steady hurling. The catcher was Harry (Farmer) Vaughn, also a Comiskey holdover and a fellow who could help out on occasion at first base.

In early May the club pieced together ten successive wins, the tenth victory sending the team into first place, but they slid back to second the next day as Rhines got trimmed by the Phils, and they never regained the lead. Their decline after that was gradual but steady, the team dropping one notch lower every few weeks, drifting downward through the twelve-club league.

But their fine start assured them of a better record than

Comiskey's last team, and they eventually landed in eighth place, with 66 wins and 64 defeats, an improvement over 1894 of eleven full games. Dusty Miller, the new outfielder, led the club at bat with a .329 mark, and Ewing, Vaughn, and Latham were all over .300. Rhines won 19 games while dropping 10. Dwyer had a record of 18 and 15, but Parrott was a disappointment, winning 11 while suffering 19 reverses.

2

Ewing determined that since the club as constituted could not seem to win with regularity, numerous changes would have to be made if the team were to hold its following in 1896. As a result, Ewing and Brush completed the first big deal ever made by the Reds. Arlie Latham, Tom Parrott, and a catcher named Morgan Murphy were shipped to St. Louis in exchange for pitcher Philip (Red) Ehret and catcher Henry (Heinie) Peitz. It was a deal that worked out advantageously. To replace Latham at third base Ewing signed Charlie Irwin of Sheffield, Illinois, who had spent two years with the Chicago club. Ehret more than made up for the loss of Parrott, so the strong pitching staff remained intact.

It was at this time in National League history that the famous Baltimore Orioles were at their height. Storming and blustering their way through the league, flashing their spikes and spewing abuse at all, they had won pennants in 1894 and 1895, and were determined to make it three in a row in 1896. Managed by Ned Hanlon, the Orioles were the most famous team of the nineties, and in 1896 they were at their best. Their infield of Jack Doyle, Henry Reitz, Hughie Jennings, and John McGraw was the finest ever seen up to that time. Willie Keeler, Joe Kelley, and Steve Brodie gave them a fearsome outfield. Wilbert Robinson, their catcher, superbly handled the fine pitching of Arlie Pond, John McMahon, and Bill Hoffer.

Cleveland had finished second to the Orioles in 1895, and was expected to give them their greatest opposition again in 1896. The Spiders, as the Cleveland club was then called, had the finest pitcher in baseball in Cy Young and a redoubtable slugger in Jess Burkett.

Faced by that sort of opposition, Buck Ewing's Reds weren't expected to fare so well, even though the big deal with St. Louis had strengthened the team. But the Reds were the surprise of the league.

In May, Cincinnati actually spent three days in first place, the Orioles biding their time in second and the Spiders a menacing third. The three clubs seesawed back and forth in June. Starting on June 24, the Red pitchers began working with cunning consistency, pitching complete games in twenty-three consecutive contests, the work being shared by Dwyer, Ehret, Foreman, and a rookie, Chauncey Fisher.

When Frank Dwyer defeated Washington on July 11 for the club's seventh straight victory, the Reds surged into first place once more, and when Ehret, Foreman, and Fisher then trounced Brooklyn three in a row, the winning streak had reached ten straight, and the rooters were in a fury of ecstasy.

It was then that haughty Baltimore came to the Rhine, determined to dispose of the upstart Reds, but in the first contest Dwyer shut them out, 5 to 0, in a duel with John McMahon, running the winning skein to eleven. The next day Baltimore broke the streak and evened the series behind the clever hurling of George Hemming, our old friend who spent his winters cooking for the lunatics.

Then the series closed on Sunday, July 19, before the biggest crowd that had ever seen a game in Cincinnati up to that time, with 24,944 laying it on the line to watch the fireworks. But it was a saddened throng that watched the vicious Orioles knock Foreman from the box and continue the assault against Fisher, winning 14 to 6.

That series should have been the tip-off, but the Reds hung on doggedly, resuming their winning ways against New York and Boston, and then knocking down Cleveland three times, beating the great Cy Young twice. But the Orioles were not to be denied. They took first place on August 6 and never gave up the lead thereafter, finishing the year with 90 wins and 39 losses, the best record they had ever made, as they won their third pennant in a row.

Cleveland then also passed the Reds in September, eliminating Cincinnati from the Temple Cup series, forerunner of the World Series, which called for a postseason set of games between the clubs that finished first and second.

But the Reds ended up in third, with 77 wins and 50 defeats for a percentage of .606, the highest mark achieved by the club since 1878, when Will White had pitched them into second place over the short route of a sixty-game schedule.

Frank Dwyer finished the season with 25 victories and 11 setbacks, and Ehret won 18 and lost 15. Eddie Burke hit .342, Dusty Miller .318, and Dummy Hoy .296, the three gardeners stealing 185 bases between them. But still the Reds were outclassed by the soaring Orioles and treacherous Spiders.

3

When Heinie Peitz, the Cincinnati catcher, had played at St. Louis for three years prior to joining the Reds, he had been part of a famous battery, Breitenstein and Peitz, that was known to the adoring fans as the Pretzel Battery. And so, when the Reds acquired Theodore Breitenstein from St. Louis for 1897 delivery, the Pretzel Battery was reunited.

Actually, another pitcher and catcher had been known as the Pretzel Battery years earlier. Charlie Getzein, a pitcher with Detroit of the National League, and his catcher, Charlie Ganzel, were called that as early as 1886. But the pair that will always be remembered as the pretzel duo was the Breitenstein and Peitz combination.

Peitz always maintained that the name originated at the Golden Lion saloon in St. Louis. After a game at the Mound City one day, Breitenstein and Peitz were at the Golden Lion, sitting in a back room and cooling off in an appropriate manner. On a table before them sat a bowl of pretzels. A fan strolled in, saw who was sitting in the back room, and shouted to John Peckington, the proprietor, and to the customers at the bar, "Hey, look who's back there. It's that pretzel battery, Breitenstein and Peitz."

The name caught on, and it was the Pretzel Battery thereafter.

Frank Foreman was let out to make room for Breitenstein, who joined the other regular pitchers, Frank Dwyer, Billy Rhines, and Red Ehret.

In another move that was destined to strengthen the club for 1897, shortstop Germany Smith, who had been a regular for the Reds for six seasons but who had reached the age of thirty-four, was traded to Brooklyn for another shortstop, Tommy Corcoran, who was six years younger.

First base was a problem, since Buck Ewing had just about reached the end of his playing days, and decided to retire. He appeared in only one game that season, his last appearance in a major-league box score. Farmer Vaughn, the catcher, was shifted to the base to start the season, but Farmer was a catcher by trade and not an adequate replacement for Ewing at first base. The season wasn't very old when Ewing found the first baseman he wanted, Jake Beckley, of the New York club. His purchase was arranged, and Beckley became a Red.

Beckley was a fine hitter, one of the most dangerous in the league. He had come to the circuit with Pittsburgh in 1888, and established himself immediately by hitting .342. He remained in the National League until 1907, hitting more than .300 in 13 of his 20 seasons. But Jake had had a bad year at the plate in 1896, hitting only .268 for Pittsburgh and New York. It was this fact that made his purchase possible.

Though a fine hitter, Jake left much to be desired afield. He was rather clumsy and had a notoriously bad throwing arm. It was his poor arm that made possible one of the strangest plays an infielder ever participated in.

Tommy Leach, the great Pittsburgh outfielder, once hit a ball down to Beckley on the ground, and Jake prepared to make the toss to the pitcher covering first. The throw was so poor that it rolled past the pitcher into foul territory. Jake ran over and recovered the ball on the rebound, but by this time Leach was almost at third base. Jake sized the situation up correctly and realized that Leach would try to score, thereby making the equivalent of a home run on his infield roller. And with his bad arm, Beckley was in no position to throw him out at the plate. So he started running home with the ball, arriving there just as Leach did, and in a final desperate flying leap, tagged him out. Leach was not only retired, he suffered three fractured ribs.

That's the way Jake Beckley played first base. But how he could hit!

The opportunity for the Reds in 1897 was ideal, because the Orioles had passed their peak, and Cleveland was also on the decline. But a new power was appearing in the league, Frank Selee's Boston team.

Boston in 1897 had a veteran team that boasted such famous names as Hugh Duffy, Billy Hamilton, Bobby Lowe, Herman Long, Fred Tenney, Jimmy Collins, Kid Nichols, Marty Bergen, and Charlie Getzein.

The Reds had a record of 25 victories and 13 defeats and were by far the best of the western clubs when they first visited the Hub. But Boston won three straight games, Kid Nichols defeating Billy Rhines, Fred Klobedanz trouncing Frank Dwyer, and Ed Lewis besting Red Ehret. The Reds went west again and continued to win, but they knew that they had met their match in the team from Massachusetts.

When the Beantowners came to Cincinnati in July, they won 2 out of 3, once more establishing their superiority. After that, it was a question of whether the Reds could finish second. But they couldn't, for Baltimore still had enough to pass them, and so did New York. The Reds ended up in fourth place, with 76 wins and 56 defeats, the best record made by any of the league's six western teams.

Little of importance happened to the Reds that year once their level was determined. On September 18 they ran into Cy Young at his greatest in a contest at Cleveland and were the victims of a no-hitter. Eight days later, at St. Louis, Jake Beckley had one of his great days at bat and connected for three home runs in a single game, the first Red to achieve that particular feat.

And also in St. Louis, on September 27, the Reds lost a

61

game to the Browns for the first time in more than two years. Later in their respective careers, St. Louis found an easy mark in Cincinnati. But from September 25, 1895, when Breitenstein pitched the Browns to a 5-to-4 decision over Tom Parrott, until September 27, 1897, when Breitenstein, by now with the Reds, lost by the same score to Francis Donahue, the Reds had beaten the Browns twenty-three times in a row.

Beckley led the team at bat with a mark of .336. The always dependable Dusty Miller hit .317, and Bid McPhee was right around there with a .307 mark for his sixteenth season with the club. Ted Breitenstein paced the staff of hurlers with 23 wins and 11 defeats, and Billy Rhines, pitching in Cincinnati for the last time, won 21 and dropped 15.

Ewing's team was consistently good, but just not good enough.

4

Previous to Ewing, no Cincinnati manager had ever lasted with the team for more than three years. Gustavus Heinrich Schmelz had piloted the American Association club for three campaigns, and Charlie Comiskey had spent a similar period of time with the city's National League entry. But three years seemed to be the limit. John Brush, however, felt that Buck had done as well with the reins as any other pilot might, so Ewing was retained for 1898.

In a move to obtain pitching strength, Dummy Hoy and Red Ehret were sent to Louisville for a moundsman named Bill Hill. Another pitcher, Emerson (Pink) Hawley, came to the team from Pittsburgh, along with outfielder Elmer Smith for Billy Rhines and a catcher, William (Pop) Schriver. Smith was the same man who had pitched for the American Association Reds, but he was by this time an outfielder.

Hawley was a native of Beaver Dam, Wisconsin, where he had been born on December 5, 1872. He had had a twin brother, and to distinguish the pair, the parents had pinned a pink ribbon on one child and a blue one on the other. It was Pink who became a major-league pitcher, Blue following other pursuits. The Reds also brought several promising players up from the minor leagues, including infielder Harry Steinfeldt, outfielder Bob Wood, and outfielder Algie McBride, who had had a previous trial with Chicago. The season was just a week old when Ted Breitenstein pitched a no-hit game against Pittsburgh, the Reds winning, 11 to 0. Cincinnati made one error and Breitenstein passed one batter. Peitz was behind the bat, of course, the Pretzel Battery functioning with precision. It was the first no-hitter for the team since Bumpus Jones pitched one as a raw recruit on the last day of the 1892 season.

Hawley's early-season pitching was also more than anyone could have hoped. Pink won his first nine games, defeating Pittsburgh twice and seven other clubs once each. He was finally defeated by Vic Willis of Boston.

The other pitchers didn't work out so well. Hill was a distinct disappointment, and Dwyer, who had done such fine work for the club ever since coming to Cincinnati with Kelly's Killers in 1891, was no longer able to pitch as frequently as before, though he was still effective when called upon.

It was the old story of not being able to beat Baltimore, Boston, and New York. The Reds had a decisive margin over the other eight clubs, but were unable to beat the top three. Selee's fine Boston club rolled on to its second pennant in a row, winning 102 and losing 47 games. Baltimore was second with a 96 and 53 record, and the Reds were third with 92 and 60. It was another year of almost!

Buck Ewing managed the Reds for the fifth and last time in 1899. The club that had hung on so gamely against Baltimore and Boston had begun to show signs of wear and tear.

One player who saved the team from the ignominy of a second-division finish was a rookie southpaw, Frank (Noodles) Hahn. A native of Nashville, Tennessee, Hahn was only twenty when he joined the club in 1899, but from the outset he demonstrated he was a major-leaguer. He won his first three starts, dropped his next three, triumphed in his next five, lost one, then reeled off seven victories in a row, and

63

continued to pitch consistently, ending the year with 23 wins against 8 defeats and finishing 32 of the 34 games he started. Noodles was a life-saver, because Pink Hawley, after his fine freshman year with the club, suffered a disastrous season, winning 14 and losing 16.

Another player who came to the majors with the Reds during that 1899 season was a nineteen-year-old rookie outfielder who promised to be one of the greatest hitters the game had ever known. His name was Sam Crawford, Samuel Earl Crawford, to be exact, and he came from the unlikely town of Wahoo, Nebraska. Son of the village barber, Sam was a big fellow, possessed of tremendous hands and feet. It took him only four months to reach the big league, once he had started as a professional. Early in the 1899 season he reported to the Chatham, Ontario, club of the Canadian League, and soon was promoted to Grand Rapids of the Western League, where the Reds first spied him. Crawford reached Cincinnati on September 10, with the team scheduled to play a freak double-header, meeting Cleveland in the first game and Louisville in the second.

Cleveland in 1899 had the saddest team that ever played a major-league schedule. That can be stated without incurring a dispute, because the club won 20 games and lost 134, spending most of the season on the road after they abandoned any idea of drawing people to the games in Cleveland. So, for the rest of the year, they swung around the loop like some sad, lost planet meandering around the solar system. The Reds, always delighted to play the poor Cleveland orphans, defeated them every time they faced them, fourteen times in all.

In the first game that day against Cleveland, Crawford made two hits off Harry Colliflower, and in the nightcap against Louisville, added three more against Bert Cunningham. He was given a regular outfield position on the strength of that performance and was able to get into thirty-one games before the season ended, making 39 hits in 127 times at bat, for an average of .308.

As the end of the year approached, the venerable Bid

McPhee announced that he was closing his career and would not take the field again in 1900. This was understandable, for Bid had been on the job continuously since 1882, playing with the Reds in both the Association and the league, and outliving any number of managerial changes. Still, McPhee remained a capable player. He hit .283 in 1899, a mark that exceeded his lifetime average, and he was still able to field his position with consummate skill.

The fans of Cincinnati, upon learning of Bid's threatened retirement, begged the club to induce the veteran to reconsider. Why, Bid was as much a part of Cincinnati as the Mohawk Canal! To have anyone else play the keystone was unthinkable.

"But I know what I'm doing," McPhee said. "The fans are never going to have a chance to urge that I be benched, or traded, or asked to retire. I'm going out while I can still play ball."

So he did. And with the departing McPhee went Buck Ewing, after five seasons of success, but still seasons of disappointment, because though the Reds finished in the first division the last four years of his reign, they never reached the top. And Cincinnati, which hadn't won a flag since 1882, was getting the pennant itch. The Reds of 1899 finished sixth, with 83 wins and 67 defeats.

⊗ 7 ⊗

JOHN T. BRUSHED OFF

1

After eight years of operating as a twelve-club league, the National in 1900 abandoned the franchises in Louisville, Cleveland, Washington, and Baltimore, and reduced to an eight-team circuit, the same eight teams that have carried on without a hitch to the present time. The reduction made for a better pennant race. It's bad enough to finish eighth today. To have finished eleventh or twelfth must have been frightful. The Reds did not do badly in the old twelve-club loop, though, finishing in the first division in six of the eight years.

Having decided not to renew Buck Ewing's contract as manager, John Brush, by way of preparing for his tenth season as president of the team, offered the post to Bob Allen, a major-league shortstop and catcher who had won a pennant managing Indianapolis of the Western League in 1899.

Allen was a native of Marion, Ohio, where he grew up as a childhood friend of Warren G. Harding. The son of a banker, Allen demonstrated a talent for business, and long after his major-league days were done he was famous as a club owner in the Southern Association. Originally Bob was a pitcher, his battery mate at Mansfield, where he started playing in 1887, being the famous Ed Delehanty. Allen next went to Kalamazoo, where he was converted into a shortstop. He served as playing manager of Davenport in 1889, and joined the Phils in 1890. He remained with that team until

1897, though he was out of the game for two years after being struck over the eye with a pitch in 1894.

He was a remarkable fielder, and in 1892 he accepted 955 chances at short, a National League record that stood until 1914, when Rabbit Maranville of the Braves handled 981.

Although Allen remained at Cincinnati only for the 1900 season, he developed a great affection for the Reds and became quite a student of their history. Late in his life, after the Cooperstown museum was built, he publicly deplored the omission of Harry Wright as a Hall of Fame candidate.

"If there is one objection I have to make about baseball," Allen stated, "it is that Harry Wright is not in the Hall of Fame. He managed the first and only unbeaten baseball team in history in 1869. That feat was the thing that brought baseball leagues into being and fostered the keen competition that has come down through the years. Harry Wright is the father of professional baseball."

Allen took his club to train at New Orleans. He went along with most of the players Ewing had left him, Heinie Peitz behind the bat, and Jake Beckley, Tommy Corcoran, and Charlie Irwin in the infield. The one spot that had to be filled was second base, and to replace Bid McPhee, Allen obtained Joe Quinn, a keystoner who had been born at Queensland, Australia, an odd place for a player to originate. Sam Crawford was expected to strengthen the outfield, and Jimmy Barrett and Algie McBride were holdovers. Two new pitchers, Ed Scott and Doc Newton, bolstered the staff that included Noodles Hahn, Ted Breitenstein, and Bill Phillips.

Allen's club hit well, but the fielding was spotty and the pitching bogged down, only Hahn continuing his good work of the year before. The team indulged in many high-scoring games, their defense not being adequate to stop the enemy from scoring. Often the Reds would tally enough runs to win, but more often they would lose. The season had not advanced far when it became obvious that the Reds were headed for a finish lower than they had achieved under Ewing.

Hahn, on July 12, pitched a no-hit game over the hard-hitting Phils, the team's third no-hitter, and the second caught by Peitz. Noodles walked two men, hit one, and the Reds committed an error, but he was otherwise invincible.

But even Noodles could not win consistently with the sliding Reds of 1900.

And as if it were not enough to lose, the Reds suffered another disaster. After the eccentric Rube Waddell had pitched Pittsburgh to a triumph over the Rhinelanders, the stands caught fire. The blaze began in the dead of night, and although groundskeeper Matty Schwab rushed to the scene —the same Matty Schwab who manicures the field today— it was too late to do anything. Most of the grandstand was burned down, and was hurriedly replaced with temporary seats so the Reds could finish their schedule. It was not rebuilt entirely until 1902, when the Palace of the Fans was opened.

In August the Reds rallied somewhat, but couldn't quite reach the .500 mark, and after that a decline set in. Cincinnati eventually finished seventh with 62 wins and 77 defeats, only the lowly Giants being beneath them. But the Giants were not to remain lowly; the Reds saw to that.

During that 1900 season, New York had purchased conditionally from Norfolk, Virginia, the contract of a young pitcher named Christy Mathewson. The asking price was $1,500, and after Mathewson had reported to the Giants in June and had lost three games, he was returned to Norfolk and the deal canceled. After the 1900 season, the Reds bought Mathewson, drafting him for $100, the small selection price that was required at the time. But no sooner had John Brush purchased him than he traded him back to the Giants in an even-up deal for Amos Rusie, the one-time Hoosier Thunderbolt, who was just about out of sparks. At the time the deal was made, Mathewson was twenty, and Rusie, though only thirty, was definitely through as a pitcher. Amos won no games in his career with the Reds, making only two appearances, while Matty went on to become immortal, winning 372 times for the Giants.

Why was the deal made? The only conclusion that can be reached is that John T. Brush bought Mathewson for the New York club to save the latter $1,400, Norfolk, of course, being the loser to that extent. At least that's the supposition. Such a deal at the time was probably considered good business, ethics in business being what they were. But as a deal, from the standpoint of Cincinnati, it was the most inequitable transaction ever made. If a worse deal was ever pulled by a club, it hasn't been recorded.

So in 1900 the Reds finished seventh in the new eight-club league, saw their ball park burn down, and lost Christy Mathewson. Small wonder that Bob Allen departed after that one season!

2

When Bob Allen left after serving as pilot of the club for one sad season, fans were almost unanimous in telling John T. Brush who should run the club in 1901. Their selection was Bid McPhee. Things hadn't seemed quite the same without the veteran infielder, and the patrons of the game, being rather quick to jump at conclusions, somehow figured that Bid's absence had something to do with the nine's low estate. So Brush, bowing to popular demand, named McPhee his manager.

The team trained at home. McPhee felt that the previous year's expedition to New Orleans had enabled the players to find pursuits that were not in keeping with conditioning. The Crescent City was always a gay one, especially in that nostalgic era. And while the players trained at home, the grandstand was being built again and the field moved around. Prior to 1901, home plate was located where the right-field corner now stands at Crosley Field. This was a poor arrangement because the sun shone directly in the eyes of the first baseman and second baseman, and sometimes the catcher and batter. It will be recalled that a game in 1892 had to be called because the sun got in the eyes of batter and pitcher alike. So home plate was moved to what had previously been the left-field corner, and there it remains today.

McPhee, not satisfied with Joe Quinn at second, put Harry Steinfeldt at the base, and also experimented with a rookie named George Magoon. Beckley was back, and so were Corcoran and Irwin. Bill Bergen was acquired to share the catching with Peitz, and Hahn, Phillips, and Newton were asked to carry the pitching load, with the help of a rookie named Archibald May Stimmel, a bald hopeful from Maryland.

The club was hopeless from the start, though Hahn's pitching prevented an immediate crack-up. It was the most amazing year that Noodles had with the team. He started 42 times and completed 41 games. In a contest against Boston on May 22, he fanned sixteen batters, a Cincinnati high throughout the years and only one strike-out removed from the modern major-league record.

Rusie started once and received a 14-to-3 shellacking from St. Louis, pitching the whole dismal route. Late in May the Reds ran into Mathewson for the first time, and he beat them, 1 to 0.

With the team going badly, McPhee got desperate and signed one recruit after another. Altogether, an even twenty players were introduced to the majors by the Reds before the campaign was finished.

Of these, the most unusual candidate was Amos Richard Scott, of Bethel, Ohio. Mr. Scott obtained his chance by the simple method of writing accounts of the games he pitched on the sand lots and mailing them to the Cincinnati papers. He was a nineteen-year-old country boy who hardly knew how to stand on the mound, yet he was signed.

What's more, he was given a starting assignment against the great Mathewson, and didn't do badly either, losing to the Giants 6 to 2. In the next series between the two clubs, Scott started against Matty again, this time bowing 9 to 3.

That wasn't bad for a boy from the wilds of Bethel, Ohio, but McPhee was running a major-league club. Scott wasn't the only one, either. In all, the team employed fourteen pitchers, and five of them failed to win a single game.

Even Hahn found it difficult to win in such surroundings,

but ended up with 22 wins and 19 defeats, a record far ahead of that of the club, which finished with 52 wins and 87 setbacks.

A hero for eighteen years as a player, Bid McPhee took on the standing of just another fellow when he assumed the managership. The club, which had not finished last since 1880, sank to that dismal abode, a single game beneath the seventh-place Giants.

McPhee was given another year to produce, however, and the team trained at home again in 1902. When the season was opened on April 17, a new grandstand greeted the populace, the Palace of the Fans.

Based on the architecture exhibited at the World's Fair of 1892 and adorned with pillars and columns, the Palace of the Fans was joyous to behold, but there was not an overabundance of seats.

The nicest feature of the new plant was a section called "rooters' row," a collection of seats extending along the first and third base lines on a level with the field, a wire screen separating the customers from the players. Beer was served the patrons of "rooters' row" by the glass, twelve glasses for one dollar. The combination of the effect of the beer and the proximity of the players led the inhabitants of "rooters' row" to shout abuse at the athletes, a practice that was studiously followed for the ten years the setup was in existence.

McPhee's club showed improvement in 1902 as the pitching straightened out. Not only did Noodles Hahn continue his excellent work, but a newcomer, Bob Ewing, took his regular turn and won.

The club smartly didn't try to contend with the other seven teams by signing amateurs, and only twenty-three players, all of them experienced men, were on the roster all season.

But Bid McPhee found that managing did not suit him. After all his years of popularity due to his sterling play, he discovered that having the burden of a team's success on his shoulders wasn't the most pleasant sort of life. On July 10 he submitted his resignation, and Brush accepted it, appointing Frank Bancroft, his business manager, as temporary helmsman. Banny had managed the old Providence club of the National League and knew every angle of the game, but he made it clear that he was only a fill-in until a permanent pilot could be obtained.

He did not have long to wait. In 1902 the National League was waging a terrific war with the American League for the contracts of players. Ban Johnson, Brush's old enemy, had succeeded in making the American League a major by 1901. And now it was open warfare with players jumping their contracts almost every day.

The Reds entered into the spirited bidding for players' contracts and announced on July 16 that outfielders Joe Kelley, Cy Seymour, and Mike Donlin were jumping their contracts with Baltimore of the American League, and reporting to Cincinnati immediately. They were among the most famous players of their time, and the announcement was a great shock to the Oriole fans. At the same time John McGraw jumped from Baltimore to the Giants, spelling doom for the Orioles, who were now completely broken up.

Two weeks after joining the club, Joe Kelley took over the managerial reins. Between McPhee's resignation and Kelley's appointment the Reds had played 16 games under Bancroft, winning 9 and losing 7. Their record for the year was 36 victories and 44 defeats.

Kelley had been one of the greatest hitters in history. He had started with Pittsburgh in 1892 and was shipped to Baltimore that same year. In six years with the Orioles he compiled batting averages of .312, .391, .370, .370, .389, and .328. In 1899 he moved with manager Ned Hanlon and other Orioles to Brooklyn, where in three years he batted .329, .318, and .309. He had joined Baltimore again early in the spring of 1902. Joe was originally a pitcher, but won his greatest fame in the outfield, though he was also a capable first baseman. There was nothing required in baseball that he could not do.

The inspiration of Kelley at the helm and the presence of

72

Seymour and Donlin in the line-up caused a quickening of interest in baseball in the Queen City, and also had its effect on the team, which immediately began to climb.

But more sensational news was brewing. On August 9 it was suddenly announced that John T. Brush had sold the club to a clique of citizens that included the Messrs. Fleischmann, Julius and Max, members of the gin and yeast family, George B. Cox, boss of the city of Cincinnati, and August Herrmann, president of the board of the waterworks commission. Julius Fleischmann, at the time, was the city's mayor.

George B. Cox headed what was possibly the most corrupt government that ever infested a municipality. Lincoln Steffens, the great political writer who spent a lifetime studying such things, at least thought Cox was the worst. The Cox gang in Cincinnati has long been through, for the regime got so bad that the people revolted, threw the rascals out, and established the city-manager form of government.

A highly reputable Cincinnati newspaperman vividly recalls the purchase of the Reds by the Cox interests, and reports that Brush was reluctant to sell until Cox said, "If you don't sell the club to us, we're going to build a street in the city that will run right through the ball park." The life and times of George B. Cox are a matter of public record, and if that is the way he negotiated the purchase of the Reds, it would still be among his more honorable transactions.

At the time the deal was made, it was announced that the new owners had assumed an indebtedness of $70,000 and paid "a large cash sum" in addition. Brush still made out all right, as he had taken the club from Aaron Stern for practically nothing eleven years previously.

The season of 1902 was brought to a conclusion with new owners, a new ball park, a new manager, three formidable new players, and new hopes. Spurred on by all the excitement, the team climbed up to the .500 mark, finishing with seventy wins and the same number of losses, a pace that placed them fourth.

8

GARRY HERRMANN AND THE YEARS OF FERMENT

1

August (Garry) Herrmann, the man who was responsible for the addition of fried pigs' feet to the breakfast menus of the staid Waldorf-Astoria, became president of the Cincinnati Reds on August 16, 1902.

Though a representative of the George B. Cox interests, Garry was fortunately free to run the ball club as he saw fit. As a result, it cannot be fairly said that the Cox machine controlled the affairs of the ball club.

It is doubtful if the Fleischmanns and Cox could have found anyone more suited to handle a Cincinnati team than Garry Herrmann. And they found him right in their own back yard, right in their waterworks, in fact.

At the time he took over as president of the Reds, August Herrmann was forty-three years old, a portly, florid gentleman who liked to wear checked clothes, and who frequently wore diamond rings on both hands.

As a boy, Herrmann had obtained a job in a type foundry, where he learned typesetting. Eventually he became the chief compositor on a legal publication and a member of the International Typographical Union.

It was at this stage of his career that he acquired the nickname Garry. Young August, a good Cincinnati German, worked for another good Cincinnati German who liked to bestow quaint nicknames upon his employees. Neither

August nor Herrmann pleased the boss, and it was his first intention to call the lad Bismarck. But unfortunately there was another Bismarck in the shop, so to avoid confusion young Herrmann was called Garibaldi, in honor of the renowned Italian rebel. And Garibaldi, of course, was soon shortened to Garry.

Young Garry Herrmann soon discovered that the way to prominence in Cincinnati was through ward politics. First he became a member of the board of education, then an assistant clerk of the city police court. He was a bright lad, and before long he was running the city hall for George B. Cox.

Today in Cincinnati the people who remember Garry Herrmann remember him with a genuine and vast affection. Garry was always more of a sport than a businessman, and as host and entertainer he was without a peer.

The parties that he threw in the quarter century that he ruled the Reds were legendary. He would attend each World Series and each major-league meeting with his entourage, often starting out at one small table. But as more and more of his friends would appear, Garry would wave them to sit down. One table after another would be added until Garry's party occupied almost the entire barroom. His very presence caused a chain reaction of mirth and good fellowship that was all-inclusive. And Garry always paid the tab.

Garry was a walking delicatessen. A connoisseur of sausage, he carried his own everywhere he went. When he presided at a hotel suite or in a bar, his party sat around one or more tables that were piled high with roast chickens, boiled hams, cheeses of every description, Thuringian blood pudding, liver sausage, baked beans, radishes, cole slaw, potato salad, green onions, and every type of fermented drink that was known to Bacchus.

How could anyone possibly dislike such a fabulous host? He was the living personification of Cincinnati culture. To remember him is to remember the outdoor beer gardens and vaudeville, the singing waiters, the foaming steins of beer, the Liederkrantz sandwiches, the belching, guffawing laughter of long-forgotten nights.

Garry once took a trip up Long Island Sound on Julius Fleischmann's yacht. He had, of course, arranged for his sausage to be delivered to the dock. Through some error it was left behind. Garry stood the trip for one night. In the morning he told Fleischmann, "I'm sorry. You've been very kind. But you'll have to let me off. I've got to get back where I can have my sausage."

During the years that Garry ran the Reds, he also served as chairman of the old National Commission, baseball's governing body until Judge Landis took over. Garry and the two league presidents actually ran baseball. There was no salary in connection with that job, only an annual expense account of $12,000.

One time, at an exhibition game at St. Augustine, the Elks, of which organization Garry was a proud official for years, staged a big show before the game. Garry, who had spent the morning drinking beer and eating sausage, was introduced to the crowd.

Modestly he stood quietly by as the master of ceremonies enumerated many of Garry's accomplishments, including the fact that he was the dignified president of the Reds and the chairman of the National Commission. Garry listened to his eulogy politely, then cupped his hands and shouted to the crowd, "Yes, and I'm the champion beer drinker and sausage eater, too!"

There were times, naturally, when Garry's decisions as chairman of the National Commission did not meet with approval in all quarters. There was, for instance, the time that Herrmann forced the San Francisco team to pay $2,500 for a second baseman, Eddie Colligan, who had been in the hospital with a broken leg at the time San Francisco had bought him. J. Cal Ewing, president of the San Francisco team, thought that this was an outrageous decision, but Garry's office took the position that Ewing should have provided himself with information concerning the condition of the player before making the deal.

76

Several weeks later, Garry received from Ewing a shipment of five barrels of sauerkraut, sent C.O.D. He paid for them, and was about to enjoy the treat when he discovered that the sauerkraut was rancid and not fit to eat. He wrote a scathing letter to Ewing about the matter, and the San Francisco official replied that Garry should have provided himself with information concerning the condition of the sauerkraut before he paid for it. Which ended the matter of Eddie Colligan.

The personality of Garry Herrmann had many facets. He loved a good time, in many affairs he was motivated by a sense of fair play, and he had a tremendous capacity for work. But Tom Swope, the baseball authority of the *Cincinnati Post,* thinks that Garry's finest quality was his ability to smile at adversity. Throughout the years there were many times that Herrmann was criticized in print. Some of the deals he made, some of his relations with players brought sharp comment. But he never complained. As a product of political gangism, he knew that official acts often brought a caustic public reaction. But he never complained. And he never worried. Ask any Cincinnatian today who is old enough to remember what it is he remembers about Garry Herrmann. The face of whomever you select will light up, and he will say, "Garry Herrmann? Do I remember him? Say, did I ever tell you about the time we went to Pittsburgh for the World Series? I was in Garry's compartment. He had one hundred gallons of potato salad along and I don't know how many kegs of beer. And there were prohibition agents on the train, and—"

Well, you know how it goes. Garry is as nostalgic a subject as the old-time player-piano.

2

Garry thought he and Joe Kelley were going to have a good club in 1903. With Seymour and Donlin and Kelley himself in the line-up, the Reds would be assured of a hard-hitting outfield, even with the loss of Sam Crawford. For when the peace terms were written between the National and American Leagues, an armistice that brought an end to the raiding of players, Sam Crawford was awarded to the Detroit club. Crawford had signed with both Detroit and Cincinnati, and since he had given his signature to the Michigan city first, he was considered the rightful property of that team.

Beckley at first base, Corcoran at shortstop, and Steinfeldt at third assured the Reds of a good infield. Second base, though, was still a problem. The team had never secured an adequate replacement for Bid McPhee. Joe Quinn had played the base in 1900, Steinfeldt in 1901, and in 1902 Heinie Peitz, the catcher, had seen service there more than anyone else, although George Magoon and a lad named Erve Beck had been used at the keystone. Now there was a newcomer, Tom Daly, to try his hand. With Daly around, Peitz could go back to his catching position, aided by Bill Bergen. The pitching seemed fairly solid, with Noodles Hahn, Bob Ewing, and Bill Phillips, and a young fellow named Jack Harper.

But the team won only one game of its first eight, and then, after closing the gap by winning six in a row, began to play in-and-out ball, never striking a winning stride that was sufficient to elevate the Reds in the race. The fans were loyal in their support, and turned out to the Palace of the Fans in large numbers, greeting the genial president, Garry Herrmann, drinking their beer, and cheering when Seymour or Kelley or Donlin or Beckley or Steinfeldt murdered the ball. For those five players all hit more than .300 in 1903, Donlin spearheading the club with a sparkling .351, and Seymour not far behind with .342.

In September the Redlegs put together eight wins in succession, and that guaranteed a finish in the first division. When the chips were all counted at the season's close, the Reds had won 74 and lost 65 and were fourth. Noodles Hahn, for the fourth time in the five years he was with the team, won more than twenty games, taking 22 against 12 losses.

In the spring of 1904, when the team was in training at Dallas, Texas, the word was freely passed around that unless the Reds could find a second baseman, they would never achieve a position of eminence in the race. The replacements for Bid McPhee during the past four seasons had been ghastly.

When told about this one day, Manager Joe Kelley pointed to a wisp of a lad fielding the ball at second and said, "See him? There's our second baseman. And he's going to be all right."

"Who is he?" Kelley was asked.

"His name is Huggins," Joe replied. "Miller Huggins. We bought him from St. Paul. He's five feet four inches tall and weighs a hundred twenty-five pounds. So go on and laugh all you want. But he's going to make all of you forget there ever was such a player as Bid McPhee."

Miller Huggins, one of the few major-league players to appear on the team representing the city of his origin, did make the grade. He roamed all over the infield and outfield, wanting to play the whole game himself, and the fans called him "Little Everywhere." Huggins had studied law at the University of Cincinnati, playing semipro ball on the side under the name of Proctor.

For some reason Kelley didn't use Hug in the opening game of the 1904 season, playing instead an athlete named Orville Woodruff. But he was in there on the next day, cinching the job by making a single and drawing two walks, stealing a base, and handling six fielding chances. He had a violent collision at second base with the aggressive Johnny Evers of the Cubs, and that night one newspaper printed the following:

"Prospective encounters between the Reds and Cubs over the alleged intentional injuring of Huggins by Evers, and the subsequent upset of Evers by Dolan, went no farther than words. Neither man was sufficiently hurt to discontinue playing the game."

Little Hug didn't scare. He won a job that afternoon that kept him in the majors as an active player until 1917, and as a manager long enough to win six pennants for the New York Yankees before his death. And the worry about a second baseman in the Rhineland was a thing of the past.

Kelley made other changes. Jake Beckley, after guarding

79

first base for seven years, had apparently reached the end of his string and was reluctantly sent to St. Louis. Kelley himself moved from the outfield to first base to fill that breach, sending Fred Odwell to the garden in his place. Two new pitchers, Win Kellum and Tom Walker, were added to the regular staff, taking the places of Ed Poole and Bill Phillips. Peitz, who was definitely slipping, was given the second-string catching job, behind George (Admiral) Schlei, and a third catcher was added, Charles (Gabby) Street, later famous as the battery mate of the great Walter Johnson at Washington. Gabby was also celebrated for catching a ball dropped from the Washington monument. But he broke into only eleven games for the Reds.

A crowd of thirteen thousand filled the Palace of the Fans when the Reds opened the season against the Cubs, winning 3 to 2, behind Jack Sutthoff, a local pitcher who started the season as if he were going to be phenomenal. Then, in early May, the Redlegs began to roll, clicking off eight straight triumphs.

At the end of May Kelley's club had won 26 and lost only 12, and the good burghers of Cincinnati were beginning to sniff a pennant. But the Giants of New York were the great obstacle.

When Cincinnati first visited them in 1904 in early June, Christy Mathewson, whom the Reds had once owned, defeated Sutthoff 2 to 1. On the next day Noodles Hahn retaliated, beating Dummy Taylor 3 to 2. The third game of the series drew the greatest crowd in the history of baseball up to that time, an assemblage of 37,223. And the fans really got their money's worth as Jack Harper and Iron Man Joe McGinnity battled to a 2-to-2 tie, called after eleven innings because of darkness.

Shortly after that the Reds almost lost their star shortstop, Tommy Corcoran. One day in St. Louis Corcoran and Orville Woodruff were walking down the street, aimlessly looking over the town as players are apt to do, when a balky horse, frightened by an early version of the auto, created a street scene that ended up with pedestrians scattered in all directions. Corcoran was pinned against a building and badly hurt, but Woodruff emerged from the affair a hero, picking up a woman who was lying right in the path of the horse and carrying her away from the danger in the nick of time.

The Reds continued their fine play in the latter part of the season, but the Giants and Cubs were too much of a twin obstacle. Beating the rest of the league handily but remaining ineffectual against the Bruins and the Giants, whom McGraw lashed into a frenzy and landed with the first of ten pennants he was to bring New York, Kelley had to be satisfied with a third-place finish, with 88 victories and 65 defeats, a full seven-game improvement over the preceding year.

Late that season, the Reds thought they had dug up a fine young catching prospect, a brainy youth by the name of Branch Rickey. He accompanied the team to Rushville, Indiana, one afternoon and performed behind the bat for them in an exhibition game. But young Rickey refused to play on Sunday, and the Reds, not being Sabbatarians, passed him up. They were to meet him frequently later.

⊖ **9** ⊖

HANLON TRIES HIS HAND

1

Beating Muggsy McGraw's Giants gave the inhabitants of the Palace of the Fans more pleasure than anything except a fight, and generally the latter was necessary to accomplish the former. McGraw would go to any lengths to win a game. He was a master at arousing a crowd, a dramatist of a high order, and the show started long before the ball game. The hated Giants used to ride out to the park at Cincinnati in huge open wagons. There still are people around the Queen City who recall watching the Giant caravan passing through the streets while not only urchins but grown men threw ripe fruit and vegetables at such outlanders as Dan McGann, Art Devlin, Roger Bresnahan, Iron Man Joe McGinnity, or even Muggsy himself.

Manager Joe Kelley of the Reds, like McGraw, was an Oriole, and he also loved to win. There was nothing sweeter to him than a victory over the haughty New Yorkers. But those victories were sweet because they were scarce. In 1904 the Reds had beaten the pennant-winning Giants only 5 times in 21 meetings. And their work against McGraw's team in 1905 was an exact replica of the previous year.

Kelley moved himself from first base to the outfield, joining Seymour and Odwell, relegating Dolan to the bench. Jack Barry was placed at first base, with Huggins, Corcoran, and Steinfeldt as holdovers at the other infield spots. Admiral Schlei once more was the regular catcher.

The principal addition to the mound corps was Big Orval Overall, a twenty-four-year-old Californian with an arm like the Village Blacksmith.

A baseball career is hazardous at best, and very frequently illness and injury play havoc with a player who, had the fates only smiled, would have known lasting fame. Such was the case with Noodles Hahn. The fine star southpaw of the Reds, only twenty-seven years old in 1905 but a veteran of six splendid seasons, severely hurt his arm, and was never the same pitcher again. After winning five and losing three, he was let out. And although Noodles tried to pitch again with the old New York Highlanders of the American League, he had lost his magic.

Modern pitchers who look anxiously at the bench whenever they are pelted for three hits in a row should consider the work of Noodles Hahn with the Reds. In the six years and part of a seventh that he was with the club, he started 225 games and pitched all the way through 209 of them, being lifted only 16 times, or an average of little more than twice a year. And with clubs that never finished higher than

AUGUST (GARRY) HERRMANN

JOE TINKER

The Sporting News

CHRISTY MATHEWSON

The Sporting News

third and were in the second division in four of the seven campaigns, he won 127 games and lost 91.

Noodles always kept himself in perfect shape. After he had retired from the game he became a meat inspector in Cincinnati, and in the afternoons he used to go out to the park and put on his old uniform and work out. As late as 1946, at the age of sixty-eight, he still performed this ritual. Although almost seventy, he would have pitched batting practice had Manager Bill McKechnie permitted.

Some of the players in the early 1940's, upon joining the Reds, wondered who he was. Unlike some old-timers, Noodles was never one to get a rookie off in a corner and tell him how baseball used to be played or should be played. He was never a mine of misinformation about the game, and was even reluctant to discuss his own career. But the players found out. Steve Mesner, who played third base for the Redlegs during World War II, happened across a faded clipping one day that told about Noodles' no-hitter in 1900 and his feat of striking out sixteen in a game the following year. Could this be that old fellow who works out with us? Mesner thought. Well, what do you know? If it hadn't been for that, the players would have considered Hahn only a "nice old guy they say used to pitch for the Reds."

So Hahn was gone. And though Orval Overall tried to take up the slack, the Red pitching was poor. Harper had a reversal of his splendid form of 1904, and another newcomer, Charlie Chech, was only soso.

The Reds did have some hitting that year, though. Cy Seymour spent a summer with the mace that tops anything in Redleg annals. During the course of the season, Seymour went to bat 581 times, and he responded with hits on 219 occasions. His total of 40 doubles, 21 triples, and 8 home runs gave him 325 total bases. No Red, before or since, ever made so many hits or collected so many total bases in a single year. He was the league's leading hitter.

The Reds also had the home-run champion of the National League. Fred Odwell, the left fielder, paced the circuit in round-trippers, with the stunning total of nine. Otherwise,

Fred was most undistinguished. He batted only .241, and he must be counted among the least-known home-run champions of all time.

Seymour's hitting kept the Reds' victory pace over the .500 mark, and they finished with 79 victories and 74 defeats, in fifth place. McGraw's rowdy Giants had won the pennant again.

2

Garry Herrmann decided that he had tried Joe Kelley long enough, so in 1906 he made his first managerial change, giving the job to Ned Hanlon, though Kelley remained as a player. On the surface it appeared to be an astute appointment, as Hanlon had almost everything to recommend him.

Ned, as a star outfielder, had played with the Detroit champions of 1887. He was a veteran even then, as he had commenced his career with Cleveland of the National League in 1880, at the age of twenty-three. He had managed Pittsburgh from 1889 to 1891, but won his greatest fame as pilot of the raucous Baltimore Orioles from 1892 to 1898. Then he had jumped to Brooklyn, taking with him the best Baltimore players. At Baltimore and Brooklyn Hanlon had won five pennants and finished second twice.

As a player, Edward Hugh Hanlon was a fast runner, and averaged over fifty stolen bases a season. He was a left-handed hitter, and was very weak against southpaws, benching himself when a port-sider was due to work. It is believed that Ned Hanlon was the first manager to use left-handed hitters against right-handed pitchers and vice versa, the practice that is so overworked in modern baseball.

But it was as a developer of players that Hanlon was best known. He made a star of John McGraw, and he taught the fine points of the game to such luminaries as Hugh Jennings, Joe Kelley, Kid Gleason, and Willie Keeler. Small wonder that Garry Herrmann thought he had landed the man who would bring a pennant to the Rhine.

But by the time Hanlon reached the Reds, he was sated with victory and inclined to be impatient with younger players. Baseball is a young man's game. Most players reach a time when they no longer go about their work with the same enthusiasm, and the same applies to managers, the remarkable career of Connie Mack notwithstanding.

Hanlon took the 1906 Reds to train at San Antonio. He saw immediately that the club, as constituted, was by no means a world-beater. There was a glaring weakness at first base; Corcoran, at short, was growing old; a southpaw had to be found to replace Hahn. John (Snake) Deal was given the first-base job; Corcoran, though by now woefully weak at bat, was allowed to remain at short for the want of a better replacement; Hahn's successor was found in the person of Jake Weimer, a twenty-four-year-old left-hander who turned out to be the most capable flinger on Hanlon's staff. The Reds secured Weimer in a deal with the Cubs, shipping infielder Harry Steinfeldt for the port-sider.

On top of this, Herrmann and Hanlon, early in the 1906 season, made a very bad trade. Orval Overall, the strong young right-hander, was sent to Chicago for another pitcher, Bob Wicker.

Overall's presence on the Chicago club made that team, which was already formidable, practically unbeatable. Boasting such stellar players as Johnny Kling behind the bat; Frank Chance, Johnny Evers, Joe Tinker, and Harry Steinfeldt at the infield spots; Jimmy Sheckard, Artie Hofman, and Wildfire Schulte in the outfield; and pitchers of the stature of Mordecai Brown, Ed Reulbach, Jack Pfiester, Orval Overall, and Carl Lundgren, the Cubs proved even more terrifying than McGraw's Giants and went on to win 116 games while losing only 36, the greatest winning record in National League annals.

Four times that year in twenty-two meetings the Reds were able to beat the Cubs. Jake Weimer took their measure, 1 to 0, in early April, and Jack Harper beat them, 3 to 2, in the same series. Weimer beat them again, 2 to 1, in late June, and in that series Chick Fraser set them down 1 to 0, all four of the Red victories being by a single run.

Against the Giants, the Reds had only slightly better luck,

winning 5 and losing 16. It was the inability to make a respectable showing against those top-notch teams that prevented the Reds from entering the first division.

Seymour, after his splendid 1905 season, made what for him was a wretched showing, batting only .257 in seventy-nine games before being shipped to the Giants. Fred Odwell, home-run hitter of the year before, could not even hold his regular left-field post, yielding the spot to an Indian graduate of Carlisle Institute, Frank Jude.

One bright note was struck by the late-season purchase of a gigantic catcher from Portland of the Pacific Coast League, John Bannerman (Larry) McLean. Towering six feet five and weighing 230, McLean gave promise of being a colossus behind the plate and a hitter of tremendous strength.

Throughout his life, McLean was in a series of scrapes that finally culminated when he was shot to death by a bartender. He was always the center of excitement. At the time of the San Francisco earthquake and fire, the Portland club was in San Francisco, so Larry did not even miss that. In fact, he was scared half to death when the earth began to tremble, and his fright mounted when he found he could not open the door to his hotel room. So he broke it down, and went out into the street in a long cotton nightgown, dragging a trunk, crammed with his earthly possessions, behind him.

In some respects, McLean resembled Ernie Lombardi, who came to the Reds as a receiver twenty-six years later. Like Lombardi, he was slow, but he could hit and throw.

Later in his career, when McLean was a member of the Giants, McGraw noticed him sitting on the bench in the late stages of an important game.

"McLean," the Giant pilot shouted, "you go up now and hit for our pitcher. I am instructing you to hit the ball into the stands."

McLean picked up a bat, shot a backward glance at McGraw, and said laconically, "Which seat, Mac?"

But Larry McLean arrived too late in the year to be of much help to the Reds, and he broke into only twelve games before the season closed with the Reds in sixth place, with 64 wins and 87 defeats, fourteen full games behind their pace of the year before.

Wicker, received in the deal for Overall, helped the decline by winning 7 times while getting trounced on 11 afternoons. Weimer was the only twenty-game winner on the staff.

Hanlon returned the club to Texas for training in 1907, shifting the proving grounds from San Antonio to the comparatively obscure community of Marlin.

The first-base problem was thought solved in the acquisition of John Ganzel, a thirty-two-year-old veteran who had played with the Cubs, Giants, and New York Highlanders. Harry (Mike) Mowrey was given a shot at Corcoran's shortstop job. John (Honus) Lobert, a remarkable base runner whose nickname was derived from his physical resemblance to another Honus, the great John Wagner of Pittsburgh, took over at the hot corner. The outfield was made over entirely with Odwell becoming a regular again, the other two positions going to rookies, Mike Mitchell and Art Krueger. Of the new men, Mitchell was by far the best of the lot and proved to be a steady fielder and batsman.

Again the pitching was a disappointment. Jake Weimer failed to follow up his good work of 1906, and the most dependable hurler was a rookie, Andy Coakley.

When the club was in Brooklyn late in July, winding up a long trip that saw the Reds win only 4 games out of 19, Ned Hanlon announced to the press that he did not intend to return as manager in 1908. At the time of the announcement, the Redlegs had won 32 and lost 49. Hanlon was tired. He was always previously associated with winning clubs, and the aroma of life in the second division was not pleasant to his sensitive nostrils. Trying to compete with New York, Chicago, and Pittsburgh with a mediocre collection of athletes was a new experience for him. He was tired and wanted to quit, and Garry Herrmann graciously told him to finish out the year.

So Hanlon finished his second season, which was almost an exact replica of his first in Cincinnati. The Reds lost the same number of games, 87, and managed to win 2 more, winding up with 66 triumphs.

Hanlon's retirement, announced more than two months before it actually took place, quite naturally caused a slump in attendance. The fans stayed away from their palace in droves.

There was only one big day, late that year. On September 10 a field meet was staged, and compared to similar events held today, it was really a gala affair. Players of all leagues were invited, Garry cheerfully paying their expenses to the Queen City.

Five events were run off, the winner of each receiving a gold medal and $100. The fungo hitting was won by Mike Mitchell, who socked the sphere 413 feet, 8½ inches. Harry McIntire of Brooklyn was second and Ed Walsh of the Chicago White Sox third.

Sheldon Le Jeune, a young outfielder who belonged to Springfield of the Central League, won the long-distance throw with a heave that startled the gallery, the ball sailing one inch less than four hundred feet.

Walter Clement, an outfielder from Jersey City, circled the bases in fourteen and one-fifth seconds, less than a second slower than the fastest man alive today could run the event. Honus Lobert of the Reds and Jack Thoney of the Toronto club were right behind him. Thoney also won the bunt-and-run-to-first, accomplishing the trick in three and one-fifth seconds. Accurate throwing by catchers was won by George Gibson of the Pirates, with Larry McLean in second place.

Four decades have not made much difference in the physical prowess of the players. Athletes of today could not improve to any great extent on the marks of Le Jeune, Mitchell, and Clement.

The Reds of 1907 had one dubious distinction. Not a single player, even a substitute in less than ten games, managed to hit .300. Mike Mitchell came closest, hitting .292, and the ponderous Larry McLean was three percentage points behind him.

Hanlon had made clear his decision not to return in 1908,

so Garry offered the managerial post to first baseman John Ganzel. It was also presumed that John would remain at his first-base post. The idea of a playing manager for the Reds was, of course, nothing new. In the team's infancy almost all the pilots were active players, and in more recent years Charlie Comiskey, Buck Ewing, and Joe Kelley had run the club while still actively participating in the games.

During this era the Reds also suffered because of the schedule. Pittsburgh and Chicago were almost always among the top three teams of the circuit, and the Reds were called upon to meet both the Pirates and the Bruins frequently at the start of each campaign. This would almost always result in a series of Cincinnati reverses that was difficult to overcome. By the time the Reds had met the weaker nines, they were already disheartened.

There were three new regulars. Rudy Hulswitt replaced Mike Mowrey at short, and two rookies, George Paskert and Johnny Kane, were sent to the outfield as successors to Fred Odwell and Art Krueger. Late in the season three more new names appeared in box scores for the first time that were to be celebrated later—Dick Hoblitzell, a first baseman, Dick Egan, a second baseman, and Bob Bescher, an outfielder. They had youth and speed and gave hope for a brighter day.

Ganzel managed the club for only that single season. Garry Herrmann considered Johnny only as a stopgap leader. But Ganzel didn't do badly at all. As the 1908 season closed amid the excitement of the incident of Fred Merkle's not touching second base in a game between the Giants and Cubs, the Cincinnati Reds, entirely lacking fanfare or exciting incidents of any variety, climbed a notch to fifth, with 73 triumphs and 81 setbacks.

🍥 **10** 🍥

THE MIDDLE-AGED FOX

1

During the first years of his reign as boss of the Reds, Garry Herrmann demonstrated a sense of fairness and decency that was remarkable for one trained in the sewer of municipal politics. In fact, one of his first official acts in connection with the club's affairs was an example of unsolicited generosity that is almost unparalleled. On the last day of the 1902 season, just a few weeks after Garry had taken over the front office, the Reds indulged in a farce of a game at Pittsburgh. Joe Kelley, then manager of the team, used his regular outfielders, Cy Seymour and Mike Donlin, and first baseman Jake Beckley as pitchers. The Reds smoked on the field, and otherwise comported themselves with anything but dignity. The Pirates walked off with the game, 11 to 2, but Garry felt that something was due the Pittsburgh club by way of apology for such shenanigans, so he returned the entire Reds' share of the gate to Barney Dreyfuss, president of the Pittsburgh club.

Herrmann didn't have to do that. It was a spontaneous act motivated by his sense of fair play. And in most of his decisions Garry seemed guided by high principle.

But some years later, in 1908, when he wanted to supplant John Ganzel as manager of the Reds, Garry acted in a way that can hardly be justified in baseball, although in some business pursuits it would merely be accepted practice.

The man Herrmann wanted as a successor to Ganzel was Clark Griffith, who had been a manager in the American

90

League, at Chicago and New York, ever since the junior circuit had become a major loop. Griffith had jumped to the American from Chicago of the National, which club had paid his salary since 1893.

Born at Stringtown, Missouri, in the heart of the Jesse James country, in 1869, Griffith had been a famous pitcher. He was known as "the Old Fox" because of the chicanery he employed on the mound. Bill Byron, one of the greatest umpires who ever worked in the National League, when asked what sort of pitcher Clark Griffith was, said, "For a little fellow he was pretty good. He used to stand out there on the rubber and spend minutes knocking the ball against his spikes, pretending there was dirt on them, and meanwhile scuffing up the cover of the ball."

Herrmann first approached Griffith about managing the Reds during the 1908 season, when Ganzel was still on the job. But Griff was loath to manage the Reds. The thought of going to the National League was repugnant to him, and he turned down Garry flatly.

At this time the Old Fox thought that he could by some hook or crook obtain Joe Cantillon's job at Washington, for he knew that Cantillon was planning to resign.

Garry then persuaded Griffith to come to Cincinnati anyway, in the role of a scout. Griff accepted this offer, reserving his decision on managing the club pending settlement of the Washington business. When Griffith came to Cincinnati, he paid his way into each game, usually viewing the contests from the bleachers. Then, afterward, he would make recommendations about the players to Herrmann. All this was done behind the back of John Ganzel.

Meanwhile, Griffith had had the foresight to make known his Washington managerial ambitions to Ban Johnson, president of the American League. But to Griffith's surprise and utter chagrin, Johnson ignored the Old Fox completely and arranged for the Washington job to go to Jimmy McAleer, pilot of the St. Louis Browns. Clark then accepted the job of managing the Reds, to take effect at the opening of the 1909 season.

Griffith took the club to train at Atlanta, and the general feeling was that the Reds had a formidable squad. During the winter catcher Admiral Schlei had been traded to St. Louis for two pitchers, Art Fromme and Ed Karger. It was a good deal, because the Reds badly needed pitching and they could dispose of Schlei because a promising young receiver, Tom Clarke, had been purchased from Montreal.

Dick Hoblitzell, at first base, and Dick Egan, at second, had won their spurs in late-season trials under Ganzel, and Griffith thought they would do. A young man named Tom Downey was given the shortstop post, with Honus Lobert remaining to play third. Bob Bescher, George Paskert, and Mike Mitchell were on hand to roam the outfield.

Fromme, the newcomer, was given the honor of pitching on opening day, and he responded with a good game, though yielding the victory to Howard Camnitz of the Pirates, 3 to 0. But the Reds turned about and slapped the Pirates down three straight times, with Bob Ewing and two youngsters, Jean Dubuc and Harry Gaspar, pitching the team to victory.

After taking two out of three from St. Louis, the Reds then went to Pittsburgh, and on April 23 became involved in what would today be called a "rhubarb."

The umpire behind the plate that afternoon was Bill Klem, "the Old Arbitrator," the celebrated man in blue who is so fond of telling people that he never made an incorrect decision in his life. Well, Bill Klem made an incorrect decision on April 23, 1909, and what's more he admitted it.

With Pittsburgh leading 1 to 0 in the sixth inning, the incident occurred that started the trouble. There is a rule in baseball that a batter may not cross home plate while the pitcher is in the act of delivering the ball. If he does so, he is out. It's that simple. With Pittsburgh batting in the sixth, the great Honus Wagner, who was up, stepped across the plate as Harry Gaspar was delivering the ball. The Reds immediately rushed from their positions in the field and from the dugout, demanding that Klem call Wagner out. This he refused to do, and Griffith played out the game under protest. Pittsburgh won, 2 to 1.

Harry Pulliam, president of the National League at the time, had not granted a protest in the seven years he had held office. But the Reds' cause was so obviously just that Pulliam consulted the league's board of directors—Charles W. Murphy, Charlie Ebbets, and George B. Dovey. Klem maintained that he did not call Wagner out "because it would be ridiculous under the circumstances."

To this, Garry Herrmann replied with telling logic, "No decision that is in accordance with the rules is ridiculous." Confronted with the evidence, Pulliam overruled Klem and ordered the game replayed. When it was played over, the Pirates won again, 4 to 3. But, just for the record, Bill Klem "missed one" on April 23, 1909.

After the protested game, the Reds pursued their chores with fair success, staying at about the .500 mark. Mitchell and Hoblitzell were doing most of the hitting. Fromme, Gaspar, Ewing, and a youngster from Dayton, Ohio, Jack Rowan, were taking their turns on the hill and pitching with steadiness.

At this time there was a man named George F. Cahill, who came from Holyoke, Massachusetts, and people around the country considered him something of a fool because he thought that baseball could be played at night. He had invented a lighting plant, a rudimentary affair that called for the temporary erection of five steel towers from which the lights were strung. He had demonstrated this system at various parks, and Garry Herrmann, hearing of it, invited him to stage a game at Cincinnati.

The contest was played on June 19, 1909, between two teams of Elks, one from Cincinnati and one from the across-the-river garden spot of Newport, Kentucky. The Reds had been shut out by the Phils that afternoon, and the players stayed at the park, anxious to see what this nocturnal nonsense was. Surprisingly, the game was played under pleasant circumstances, and the spectators had little trouble in following the ball, although high flies, hit above the range of the lights, created a problem.

Garry Herrmann, with perhaps more prescience than he

realized, said, "Night baseball has come to stay. It needs some little further development, but proper lighting conditions will make the sport immensely popular."

Clark Griffith's reaction to the experiment was considerably less enthusiastic. And years later, when Larry MacPhail introduced night baseball to the major leagues in 1935, Griffith, then president of the Washington club of the American League, was inexorably opposed to it. A few years later Griff had lights in his own park, and became the first big-league magnate to beg for the privilege of playing most of his games at night.

But who remembers George Cahill and his dream of 1909?

A midseason injury to big Larry McLean ended any pennant hopes the Reds may have had in 1909. The same old trio, Pittsburgh, Chicago, and New York, was still too much for the Reds to cope with. And when the other two receivers, Tom Clarke and Frank Roth, became crippled, Griffith had to sign two untried recruits, Clare Patterson and a young man with the engaging name of Simon Pauxtis.

But despite the deficiency behind the plate, Griff's team held on and finished fourth, with 77 victories and 76 defeats.

Toward the end of the campaign, Garry brought in a vast horde of rookies, specializing in pitchers whose names began with the letter "C." At least, four young men named Tom Cantwell, Chester Carmichael, Roy Castleton, and Bill Chappelle saw service on the slab. The Old Fox, then middle-aged, even broke into one box score himself, going the route against St. Louis on October 3, and getting a trimming, 8 to 1, in a contest called at the end of six innings.

2

Moving the training base from Atlanta to Hot Springs in 1910, Herrmann and Griffith decided, however, not to move any of the players. The Reds stood pat. They took the field with the same athlete at each position as the one who had manned the spot the year before. It was felt that superior replacements were not obtainable and that barring a repetition of an injury to a key man, such as the 1909 side-lining of

94

Larry McLean, the team should do even better. After all, they had just achieved a first-division berth for the first time in five years.

Three new pitchers, George Suggs, Fred Beebe, and Bill Burns, were given starting roles, along with Harry Gaspar. Bob Ewing had come to the end of his string and was shunted to Philadelphia. Fromme demonstrated early in the year that he was ineffective, a circumstance that gave the new men a chance. But outside of the pitching, it was the same team.

Bescher, Paskert, and Mitchell formed a really capable unit in the outfield. Bob Bescher, in many ways, was quite remarkable. A big fellow, standing over six feet and weighing two hundred pounds, he was extremely fast, and could beat most of his contemporaries in a race. Though never a .300 hitter, he was often close to that figure because his excessive speed enabled him to beat out numerous infield hits. He was an Ohio boy, a graduate of Notre Dame, and had played with Dayton of the Central League before joining the Reds late in 1908. Griffith let Bescher run in 1910, and he swiped a total of seventy bases.

Not only were the Reds of 1910 similar to the club of the year before, but their work on the field was almost identical. They proceeded through their schedule with considerable aptitude. Not until July were they able to put together as many as four triumphs in a row, and they never repeated with that many, but only once did they lose four straight. It was another average team, one that would win today and lose tomorrow, depending chiefly on the opposition. Pittsburgh had won the pennant in 1909, but now the Cubs were on the rampage again, and they eventually finished on top. The Giants were second, the Pirates third, and late in the year the Phillies slipped ahead of Cincinnati into fourth place, demoting the Reds to fifth, where they closed hostilities with 75 victories and 79 defeats, only two and one-half games off their pace of the year before, but one position lower in the standings.

After standing pat for that one year, Garry decided that a big deal was in order, and he managed to swing one with

Philadelphia, sending pitchers Fred Beebe and Jack Rowan, infielder Honus Lobert, and outfielder George Paskert to the Phils for pitchers George McQuillan and Lew Moren, infielder Eddie Grant, and outfielder Johnny Bates. This trade didn't work out very well for Cincinnati, because although Eddie Grant—Harvard Eddie, who was killed in the Argonne Forest in World War I and whose monument lies in center field at the Polo Grounds today—was a very capable player, Paskert had the edge on Bates, and Lew Moren injured his arm and never threw a ball for the Reds. The other pitcher, McQuillan, was suspended for breaking training and won only two games.

The players added to the Reds of 1911 who caused the most comment were not established major-leaguers, but two citizens of Cuba, outfielder Armando Marsans and infielder Rafael D. Almeida. Today it is almost impossible to realize what a furor the signing of two Cubans caused in 1911.

Americans have long had a curious attitude toward people from other lands. As far back as 1882 the Providence team of the National League introduced the first Cuban player, a catcher named Vincent Nava. The first time he appeared around the circuit he was greeted by friendly jeering, and his appearance caused the xenophobes of the land considerable merriment. One newspaper, the *Detroit Free Press,* in the manner of Gilbert and Sullivan, expressed its rather amused estimate of Nava in lyrics, as follows:

Solo
I am the catcher of the Providence club.

Chorus
And a very good catcher too.

Solo
I'm very, very good
And be it understood
There's one thing I won't do.

Chorus
He's very, very good
And be it understood
There's one thing he won't do.

Solo
Tho' at wielding the ash
I seldom make a dash
And sometimes pop an easy fly,
When I don my little mask
I'm all that you can ask
For I NAVA let a ball go by.

Chorus
Hardly Ava lets a ball go by.
Then give three cheers and a rub, dub, dub
For the Spanish catcher on the Providence club.

After Nava, few Cubans had appeared in the major leagues until Herrmann signed Marsans and Almeida. Frank Bancroft had seen them play winter ball in Cuba, and had liked them very much. Early in 1910, a certain Dan O'Neil, who operated the New Britain club of the Connecticut League, imported four Cuban players, among whom were Marsans and Almeida. They were purchased by the Reds from New Britain on the recommendation of Bancroft, and there was criticism of the Reds from some elements of the populace.

Of the two players, Marsans proved to be the better, though in 1911 he was not able to break into the regular outfield, with Bescher, Bates, and Mitchell on the job. And Almeida could not displace Eddie Grant at third, though both players broke into the games as utility men.

A crowd of almost twenty thousand turned out for the opening game of the 1911 season and saw the Reds receive the worst trimming they have ever suffered on getaway day. The Pirates really poured it on, 14 to 0, Babe Adams winning the rout, with Art Fromme suffering the loss. Toward the end of the game, Jesse Tannehill, who had been signed that spring at the age of thirty-six after being away from the club since 1894, finished out the game.

Continued inability against the Cubs, Pirates, and Giants kept the Reds in the second division, however, and although the club won seven contests in a row in May, eventually the Reds found their proper level.

One notable event of the season was a victory by Griffith's team over Christy Mathewson. The famous right-hander of the Giants trounced the Reds twenty-two times in succession until Art Fromme managed to beat him, 7 to 4, on August 19. Mathewson's record of twenty-two successive wins over one club constitutes a National League record.

Another memorable event took place on September 30, when Cy Young, who had pitched in the major leagues since 1890, made his last appearance on the slab by bowing, 4 to 1, to a twenty-one-year-old southpaw the Reds brought up from Carolina, John (Rube) Benton.

Griffith's Cincinnati teams had grown progressively worse. He had finished fourth in 1909, fifth in 1910, and in 1911 he ended up sixth, the Reds winning 70 and losing 83 games. Garry Herrmann decided that another managerial change was in order, and he supplanted Griffith with Henry (Hank) O'Day, who had been an umpire in the National League since 1895, and whose knowledge of baseball was impressive.

O'DAY TO TINKER TO HERZOG

1

Henry (Hank) O'Day, the old pitcher and umpire chosen by Garry Herrmann to manage the Reds in 1912, was about as odd a character as the game has ever produced. O'Day lived his long life in solitary silence and was as close-mouthed and mysterious as some strange mollusk one might find on a beach. As crusty and self-contained as a chambered Nautilus, he eschewed publicity and apparently had no interest in anything in life except baseball. In his late years he sometimes visited Bob Emslie, another umpire and a contemporary, at the latter's home at Fort Thomas, Ontario, and on these occasions his greatest pleasure was to sit in silence on the porch.

Cullen Cain, formerly the publicity director of the National League, once had occasion to call upon O'Day for some information. A story was to be prepared that would carry the veteran arbiter's picture. O'Day flatly refused to co-operate in any way until ordered to do so by John Heydler, president of the circuit. Finally, Hank reluctantly brought the picture to Cain's office.

The publicist, smiling and looking up, greeted his guest pleasantly and said, "Well, this is Hank O'Day, isn't it?"

"This is Mr. Henry O'Day," the umpire said in correction.

Like so many baseball people, O'Day was a great lobby sitter. He would find a spot in a hotel lobby off by himself where he could read the newspaper accounts of the games. He never read anything else. Once he was sitting in a hotel lobby, reading a description of a game he had umpired. A fan, recognizing him and anxious for an inside glimpse of the baseball world, sat down alongside Hank and said, "I see you're reading about the game. It was a great game, wasn't it?"

O'Day responded by glancing up, clearing his throat, and saying nothing.

The fan sized up the situation, but hoping to have better luck by using a different approach, replied, "I say, it was an excellently umpired game yesterday."

Hank raised his eyes from the paper, regarded the stranger, and said, "Just what does one do for privacy in this hotel, anyway?"

Everything about O'Day was a mystery, even his age, about which he was as sensitive as a fading actress. In a way, it's a shame that Hank was so laconic, because his career had been a long one, rich in anecdotal material that would have provided many a footnote to the history of the diamond.

The best evidence seems to indicate that Hank was born at Chicago in 1861. He began pitching at Council Bluffs in 1882, and the next year was with Bay City. In 1883 he pitched Toledo to a pennant in the old Northwestern League, and when in the following year Toledo entered the American Association, Hank stayed on with the club, becoming a pitching mate of Tony Mullane. His catcher at Toledo was the first Negro who ever played major-league baseball, Moses Fleetwood Walker. Walker, the son of a slave, had been born at Mount Pleasant, Ohio, which had been an important stop on the underground railroad before the Civil War. He was a young man of remarkable courage who succeeded in spite of great obstacles. Neither O'Day nor Mullane liked Walker, and each did his best to throw the ball so hard the catcher would be injured. But they never succeeded in forcing him off the team.

O'Day bobbed up again in 1886 with Washington of the National League, where his catcher was Connie Mack. Three years later he caught on with New York and helped win the National League pennant, then won two games from Brooklyn of the American Association in the World Series of 1889. Jumping to New York of the Players' League, Hank had his best season in 1890, winning 21 and losing 12. He then drifted back to the minors, doing his last pitching for Erie in 1893.

It was as an umpire that Hank came back to the National League in 1895, and he had been on the job every year since that time when Garry Herrmann made him manager of the Reds. O'Day had officiated in many important games. He was behind the plate the day that Merkle failed to touch second base, costing the Giants a pennant in 1908.

It would be difficult to imagine a president and manager more dissimilar than Garry Herrmann and Hank O'Day. The latter's peculiar conception of conviviality did not include sausage eating in public. But Garry did not make a practice of hobnobbing with his managers, and O'Day's work was limited to what went on on the playing field.

The Palace of the Fans also passed with Clark Griffith, for when O'Day's team opened the 1912 season, the Reds had a magnificent new grandstand, the same structure that is used today. It had a seating capacity of almost twenty-five thousand with room for several thousand standees. Gone were the days of rooters' row with the installation of the new plant.

The Reds opened their new park on April 11, 1912, with the Cubs supplying the opposition, and a throng of 26,336 watched the Reds win, 10 to 6.

O'Day fielded a team with three new regulars, Armando Marsans beating out Johnny Bates for the center-field post, and two recruits, Jimmy Esmond and Art Phelan, taking over the shortstop and third-base jobs, respectively.

Early in the year O'Day's club demonstrated a liking for the fine new park and won games at a surprising but agreeable pace. The team won its first four tilts, lost two, picked up four more triumphs, dropped one, then won six in a row for 14 victories and only 3 defeats. After splitting a pair, they won five more, bringing the record to 20 wins against 5 setbacks.

Other clubs, amazed by the Reds' early spurt, accused

O'Day, an old umpire, of having influence with the arbiters. It was assumed that, all other things being equal, it would only be human nature for umpires to give the close decisions to one of their graduates.

But the hue and cry died down as the Reds proved unable to continue their early-season heroics. The slide began in June, and by mid-July the Reds were back at the familiar .500 mark. Five straight losses to the Giants in early August submerged O'Day's boys, and they never got back to .500, except for a day or two at a time, finishing with 75 victories and 78 defeats, though still in the first division, a game and a half ahead of the fifth-place Phils.

Actually, O'Day's record as a manager wasn't bad at all. He went back to umpiring in 1913, and the following year had a fling as pilot of the Cubs, finishing fourth with them also.

2

O'Day's record as a manager of the Reds was similar to that of John Ganzel. Like Ganzel, he was at the helm just one season, and during that season Garry Herrmann was casting his eyes elsewhere. When Ganzel managed the Reds, it was Clark Griffith at whom Garry was gazing smilingly. And when O'Day bossed the Rhinelanders, the object of Garry's affections was Joe Tinker, the celebrated shortstop of the Cubs and party of the first part in the legendary "Tinker to Evers to Chance" double-play combination that made the Bruins such a potent force in National League play.

Just when Garry started romancing Tinker isn't clear, but as early as 1911 Tinker had approached Garry and said he thought he would like a managerial appointment. Joe already had the promise of the Chicago officials that they wouldn't stand in his way, in the event of a good offer. Herrmann said he thought he might be interested, but as it developed, he appointed Hank O'Day instead.

Then, in 1912, when Herrmann promised Tinker the Redleg job for 1913, Joe found he had a hard time getting Charlie Murphy, president of the Cubs, to live up to his word. Murphy suddenly became very disinterested in dealing Tinker to Cincinnati. Tinker kept insisting he be traded, and finally cornered Murphy in the Pennsylvania Station in New York City, as the latter was en route to the funeral of John Brush. At that time he told Murphy that he absolutely would not play in 1913 except as manager of the Reds. That did the trick, and Murphy and Herrmann got together on December 11, 1912, the Reds sending Mike Mitchell, Red Corridon, Art Phelan, Bert Humphries, and Pete Knisely to the Cubs for Tinker, catcher Harry Chapman, and pitcher Grover Lowdermilk.

Tinker took the Reds of 1913 to train at Mobile, where the team had pitched its first training camp under Buck Ewing in 1895. It was Joe's thirteenth season in the majors, and when he got to the clubhouse he found he had been assigned to Locker No. 13. So just to be consistent he asked Frank Bancroft to assign lower berth No. 13 to him whenever the club traveled.

In April, shortly after the opening of the season, Herrmann managed to swing a big trade with the Giants, sending pitcher Art Fromme and infielder Eddie Grant for Leon Ames, a veteran pitcher, Josh Devore, an outfielder, and Heinie Groh, a young second baseman. This turned out to be one of the best deals ever made by the club, for Groh alone proved to be worth much more than the two men lost, though at the time he was a twenty-three-year-old recruit. Tinker's team got off to a wretched start, winning but 2 of the first 14 games. Being with a loser was a new experience for Joe, just as it had been for old Ned Hanlon, and he didn't particularly relish it.

When the Reds went on their first eastern trip, they opened in New York. The Yankees were also in town, playing a final game before departing for the West, and they were managed by Frank Chance, Tinker's old pal and fellow collaborator on twin killings. Tinker went out to the park to see Chance, but received a dolorous greeting.

"Joe, I'm glad you came here," Chance said. "I want you

to meet one of my pitchers, Ray Keating. He's the only pitcher I have who has won a game yet."

"I know just how you feel," Joe replied. "I've had the same experience. I have a big Indian pitcher named Chief Johnson, and he's the only fellow who can win for my Reds, too."

"Well, I'm sorry our train's leaving tonight," Chance told his old buddy. "I'm sorry I can't stay here with you this evening and tell you how to run your club, and I know you could tell me how to run mine. I know I can't run it myself."

Joe stuck it out with a losing club, and if the cares of managing had any effect on his shortstop play, it certainly didn't show in the averages. Tinker hit .300 for the only time in his life in 1913, finishing at .317. The Reds have not had a shortstop hit .300 since. And Tinker teamed up excellently with Heinie Groh, the young second baseman, who had a .282 mark to show for his first year in the big time.

The Red pitching was in and out. Tinker had brought Mordecai (Three-Finger) Brown to Cincinnati with him, and the veteran didn't do badly, winning 11 and losing 12. But George Suggs had a sorry season, and the big Indian, George Murphy Johnson, soon demonstrated an off-the-field weakness that caused him to be suspended from time to time.

When the Reds were in the East in August, Tinker, feeling low of spirit, talked a bit too frankly about the affairs of the club to Jack Ryder, baseball writer for the *Cincinnati Enquirer*, implying that Garry Herrmann was responsible for the decline. When Ryder printed the interview with Tinker, Herrmann, boiling mad, wired Joe that he had violated baseball law by his statement.

Upon receiving this information, Tinker replied to his boss, through Ryder's column, "I don't know what law I have violated. If there is a law requiring nothing but pleasant compliments to be handed out about the officials of the club, perhaps I am a lawbreaker."

It might be thought that such an exchange of pleasantries between Tinker and Herrmann would have sealed Joe's fate. But actually, he could have managed the club again in 1914, had he so desired. Immediately after the season was over, the Reds finishing seventh with a 64 and 89 record, the club's board of directors met and voted to retain the skipper for another year. This pleased Joe immensely, as he felt that he could vastly improve the club's fortunes with more experience and with another chance. The directors informed Tinker that he would be offered a contract when he attended the minor-league meetings at Columbus.

But just at this time Tinker discovered that Garry had created a new job on the club, that of stool pigeon and house dick. The post was to go to one Harry Stevens, whose baseball experience was exactly nil, but who happened to be a good friend of the Fleischmanns. It was to be Stevens' duty to travel with the club and see that the players took good care of themselves, both on and off the field, and to make out lengthy reports on what was and was not beneficial for the players.

Tinker rebelled, saying that he absolutely refused to have a person employed in such a capacity, and that Stevens, lacking baseball experience, was not the proper person to have around a ball club. So Joe left the minor-league meeting without signing a contract, and the board of directors met once more, this time to appoint a new manager.

Shortly afterward, in the barroom of the Waldorf-Astoria, Herrmann sold Tinker to Brooklyn. But Joe never reported to the Dodgers. Angered because he couldn't find out whether he would receive part of his purchase price, as promised, he jumped instead to the Chicago Whales of the newly formed Federal League.

At the same December meeting, Garry obtained his next manager, Buck Herzog, from the Giants, in a deal for Bob Bescher.

☗ **12** ☗

HERZOG AT THE HELM

1

The Federal League invasion was much more formidable than any previous attempt to undermine the National League, with the exception of the American League's birth pangs. But the American League issue was settled because there was room for another major circuit by 1901. There was definitely no room for a third by 1914, nor is there yet. But the backers of the Federal League had plenty of money, and they had the ball parks necessary for operation. Getting Joe Tinker, the first big star to jump, was a feather in their cap. After Tinker made the leap, he was followed by such established players as Hal Chase, Mickey Doolan, Otto Knabe, Ward Miller, Russell Ford, Claude Hendrix, and Leslie Mann. Even the great Walter Johnson threatened to jump from Washington, a state of affairs that so frightened Clark Griffith, who had at last obtained the Washington club, that he made a frenzied winter trip to Kansas and by some means induced Walter to repudiate his contract with the Feds and sign a new one with the Senators.

As far as the Reds were concerned, they weren't hurt too badly by the Federals. They lost catcher Grover Hartley, who was to have come to Cincinnati with Herzog in the deal for Bescher, and they lost outfielder Armando Marsans. Also among those who vaulted into the Fed camp from Cincinnati was Chief Johnson, the Indian pitcher. Garry felt especially bitter about Johnson, for he had been remarkably tolerant of the hurler, and he tried to restrain the Chief from pitching for his new club, Kansas City, through court action.

Charles Lincoln (Buck) Herzog, who was Garry Herrmann's seventh managerial appointment in Cincinnati, was as forceful a character as many of his predecessors, and also a well-known shortstop.

A Lutheran whose grandfather was a minister, and a product of the University of Maryland, Herzog is perhaps best remembered for his peculiar relationship with John McGraw. For Herzog's career was as intertwined with McGraw and the Giants as was Damon's with Pythias. Not that the relationship was similar. On the contrary, the fiery pilot of the New York team had no use for Herzog personally, a feeling that Buck made mutual. But McGraw had such tremendous admiration for Herzog's talents that he was always selling his contract and then buying it back.

Herzog first reported to New York in 1908, after being drafted from Reading of the Tri-State League. In 1910 McGraw traded him to the Braves, then bought him back after the 1911 season for catcher Hank Gowdy and infielder Al Bridwell. He had by no means made his final appearance for McGraw, either.

Buck gave the Reds their second successive shortstop-manager, and the feeling was that if he could perform at the position with the same skill Tinker had shown, the team might possibly be a factor in the pennant chase.

But weaknesses developed in the club, in training at Alexandria, Louisiana, that were rather serious. For one thing, Dick Hoblitzell, at first, after six years as a regular, was apparently on the downgrade, and a good first baseman was not easily obtained. The only replacements Herzog had at the position were two rookies, Bill Kellogg and Dawson (Tiny) Graham. Groh at second and Herzog at short promised to be a capable duo, and Bert Niehoff seemed satisfactory at third. Tom Clarke was back to do the catching. Herzog hoped to build his pitching staff around Leon Ames, young Rube Benton, Shufflin' Phil Douglas, and Earl Yingling. The outfield presented a major problem, especially after Marsans jumped to the Feds shortly after the season got under way. During the year the Reds did not have a single outfielder who appeared in as many as one hundred games. Among those tried in the gardens were Roy Miller, Bert Daniels, George Twombly, Wade Killefer, Maurice Uhler, Howard Lohr, and Harry La Ross, in addition to Marsans. Of those named, Killefer was possibly the best known. And there's an interesting angle to the inclusion of Twombly.

Harry Stevens, the watchdog that Herrmann added to the club much to the disgust of Joe Tinker, and whose chief claim to a job was the fact that he knew the Fleischmann family, was able to pursue his duties freely with Tinker out of the way. One of the tasks to which Herrmann assigned him was a scouting expedition at Baltimore, though why Harry Stevens should have been selected to judge ballplayers is difficult to understand, to say the least. But the Reds had a working agreement with Baltimore, and the terms of it were that Cincinnati had the right to choose two players from the Oriole roster. Stevens was the man selected to make the pick. Possibly consulting a crystal ball or astrological chart, or perhaps conferring with a few fans in the washroom at the Baltimore ball park, Stevens proudly came home with short-stop Claude Derrick and outfielder George Twombly. He had looked at but was apparently not impressed with two young pitchers named Ernie Shore and Babe Ruth.

Of course, in the career of any great player, or any mediocre one, for that matter, there are pranks of fate and wisps of fortune that seem unimportant at the time, but that change the whole course of the game. Babe Ruth might have been a member of many clubs. He came close to being a Giant. It is idle to look back on a career such as his and speculate as to what would have happened had he chanced to wear a different uniform. But the point is that the Reds had their pick of the Baltimore club, and Harry Stevens made that pick. Stevens was the man Herrmann chose to do his scouting. Stevens knew next to nothing about baseball, so he overlooked Ruth and Shore. It was as simple as that. But as far as Cincinnati was concerned, it was the saddest mistake made since John T. Brush, who, however, knew what he was doing, traded Christy Mathewson for Amos Rusie.

108

Claude Derrick's career as a Cincinnati shortstop lasted exactly three afternoons before he was traded to Chicago for Fritz Mollwitz, the first baseman the Reds needed so badly. Twombly remained throughout the summer, appeared in sixty-eight games, and batted .233.

Herzog got surprising results from the club early in the 1914 campaign, especially when it is considered what material he was given to work with and the type of scout employed by the front office. The team was over the .500 mark when it headed east in June, but the National League race was a dandy, with all eight clubs neck and neck.

When the Reds first visited New York, admirers of Buck Herzog decided to give him a "day," designating a certain game to honor the Redleg manager and former Giant. John McGraw put a quick stop to their plans by refusing permission for such an event, thus showing his love for the Marylander. Undismayed, Herzog's followers then made arrangements for a "Herzog night" at a theater, but they had underestimated the influence Muggsy had in Manhattan, for he prevented the staging of that performance also. Herzog's coterie then gave up the ghost. But McGraw, not yet satisfied, tried to undermine Herzog's hold on his own club, saying all the uncomplimentary things he could think of about Buck to Tom Clarke. Naturally, Tom reported this to his manager, and the Reds, worked up to a froth, were determined to trounce the New Yorkers.

But an angry flea can do little to a Giant except sting him, and McGraw's team turned on the Reds with a vengeance, beating them three straight behind the excellent hurling of Rube Marquard, Jeff Tesreau, and Christy Mathewson.

As July rolled around, the Reds were still in the first division, in fourth place, but were beginning to slip. They sank to sixth on July 10.

Any baseball fan of today who remembers 1914 recalls it as the year that George Stallings and his "miracle team" of Boston Braves rose from the indignity of the cellar in July, swept to the National League pennant, and then bowled over Connie Mack's hitherto invincible Athletics in four straight

World Series engagements. That was unquestionably the greatest Frank Merriwell stunt of all time, and the Braves did it with just three winning pitchers—Dick Rudolph, George Tyler, and Bill James. But the game that enabled the Braves to escape from last place that year was played in Cincinnati on July 19, and the man who pitched Boston to victory was not Tyler or Rudolph or James, but a young kid named Paul Strand.

The game was the last of a series of three. On July 17, the Braves, behind James, had beaten the Reds, 1 to 0, Rube Benton losing the contest, though yielding in the latter frames to a recruit from the Pacific Coast, Pete Schneider. On the following day, Boston had again taken the measure of Herzog's crew, 6 to 3, Rudolph besting Leon Ames, with King Lear, a graduate of Princeton, finishing on the slab for the Rhinelanders. Then came Strand's game. He beat Earl Yingling, 3 to 2, and on the strength of that, Boston crept out of their eighth-place mustiness, relegating the Pittsburgh Pirates to that abode.

As September dawned, the old National League was engaged in the greatest cat-and-dog fight of its history. Boston, New York, St. Louis, Chicago, Brooklyn, and Philadelphia were all in the heat of it. And that was the moment Cincinnati chose for the longest losing streak in its history.

When Phil Douglas beat Larry Cheney and the Cubs, 4 to 2, on the afternoon of September 4, the Reds were only nine games under the .500 mark and gave promise of finishing fifth or sixth, possibly better, considering the peculiar race. But then the avalanche began.

The team dropped two games to the Cardinals at Cincinnati, then went to Chicago and lost three more. Once more the Cardinals came to Cincinnati and took four straight, extending the losing skein for Herzog's men to nine. Next, the club went east, losing a single affair at Pittsburgh, three more in New York, and five in Brooklyn. Boston was the next port of call, and Stallings took the first of the series, 3 to 2, with James pitching, and the total of nineteen had been reached. On the next day, King Lear, possibly employing scientific stuff that he had learned among the arches of Princeton, ended the horrible business by shutting out the Braves, 3 to o.

By this time, of course, the Reds were in the cellar. And there, for the first time since 1901, they closed the season, with 60 victories and 94 defeats.

2

When Herzog took his men to Alexandria again in the spring of 1915, he felt certain that the fates could not possibly be so cruel as they had been the year before. The thing that had annoyed him most in his first season at the helm was that just when the team was in a position to gain in the race, it went on the most prolonged losing jag in club history.

The outfield had to be revamped entirely, and most of the various characters who had posed as gardeners in 1914 were summarily dismissed. Two new ones were acquired in the month before the team went south—Tommy Griffith, who was purchased from Indianapolis, and the veteran Tommy Leach, who was almost thirty-eight and who had been signed after the Cubs had cut him adrift. Leach had spent most of his career with the Pirates, first as a third baseman and later as a fly-chaser. Tommy was about through, but it was felt that a man of his talents, even though in the grip of comparative senility, would be a vast improvement over the haphazard assortment of players who had masqueraded as outfielders in the 1914 steeplechase.

A deal was also swung for a catcher, the Reds sending Mike Gonzales to St. Louis for Ivy Wingo, in a three-cornered arrangement that transferred outfielder Bob Bescher from the Giants to the Cardinals. Another catcher was obtained when Herrmann and Herzog dealt infielder Bert Niehoff to Philadelphia for Charles (Red) Dooin, a thirty-six-year-old veteran who had spent most of his adult life with the Phils. To replace Niehoff, Herzog simply moved Heinie Groh from second base to third, a shift that proved wise indeed, as Heinie soon blossomed into the best guardian of the hot corner in the circuit.

As is customary in the National League, the 1915 race was a tight one. The defending champions, the Braves, ran up against unexpected opposition from two clubs that had finished in the second division the year before, Philadelphia and Brooklyn. The play of the Phillies under the wise old catcher, Pat Moran, was startlingly good. Moran was an expert with pitchers, and he built a staff around Grover Alexander, Al Demaree, George McQuillan, Erskine Mayer, George Chalmers, and Eppa Rixey that was powerful.

Pitching in Cincinnati, however, was a problem. Herzog had Ames, who was fading rapidly, Rube Benton, and King Lear, who had bad seasons, and three young hurlers who were still improving, Gene Dale, Pete Schneider, and Fred Toney. The last-named didn't make his first start until June, but after that he was a bearcat, winning 17 and losing only 6.

By July, though, the Reds were in fifth place, and more help was needed. A young outfielder named Ken Williams was purchased for $4,000 from Spokane, and a second baseman, Wilbur (Raw Meat) Rodgers, was secured from the Boston Red Sox. Williams was given an immediate shot in the outfield, the aged Tommy Leach being rested.

By August 15 the Reds had sunk to last place, but so close was the race that they were only nine and one-half games from first. Then, after winning three in a row, they were only seven and one-half contests behind, but were still last. Eventually, of course, the gaps between the clubs widened, and the Reds improved their position slightly, emerging from the cellar to finish seventh, with 71 victories and 83 defeats. The club below them, oddly enough, was the Giants, who ended in the coal hole for the first time since McGraw had taken over the club in 1902.

The Reds of 1915 played more baseball than any other Cincinnati club. In addition to numerous extra-inning games, they indulged in six ties, competing in 160 contests before it was all over. Outfielder Tommy Griffith and third baseman Heinie Groh appeared in every game, Griffith leading the club at bat with a mark of .307, and Heinie hitting .290.

Following the 1915 campaign, the Federal League went out of business as a competitor of the National and American, and baseball's latest war was over. Players began to drift back to the legitimate circuits in hordes. The Reds, however, purchased a player from the Feds, a pitcher named Earl Mosely. Garry Herrmann, perhaps in a Christmas mood, paid the Newark Federals $5,000 for the young hurler, on December 23, 1915. Another player, second baseman Bill Louden, was secured from the Buffalo Feds.

But the most famous player who came to the Reds via the Federal League was first baseman Hal Chase. Generally accepted as the greatest fielding first sacker who ever lived and a fine hitter in addition, Chase was thirty-three when he came to Cincinnati, and had several good years of baseball ahead of him. In spite of this, he was *persona non grata* because of a series of shady circumstances surrounding his play. He had for years been a controversial figure in the American League, both with the Yankees and the White Sox, and when the Federal League blew up and he was let out, the Reds were the only club in either major to express interest in him.

Chase reported to Cincinnati on April 16, 1916, on the fifth day of the league season. The Reds had lost the opener to Chicago, and had then taken three straight from the Cubs. Pittsburgh was the visiting team on the day that Hal made his appearance.

Fritz Mollwitz was at his accustomed first-base position that afternoon as Chase rode the bench, but in the third inning Fritz objected so strenuously to a called second strike that he was banished from the park by the umpire, and Chase was sent in to take his place.

The count was two strikes and no balls when Hal strode up to the plate, and he promptly slapped the first pitch over third base for a double, then, on the next pitch, stole third. Tom Clarke was the hitter, and he eventually walked. At this point, a signal was flashed and the double steal was on, Chase sliding safely home in a cloud of dust. In less than three minutes he had made a double, stolen two bases, and scored a run. If any player in the history of baseball ever made a more spectacular debut, it is not recorded. Chase had demonstrated immediately why he was regarded as a super-player, and the galleries had a new hero—for a time.

That was the end of Fritz Mollwitz as a regular with the Reds, for Chase at once became the first baseman, rounding out the infield with Bill Louden at second, Buck Herzog at short, and Heinie Groh at third.

As the season progressed, the Reds were little better than the year before. The fans, after so many lean years, were running out of patience. Ned Hanlon, John Ganzel, Clark Griffith, Hank O'Day, Joe Tinker, and now Herzog—all of them had been unable to elevate the team from the mire. Each spring had brought new hopes, each autumn more bitterness. Was there no hope? Were the Reds destined never to finish on top? Sure, they'd won a pennant—back in 1882 in the American Association. But in 1916 one had to be a middle-aged man to remember that.

As the season wore on, there were the usual rumors that Herzog was to be let out. Such is always the case with a losing club, but sometimes rumors increase in tone and clamor for denial.

Lou Widrig, treasurer of the Reds, in commenting on the reports, said on July 13, "There is absolutely no truth in any statement to the effect that Manager Herzog will leave the Reds this season."

Within a week it was announced that Herzog and out-fielder Wade Killefer had been traded to the New York Giants for Christy Mathewson and two obscure performers, an infielder named Bill McKechnie and an outfielder named Edd Roush. It was also announced that Christy Mathewson was the new manager of the Cincinnati Reds.

PAT MORAN

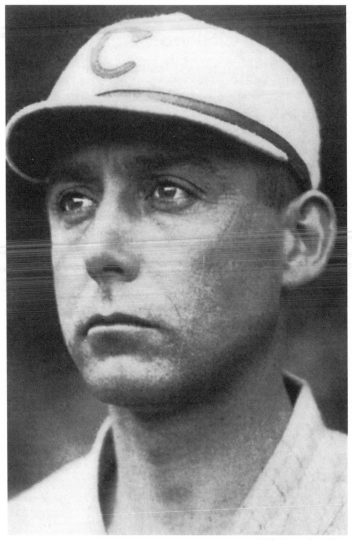

The Sporting News

EDD ROUSH

13

THE YEAR THAT BELONGED
TO FRED TONEY

1

Garry Herrmann laid the groundwork for the Herzog-Mathewson deal, not at the barroom of the Waldorf-Astoria, but amid the much more frivolous surroundings of the Elks convention at Baltimore, to which conclave he summoned the manager of the Giants.

The deal was completed in its final form on July 20, and announced the following day. But there had been a leak, and a report had spread that Herzog had been traded, and that Hal Chase had been named manager of the team. When the Reds played a double-header against Philadelphia on July 20, the fans applauded Chase every time he made a move, laboring under the impression that he was the manager. Actually, on that one day, Ivy Wingo, the catcher, was charged with running the team's affairs, but on the next afternoon, Matty, McKechnie, and Roush reported, ending the confusion.

The career of Christy Mathewson is probably as well known as that of any player who ever trod the diamond. Born at Factoryville, Pennsylvania, on August 12, 1880, Matty was educated at Bucknell University before he took up baseball as a livelihood. His work with the Giants from 1901 to 1916 has made him one of baseball's true immortals. He pitched three shutouts in the World Series of 1905 against the Athletics and won just about every pitching honor there

115

is, ending his career with a record of 373 victories and 188 defeats in 17 seasons.

One of the most pleasant aspects of the deal from a Cincinnati standpoint was that the Reds were no longer called upon to face the wizard of the mound. Of all the hurlers the Reds have ever contended with, Matty was the toughest. He beat them 1 to 0 the first time he was pitted against them, and before he was done he had defeated them 64 times while taking only 18 lickings in return, once running up a streak of 22 consecutive victories over them.

At the time the Reds made the deal for Matty, he was just about through as a pitcher, however. For the Giants in 1916 he had won 3 games and lost 4, and hadn't worked more often because of pain, not in his pitching arm, but in his left side. Matty was not quite thirty-six, and should have had several years of pitching left. But every time he took his wind-up, he would get sharp, shooting pains in his left arm, shoulder, and side.

Mathewson's first announcement to the fans of Cincinnati was that he would not attempt to pitch any more, but would pilot the club from the bench. This was a source of sorrow, because followers of the Cincinnati team, having seen Matty win with such regularity, were hoping that he would bolster the club not only with off-stage strategy but with his strong right arm. But Matty remained adamant.

There was just one exception. In the second game of a double-header at Chicago on September 4, Matty was prevailed upon to take the hill once more, against his arch rival, Mordecai (Three-Finger) Brown, who, after many a stirring duel with Matty in the National League, had pitched in the Federal before rejoining his old team, the Cubs. Like Mathewson, Brown was just about through, and the game in which they hooked up, which was probably the most sentimental hurling duel ever staged, was the last for both. Matty staggered through to a 10-to-8 triumph, but his pitching made it clear that he was definitely washed up.

"Boys, I thought I could pitch a few more games," Matty told the Redleg players in the clubhouse after his farewell appearance, "but I find I haven't got the stuff any more. I shall never attempt to pitch in a championship game again. If I ever go into the box again, I will buy every one of you a suit of clothes."

Matty's record of 373 victories is tops for the National League, though Grover Alexander of the Phils, Cubs, and Cards won exactly the same number. That last victory, No. 373, was pitched in a Cincinnati uniform. And if John T. Brush hadn't entered into collusion with the Giants to deliver Matty to New York, all his triumphs could have been notched in a Redleg livery.

In finishing that last game, 10 to 8, Matty's final big-league pitch was hit by Fritz Mollwitz, and a lazy fly to Alfred (Greasy) Neale resulted in the third out. Matty's final third out. And, as usual, he won.

At the time that Matty took over management of the Reds, the team had won 35 and lost 50. For the balance of the year there was slight chance of improving the team's finish in the league race. In reality, the club played worse ball than it had under Herzog, but Matty was taking his time, looking at his younger players, especially the pitchers, and making an analysis of what was needed to make the team a contender in the years to come.

As the season closed, the Reds played 25 games on the road, winning 10 and dropping 15 before coming home for a final contest on October 1. In Philadelphia on September 23 they ran into Grover Alexander, then a strong young right-hander who could make the ball sing. He pulled the iron-man trick against the Reds that afternoon, beating Al Schulz, 7 to 3, and then shutting out Fred Toney, 4 to 0.

When the Reds entertained Pittsburgh on the campaign's final day, they needed a victory to tie St. Louis for seventh place and escape the ignominy of a cellar finish. Fred Toney saw that they achieved it, as he shut out the Smoketowners and Wilbur Cooper, 4 to 0.

There were bright aspects of the 1916 season, however. Hal Chase, the remarkably skilled first baseman whose debut had been so sensational, was the league's leading hitter, with a mark of .339. And Edd Roush, the young outfielder who had been thrown in as an extra in the Herzog transaction, gave every indication of becoming a star. Roush took over Wade Killefer's outfield job upon reporting to the Reds. And in his debut he smashed three hits in five trips to the dish, including a ninth-inning triple off Eppa Rixey of the Phils. Yes, Roush would do. He batted .287 in sixty-nine games and had all the confidence of a veteran.

2

It was pitching that Matty knew most about, and so when he went about the task of improving the Reds' lot, his emphasis was on the mound corps. In 1916 the Reds had depended chiefly on pitchers Fred Toney, Pete Schneider, Clarence Mitchell, and Al Schulz. Matty saw at once that this quartet would never do. Toney was a star and the man around whom the new staff was to be built. Schneider and Mitchell, the latter a southpaw and spitball artist purchased for $3,000 from Denver, might do. But Schulz was definitely a flop and would have to be replaced, and more flingers would be required, youngsters with their careers ahead of them. During 1917 the Reds secured four pitchers who proved infinitely valuable, though all did not come around at once: Walter (Dutch) Ruether, Jimmy Ring, Horace (Hod) Eller, and Rube Bressler. Ruether, a southpaw and as canny a moundsman as they come, was picked up on waivers from the Chicago Cubs. He was only twenty-four years old. Ring, a fast-baller with previous tryouts with Brooklyn and the Yankees, was purchased from Buffalo, much to the surprise of the Yanks, who in those days of irregular practices thought they had him safely tucked away for future use. He was twenty-two. Bressler, who had had brief trials with the Philadelphia Athletics, later found his real niche as an outfielder. He was also a southpaw, and was twenty-three. Eller, who employed a strange delivery called the shine ball, was drafted from Moline. He was also twenty-three.

The rest of the team seemed well set, with Ivy Wingo and

Tom Clarke behind the bat; the great Chase at first; Dave Shean, a veteran purchased from Providence, at second; Larry Kopf, who had had a previous trial with the Athletics, at short; and Heinie Groh at third. Tommy Griffith, Edd Roush, and Greasy Neale combined to form a substantial outfield.

Matty started the season with his young pitchers Eller and Ring used chiefly in relief roles, watching Toney, Schneider, and Mitchell take their regular turns. And what these youngsters saw on the afternoon of May 2, 1917, must have made their eyes pop.

It was just a routine game between the Reds and Cubs, with Fred Toney starting for the Reds and Hippo Jim Vaughn for the Bruins. It was a bitterly cold Wednesday afternoon at Weeghman Park, with only about 2,500 in the stands.

How often it is that small crowds witness some of baseball's greatest doings. Toney and Vaughn that afternoon became matched in what turned out to be the greatest pitching battle of all time. At the end of nine innings the contest was not only runless but hitless! This was absolutely unheard of. Pitchers had pitched no-hitters before, of course, but never in opposition to each other in the same ball game. In nine innings Toney had been suberb. He walked Cy Williams, the Chicago center fielder, in the second inning and again in the fifth, the only Bruin to reach base. Vaughn had pitched on a par with Fred, walking Groh twice and each time seeing him erased on a double play. Neale also reached base on a fumble by Rollie Zeider, the Cub shortstop, but was out attempting to steal. As the game went into the tenth inning, the crowd, sensing the history that was being made that afternoon, forgot about the cold and sat in rigid astonishment. Then, in the tenth frame, the spell was broken. After Gus Getz, the Red second baseman, had been retired to start the tenth, Larry Kopf shattered Vaughn's record with the first blow of the game, a line single to right field. Chase then socked a line drive to center that Williams muffed after getting both hands on the ball, Kopf going to third. Jim

Thorpe, the Indian who won his greatest fame on football fields and in the Olympic Games but who was a reserve outfielder with the 1917 Reds, then scratched a hit in front of the plate, and Kopf raced across the plate with a run. Thorpe's hit was one of those balls that, when topped, bounce high in the air in front of the plate. Vaughn rushed in on the hit, saw Thorpe was nearing first, and realized his only play was at the plate. But Art Wilson, the Bruin receiver, was caught off guard, and missed Vaughn's toss as Kopf crossed over. That was the ball game, as Toney retired the Chicagoans in order in their half. Vaughn fanned ten batters and Toney only three.

That game was one of those "once in a lifetime" affairs, but for Fred Toney, whose career seems to have been touched with some rare enchantment, it was not even his longest no-hitter. Back in 1909, pitching in his first year of professional baseball for Winchester, Kentucky, of the Blue Grass League, against Lexington, Toney pitched a no-hit game that went *seventeen* innings. The date was May 10, 1909, and Winchester scored the only run of the contest to win, 1 to 0, in the last half of the seventeenth. Toney walked only one batter over the entire route, though his Winchester mates made four errors behind him. When inning after inning of that game unfolded and word spread of what Toney was doing throughout the little Kentucky town, citizens rushed to the park, deserting supper tables laden with fried chicken and Kentucky corn bread, and engineers in the railroad yards, learning about the proceedings, started their whistles going.

Throughout May and June the Reds, after a slow start, began to show improvement under their masterful manager. Matty began to use his young pitchers more and more. Playing at home against the Cubs on June 19, he even let Hod Eller essay the iron-man stunt. After dropping the lid-lifter, 2 to 1, to Jim Vaughn, Hod defeated Vic Aldridge, 6 to 2, in the six-inning nightcap halted by darkness. Matty tabbed the "shine ball" boy as a comer on that afternoon.

Fred Toney, not yet out of heroics, and inspired by Eller's performance, asked Matty for a chance to become an iron man too. So on the afternoon of July 1, against the Pittsburgh Pirates, Fred pitched and won both contests of a twin bill, 4 to 1 and 5 to 1, both nine-inning affairs, and remarked that he could have pitched and won a third game, if necessary. And when the Reds won again the next day, they reached the .500 mark for the first time.

The Reds continued to play good baseball, both at home and on the road. For the first time since 1903 they were able to hold their own with the hated Giants, holding McGraw's club to an even split of the twenty-two games. And every time Christy Mathewson made his appearance at the Polo Grounds, he was cheered to the topmost rafter.

Sunday baseball in New York had always been outlawed, and usually when the Reds were in the East they took advantage of off Sundays to go over to New Jersey and pick up some change by playing exhibition games. In these exhibitions young Bill McKechnie, the infielder who came to the Reds along with Matty and Roush, served as the team's manager. McKechnie had managed the Newark team of the Federal League for Harry Sinclair in 1915, and Matty recognized him as one of the smartest young players in the game.

But on one Sunday afternoon—August 19—the Reds and Giants staged a championship National League game, in defiance of the law. Toney pitched another shutout, 5 to 0, over Al Demaree, and immediately afterward the two managers, McGraw and Mathewson, were forced to appear in police court to explain why baseball had been played on Sunday at the Polo Grounds for the first time in history.

Jack Ryder, the able baseball scribe of the *Cincinnati Enquirer*, who always spiced his columns with gentle sarcasm, sly digs, and subtle quips about life in general, wrote:

After the game Matty and McGraw had to appear in Washington Heights Police Court to answer the terrible charge of instigating a game of baseball on Sunday. The summons was issued by the so-called Sabbath Society. Magistrate Frothingham dismissed the case and complimented the managers for providing enjoyment for soldiers who were in the stands. As a comment on the hypocrisy of human nature, however, it was necessary for him to announce that he let them off because the money taken in at the gate was paid by the fans to hear the alleged sacred concert which preceded the game, and not to see the contest. It's a queer world!

The Reds slumped a little as the season matured, but Toney went on winning, and at the end of the line the Reds were in fourth place, with 78 wins and 76 defeats. Matty had done a noble job with a club that had barely escaped the cellar the year before.

Another remarkable feature of the season was the work of Edd Roush, who in his first full year in the major leagues replaced Hal Chase as batting champion, with a mark of .341, giving the Reds the hitting championship for the second successive season.

But the year was really Fred Toney's year. Not only did the big right-hander pitch his ten-inning no-hit game and pull the iron-man stunt, but he won 24 games and lost 16, notching more victories for the club than any hurler since Pink Hawley in 1898.

When the great pitchers of the game are named, you don't often hear of Toney, but the Tennessean, on occasion, was the equal of any. After his stunning seventeen-inning no-hitter with Winchester in 1909, Fred had climbed to the majors in 1911 with the Cubs, but he drifted back to Louisville in 1912. Drafted from the Falls City team by Brooklyn after the 1914 season, he found himself unable to come to terms with the Dodgers, and the Reds were able to purchase his contract in February 1915.

Still another pleasant surprise was the late-season work of the veteran outfielder Sherry Magee, who filled in for Greasy Neale. Sherry hit .324 in forty-five games.

SHERRY MAGEE, EDD ROUSH, AND
EARLE (GREASY) NEALE

EUGENE (BUBBLES)
HARGRAVE

CHARLES (RED) LUCAS

⊗ 14 ⊗

HAL CHASE: ENIGMA

1

When the Reds returned from their training base at Montgomery, Alabama, to open the 1918 season, Matty felt that the club would be improved because of the addition of a second baseman named Lee Magee. In 1917 Dave Shean had failed to be a ball of fire at the position and hit only .210. So in April, the Reds traded catcher Tom Clarke, who had been with the club for a decade but who was no longer needed with Ivy Wingo doing most of the work, to the Giants for Magee. The new man's real name was Leopold Hoernchemeyer, but he had shortened it for box-score purposes, to the eternal gratitude of members of the printing craft. Magee, a native Cincinnatian, was twenty-nine when he joined the Reds, after launching his major-league career with the Cardinals in 1910. He had been another of the many players who had jumped to the Federal League, and had served as manager of the Brooklyn team of that circuit. After peace was made with the Feds, Lee became a Yankee, put in a season with the Browns, and had just joined the Giants when the Reds swung the deal for his services.

Otherwise, the Reds were much the same team as took the field in 1917, a young club that gave promise of improvement, especially in the pitching department.

There were a few changes brought about by the fact that the country was at war. Since the drafting of men into the Army was not universal in World War I, the lot of the ballplayer was an unpleasant one, with fans wondering, often quite loudly, why able-bodied men were not in uniform. Dutch Ruether, the promising young southpaw, pitched only two games before joining the Army. Larry Kopf, the shortstop, spent the season working in the shipyards, and he was replaced with a veteran fill-in, Russell (Lena) Blackburne. Ruether's departure was more easily accepted, as it meant only that Toney, Schneider, Eller, Ring, and Bressler would get more work on the slab.

The Reds were a first-division club now, rid of all the feelings of inferiority that accompany chronic losers, and early in May they went on an eight-game winning streak that put them up in the race, along with the Cubs and Giants. Roush was hitting the ball with all his certitude, Groh had by this time become a .300 hitter, and Chase, still a dazzler around first base, had his good days at bat.

That team of 1918 Reds might have been good enough to win the pennant had it not been for the gradual appearance of an unforeseen cloud of the strangest possible variety.

Sometime during the summer Christy Mathewson came to the conclusion that Hal Chase was acting in a most peculiar manner. Though he was still one of the greatest players in the game, his work at times was so bizarre that Matty could only conclude he was not playing to win. That was a serious charge, and because it was so grave a thing, the manager remained quiet and just watched. Chase and Lee Magee were great friends off the field, and were often observed in hushed conversations. That seemed meaningless, though Chase was not one to inspire close friendship.

The play that Chase consistently made that aroused his boss's suspicion was when he retrieved a ground ball and made the toss to the pitcher covering first base. Matty had been a pitcher all his life, and he had engaged in this play so often he knew exactly how it should be executed. And Chase, being a wizard at all phases of first-base work, knew the mechanics of the play to perfection. But Matty noticed that Chase would often make his throw to the pitcher just erratic enough so the play would miss, and the batter would be safe.

124

To all appearances, when this play went wrong, the fault was with the pitcher. But Matty knew better.

Finally, in a series at Boston, Chase's work became so erratic that Matty, knowing full well what was implied when he took action, conferred with Garry Herrmann. A statement was issued in which it was said that Chase was suspended without pay. Hal left the club, and Sherry Magee was brought in from the outfield to take over first base.

In the next few weeks the incident was temporarily forgotten in the face of what appeared to be more important news. Matty was leaving the team to accept a commission as captain in the Chemical Warfare Division of the Army. He managed the club for the last time on August 27, in a doubleheader in Cincinnati against Boston, the teams splitting the contests. The Reds had won 61 and lost 57 and were in third place.

Third baseman Heinie Groh was made manager of the team, but the understanding was that it was a temporary appointment, made only for the balance of the season. And the balance of the season didn't amount to much because the nation was by this time operating under the "work or fight" edict. That order meant the end of baseball for 1918, and the magnates sensibly decided to abbreviate the season, ending hostilities on Labor Day.

Groh's record as manager of the Reds was most unusual. There were only ten games left to play under his guidance, and the team won seven of the ten, ending the campaign with six consecutive victories. Even stranger was the fact that in Groh's entire managerial career—ten games—every pitcher he selected to start finished his game. One of them, and the man who closed the season with a 1-to-0 triumph over the Cardinals, was a young right-hander, a Cuban, named Adolfo Luque, who had been purchased in July from Louisville for $7,500. The Reds finished third with 68 victories and 60 defeats.

That winter Garry Herrmann brought formal charges of throwing games against Hal Chase, filing them with John Heydler, president of the National League. Heydler held a meeting behind closed doors, January 30, 1919, at which the evidence against the player was presented. The weakness of the club's case against Hal was the fact that the most important witness against him, Christy Mathewson, was in France. Matty, however, was represented by affidavits in which the charges were outlined. Pitchers Jimmy Ring and Mike Regan, of the Reds, were called as witnesses. John McGraw, manager of the Giants, Poll Perritt, a pitcher on the New York club, and Sid Mercer, a sports writer, were also summoned to testify.

The upshot of the investigation was that Heydler acquitted Chase completely, saying, "In one game in which it was intimated that Chase bet against his club, the records show that in the sixth inning, with two men on base and the score two to nothing against his team, Chase hit a home run, putting Cincinnati one run ahead."

The probability is that John Heydler cleared Chase because he felt the case against the player was weak, the publicity was bad for the game of baseball, and there was always the danger of lawsuits.

But one of the strange aspects of the matter is that during the course of the inquiry, John McGraw announced that if Chase were declared innocent, he would hire him to play for the Giants. This was actually done, and after the acquittal McGraw obtained Hal in a deal for catcher Bill Raridan.

But Chase failed to last long with the Giants. John Heydler, still intrigued by the case, continued his investigation and happened onto some information furnished by a Boston bookmaker, along with some canceled checks that indicated Chase had bet against the Reds. Chase was then dropped by the Giants. He had come to the end of the road in organized baseball.

Hal's career had long been tinged with mystery. A product of California, he had attended Santa Clara University and had started his professional career on the Coast in 1903. He attracted immediate attention by the startling cunning of his play. A left-handed thrower, he strangely batted right-handed, and he liked to slide into bases headfirst. Clark Griffith, at

126

that time manager of the Highlanders, as the New York Yankees were then called, drafted Hal from Los Angeles and installed him at first base in place of John Ganzel. His wizardry was immediately noticed, and he was dubbed "Prince Hal."

But as the fans daily had occasion to marvel at his work, his fellow players had little love for him. Hal had a superior air, and made no secret of the fact that he considered most players inferior in intelligence. Other infielders would frequently try to show him up by making their throws as hard as possible and designed to arrive at a difficult angle. But Hal would always smile and dig the ball out of the dirt or out of the air, emerging from the play looking better than ever.

Chase's first difficulty came in 1908, when he jumped the Highlanders and finished out the season at Stockton, California, in an outlaw league. For this offense he could have been barred from the pastime for five years, but the fans clamored for him and he was reinstated during the winter. He was even made manager of the Highlanders in 1910, a rather absurd choice, for although he was blessed with individualistic genius, he was anything but a leader of men. He was let out as pilot after two seasons, but remained as a player, first under Harry Wolverton and then under Frank Chance. It was Chance who first suspected that Hal was not giving his best efforts, and he had him transferred to the Chicago White Sox.

In every baseball contract there is a clause that a club can release a player upon ten days' notice. Hal Chase felt that in order to be equitable, this should work both ways. So when the Federal League came into existence, Chase simply gave the White Sox his ten days' notice and jumped to Buffalo. Charlie Comiskey, the White Sox owner, decided to take court action and restrain Hal from playing with another club. The result was that the courts upheld Chase's version of what was an equitable contract and severely criticized the whole structure of baseball law. But when the Feds blew up, the Reds were the only club to show an interest in Hal.

Chase was well paid in Cincinnati, his salary being $8,333.33 per season. Those writers who imply that when players have been suspected of dishonesty the real fault lay with parsimonious magnates who underpaid them simply do not have a case. Hal Chase's problems were not financial in nature, but were problems of personality.

When John McGraw dismissed Hal late in the 1919 season, it was the beginning of a sad chapter in his career. He went west and became a drifter, playing baseball in the outlaw circuits of the desert region, the wildcat copper loops and semi-pro circuits around the Mexican border. His number was definitely up when it was revealed that he had guilty knowledge of the scheme to throw the 1919 World Series. As a crowning indignity he was barred from the parks of the Pacific Coast League.

The new generations of fans, knowing of Hal Chase only by hearsay, are familiar with the fact that he was probably the greatest first baseman who ever lived and a man who left the game under a cloud.

But Hal Chase was by no means a hoodlum. He was simply completely amoral. He had no sense whatever of what constituted right and wrong. After his banishment from baseball, he began to depend heavily on alcohol. He used it in ever increasing quantities, and since the United States was at this time embarking on a "noble experiment" to legislate morality, the quality of the stuff he poured into his stomach made certain his oblivion.

All through the twenties and early thirties he continued to play outlaw ball, and toward the end the price for his services was only a couple of drinks. He became a wanderer of the wasteland, an itinerant among the cactus leagues, exhibiting his genius as long as his body could stand it, and then relaxing with the temporary nepenthe of tequilla, crawling at night to the blurred oblivion of deep sleep in some tourist camp or wretched desert filling station. And who knows what his thoughts were as he lay in some drab bunk, looking out at the sagebrush as the Big Dipper winked down at the sand?

Eventually he fell heir to beriberi, that strange disease which often comes to people who drink and do not eat. His system wrecked with vitamin deficiency, he finally died at Colusa, California, on May 18, 1947.

As the end approached he showed signs of wanting to make a clean breast of things, but even so, he was still utterly unable to tell the whole truth.

"I knew it years ago," Hal said on his deathbed, "and I know it more clearly now—that my life has been one great mistake after another." But he gave no details.

One mistake Chase made was not continuing an interesting correspondence he had with Judge Landis. In one of the lucid moments of his latter years, he wrote to baseball's commissioner, vaguely admitted that he had made some mistakes, and asked what his status was. Landis replied that so far as he knew, the Commissioner's office had nothing against him, but what, by the way, were the mistakes he referred to? Chase never answered the letter.

Amoral though he was, Hal was apparently a good judge of character in others. For he once said of Judge Landis, "I wonder how many people realize what Landis has done for baseball. Where would the game be without him? His consistent championing of the underdog and his determination to see that justice prevails, no matter what the cost, has made him, in my opinion, the most valuable member of the whole baseball fraternity."

Hal blamed much of his trouble on leaving his first wife, after four years of marriage, in 1912. But it is doubtful if sticking with her would have headed off disaster. The trouble with Hal Chase was innate.

The career of Chase is a tragedy, of course. If he were to be judged solely on his ability as a baseball player, he should, naturally, be included among the immortals at Cooperstown. But one of the requirements for inclusion among that exclusive fraternity is integrity. Hal Chase was one of the most talented, remarkable, and interesting personalities the game has ever known.

The Armistice brought peace, and with it the assurance that baseball would carry on. But major-league magnates were still timid, and arranged for only a 140-game schedule for 1919.

Garry Herrmann had numerous problems, the first of which was inability to get in touch with Christy Mathewson, who was still overseas with the AEF. That left the Reds without a manager for 1919. After sending one cable after another without success, Garry finally determined to seek a pilot elsewhere. He found his man in Pat Moran, who had managed the pennant-winning Phillies of 1915. Moran, a veteran catcher, had bossed the Phils through 1918, but had resigned because of difficulties with the front office, signing with the Giants as a coach. McGraw readily agreed to permit him to come to Cincinnati to take over management of the Reds.

⊖ **15** ⊖

RAINBOW'S END

1

In all the years that Garry Herrmann had been trying to build a pennant-winner in Cincinnati, he had met with one disappointment after another. To his friends and to the pestiferous acquaintances who always come within the radius of a ball club's front office, he kept insisting, "Someday we will win." Garry had been forty-three when he became president of the Reds. In the spring of 1919 he was almost sixty. The best years of his life had been devoted to the cause of bringing Cincinnati a championship, but after seventeen years of work, the pennant was still a dream. Frank Bancroft, the devoted business manager, had given even more of his life to the same cause. When Banny first moved to the Queen City with

Kelly's Killers in 1891, he had been forty-five. In the spring of 1919 he was almost seventy-three.

That pennant still seemed far away when Pat Moran, the new manager, gathered his flock of hopefuls for spring training at Waxahachie, Texas. It was a dismal setting for a camp. During the first few days it rained, and the players worked out in such odd settings as the railroad tracks and the platform of a cotton mill, and eventually utilized the town graveyard.

Moran shook his head sadly over the club. There was no proven shortstop or second baseman. Lee Magee had refused to report. The sale of Fred Toney to the Giants by the front office had left the pitching uncertain. Edd Roush, the star of the club, who was always reluctant to begin a new season, had announced his retirement, as was his annual custom. The dismissal of Hal Chase left the team without a first baseman, as Walter Holke, a first sacker obtained with catcher Bill Raridan in the deal for Chase, had been peddled to Boston for a reserve infielder, Jimmy Smith, later famous for having a fight with his son-in-law, boxer Billy Conn.

But Moran quickly took steps to improve the club's personnel. Lee Magee's contract was sold to Brooklyn for shortstop Larry Kopf, who had been with the Reds in 1917. The second-base job was given to Morris Rath, who had been drafted from Salt Lake City. Never much of a hitter, Rath proved to be fast and was used as lead-off man in the batting order. He was exceptional on double plays.

The best transaction of all was made with Brooklyn, which club was having contract trouble with Jake Daubert, the veteran first baseman. Daubert made the Brooklyn president, Charlie Ebbets, so angry over his salary demands that Charlie convinced himself that Jake was slipping and transferred him to the Reds for outfielder Tommy Griffith. That gave the Reds an inner works of Daubert, Rath, Kopf, and Groh that was superb.

The key to the whole club was Roush, and when Edd decided to report, the team's outlook visibly brightened.

Roush, in many ways, is one of the most interesting athletes

131

who ever wore Redleg livery, and certainly one of the greatest. He is a native of Oakland City, Indiana, and his correct full name was and is Edd J. Roush. Roush knows of no particular reason for the two d's in his given name, but that is his name, nevertheless. You can find it painted on barns in rural Indiana to this day, a relic of the time when Edd was without a peer among the outfielders of baseball. His middle initial of J. is also correct. Roush had two uncles, one named James and the other Joseph, and rather than show partiality, his parents gave him the J. to stand for both of them.

There is a legend about Roush to the effect that he was originally a right-handed thrower, but broke his arm and then learned to throw with his left. This legend was started by an Indiana barber, one of those Ring Lardnerian characters with a vivid imagination, who passed the yarn on to Dick Kinsella, a famous baseball scout of his day, who happened into the region where tales of young Roush abounded. Actually, Roush always was a left-handed thrower. But as a child, when he played around the small Hoosier towns, there were no gloves suitable for southpaws. Rather than wear a glove on the wrong hand, Roush tried to be a right-hander, wearing the only glove obtainable on the hand for which it was designed. Then, as soon as he was old enough to afford a glove of his own, he managed to buy one that fitted on his right hand and permitted him to throw in the southpaw style that was natural to him.

Edd's first big-league club was the Chicago White Sox, but it was with Newark of the Federal League that he first attracted attention. Roush was by far the best player developed by the Federals, though the most publicized was outfielder Benny Kauff. Both were sold to the Giants, Kauff for $35,000, Roush for $7,500. There was a reason for the difference.

"Germany" Schaefer, who had played second base for the Newark Feds, was one of the first to see Roush's promise, and he became one of Edd's biggest boosters. Schaefer told Fred Lieb, the veteran baseball writer, "Roush is by far the best player we had."

But Kauff, a flamboyant strutter with a good sense of

132

publicity, was the batting champion of the Federals, and when Harry Sinclair, the team's owner, began to peddle his stars to the majors, Kauff was the first one they asked about. McGraw bought not only Kauff and Roush, but Bill McKechnie and Bill Raridan from the Newark club.

When Roush and McKechnie were thrown in the Mathewson-Herzog deal in 1916, many people felt that McGraw had misjudged Edd. It is often said that selling Roush was one of McGraw's few mistakes in judgment. But it wasn't really a mistake in judgment at all. He had Kauff at the time, and had paid so much for him that he felt an obligation to use him.

After arriving in Cincinnati, Roush did not wait long to prove his worth. He won the batting championship of the league in 1917, and failed to repeat in 1918 by only two percentage points, losing out to Zack Wheat of Brooklyn, .335 to .333. By the spring of 1919 Roush was accepted as one of the league's greatest stars.

He was a remarkable fielder, his only weakness being on ground balls. He specialized in circus catches, and the memory of Edd tearing across the outfield to snare hits that were tagged as doubles or triples is one of the proudest recollections of Cincinnati fans. He was a left-handed hitter who liked to poke the ball to all fields, and he constantly moved around in the batter's box. Pitchers who tried to pitch him outside were apt to find him perched on second base after slashing a safety down the left field line. If they pitched him inside, he pulled the ball to right field. He was also a guess hitter and delighted in imagining what the next pitch would be, setting himself accordingly.

His annual custom of not reporting to training camp was twofold in origin. First of all, Edd was a cagey individual with a dollar bill. Baseball will never need to hold a benefit for him. He always had a high estimate of his services, and he usually ended up by signing for his original demand. But it was more than that. Roush simply hated to play baseball when nothing was at stake. Exhibition games bored him. And he felt that the long training grind each spring was unnecessary. Often Roush would announce his holdout campaign, sit at home at Oakland City, then report two or three days before the opening game, after taking only a few practice swings.

"No player should require more than a week or ten days to get in shape," Edd often said. But in that respect he was a freak. He always took care of himself, and, outside of a tendency toward charley horses, he was always in shape to play. That common baseball muscle injury, however, frequently kept him from the line-up.

Next to Roush, the star of the club was Groh, and there is something of a parallel in the careers of the two. Like Roush, Groh had come to the Reds as a throw-in in a deal with the Giants. He had been a young second baseman when the Giants shipped him to the Reds in 1913 with pitcher Leon Ames for outfielder Josh Devore and pitcher Art Fromme.

At the time that Groh played third base for the Reds, he was the best guardian of the hot corner in the league, and a very capable batter. He is remembered chiefly because he used what was called a "bottle bat," a war club with a very short handle, and an extremely plump meat end. The origin of the "bottle bat" was unusual.

Unable to hit a curve when he started playing professional ball, Groh decided he needed a bat with plenty of hitting space. But the big bats that he would have liked to use were unsuited to him because he could hardly swing them. So he started cutting down the size of the handle, until the bat was light enough for him to swing.

One day a teammate shouted, "Hey, Heinie, what are you using, a bottle?" and there it was. The handle was only about six inches long, but the bat weighed forty-one ounces.

Groh was a right-handed hitter, and he always stood with his feet facing the pitcher, far up in the box, hitting the curve before it could break. After Heinie was a famous player, the bat manufacturers were glad to design a stick that met his specifications, and variations of his model are still occasionally seen in the major leagues.

Pat Moran knew that any club with Roush and Groh in the line-up could be a pennant threat provided the pitching held up. And it was with pitchers that Pat worked his greatest

134

magic. An old catcher himself, he had come to the National League in 1901, joining Boston from Montreal. After five years with the Braves, he moved on to the Cubs and spent four and one-half seasons at Chicago before joining the Phils in 1910. Made manager of the Phillies in 1915, he won a pennant that first season and finished second in 1916 and 1917, slipping to sixth in 1918, with Eppa Rixey, one of his best pitchers, in the Army.

Pat didn't know what to think of his Cincinnati pitchers, and instead of four starters, he had six. Dutch Ruether and the veteran Slim Sallee were the southpaws, Hod Eller, Ray Fisher, Jimmy Ring, and young Dolf Luque the right-handers. All were capable of winning if at their best, but it was the sort of staff that might easily become disorganized. And giving each of the six enough work to be effective was another problem. Rube Bressler, who had been a pitcher, was given a trial in left field, making up for the loss of Tommy Griffith. Roush was in center, of course, and Greasy Neale in right. Wingo and Raridan and a newcomer, Nick Allen, were the catchers.

2

On opening day a throng of 22,462, delighted that another season had begun but afraid that another pennantless year was in store, watched the Reds defeat St. Louis, 6 to 2, Luque relieving Ruether to receive credit for the win. Then, on successive days, Fisher handed a second defeat to the Cardinals, 3 to 1, Eller bested them 5 to 1, and Luque also trimmed them 5 to 1, the Reds sweeping the four-game series, opening the year with four consecutive triumphs for the first time since Hank O'Day's 1912 club had won the first four contests played at Redland Field. The fans began to wonder about the club.

The wonder grew when Pittsburgh came to town and the Reds won two more behind Ruether and Fisher. Then the team hopped to St. Louis and, after Eller had won his second outing, the streak was finally ended at seven, with Oscar Tuero, a Cuban youngster, beating Ruether.

Against St. Louis on May 11 Hod Eller gave the home fans more to cheer about when he came through with a no-hit effort, beating a young southpaw named Jakie May, 6 to 0. Toney's famous double no-hit job in 1917 had been pitched in Chicago, and Eller's was the first no-hit game by a Redleg pitcher seen by the home fans since Noodles Hahn hurled one against the Phils in 1900.

Eller was a deceptive hurler whose deception was due to a freak delivery. Employing what was known as the "shine ball," he was reluctant to divulge exactly what it was he did to the ball to make it take a peculiar course toward the batter. But using paraffin or talcum, or perhaps both, Eller smoothed one side of the ball up so much that it arrived at the plate swirling crazily, and when he could control the delivery, it was almost impossible to hit.

When Babe Ruth glorified the home run to such a degree that magnates looked for ways and means of increasing the frequency of the four-baggers, one of the first things they did was make pitchers stop using freak deliveries. Thus it was that in 1920 the "shine ball" was barred, and Eller's effectiveness was at an end. That was a tough break for the hurler, for without the "shine ball" he was just another pitcher. When the freak deliveries were barred, an exception was made in the case of spitball pitchers, and those already equipped with the moist delivery were permitted to continue to use it. But the "shine ball" was definitely ruled out, and the batters were mighty glad of it.

The next time Eller took the mound after his no-hit effort, he pitched a game that was even more remarkable in some respects. Four days after blanking the Cardinals, he was thrown in against Brooklyn, the first stop for the Reds in their first invasion of the East. The game immediately developed into a duel between Hod and Al Mamaux, the Dodger hurler who was also celebrated for his singing ability. Inning after inning passed without a score, and the game was still a runless deadlock when the Reds went to bat in the thirteenth frame. Then, without any warning whatever, the Reds exploded, knocking the ball to all portions of Ebbets

136

Field. Before the carnage was over, ten runs had crossed the plate, and when Eller retired the Dodgers in their half of the thirteenth, one of the strangest extra-inning shutouts of all time, 10 to 0, was recorded.

Next port of call was New York, and the skeptics who had viewed the team's early success with a lifted eyebrow predicted that the Reds would fold. How often the Reds of the past had been able to do well until they crossed bats with McGraw's hated Giants!

The first contest between the Reds and Giants saw the Giants triumph, 5 to 0, Rube Benton defeating Slim Sallee in a battle of southpaws. But on the following day Dolf Luque, who was to plague the Giants so many times in the coming years, evened the series by downing Jess Barnes, 6 to 4. The odd game of the series was a free-hitting affair, with the New Yorkers coming out on top, 7 to 5.

By the first of June, New York was in first place, with a five-game margin over the Reds, but the latter club was now set for a long stretch of games on home soil. And the Reds were able to gain on McGraw by the careful use of a McGraw method. It was long a theory with the manager cf the Giants that if a team could smash the daylights out of the second-division clubs, it could win pennants by simply playing .500 ball against the other contenders.

So the Reds started working on the league's second division, Brooklyn, Boston, St. Louis, and Philadelphia, showing no mercy against them, hoping they would be able to gain a standoff with the Giants, Cubs, and Pirates. And the system worked to perfection.

Improving their work during the long home stand, the Reds cut the Giants' first-place margin to two and a half games by June 17, and a game and a half by July 1, and to five percentage points by July 15. For the first time in years it dawned on the loyal Cincinnati rooters that at last the team was in the race and had an excellent chance of winning.

Interest in the club was at a fever pitch, not only in Cincinnati, but throughout the adjoining states. In those days before the radio, farmers stood beside their plows, awaiting

137

from rural mailmen news of the latest game played by the Reds. The results of games were posted in the villages, and telephone wires were kept busy until late at night. The rural circulation of Cincinnati newspapers got a terrific boost.

New York came to Cincinnati on August 1, and the Reds were in such a position that they could take first place by winning the first game of the series. Moran chose Jimmy Ring as his pitcher for the all-important game, McGraw countering with Fred Toney. It was the chance of chances, and the Reds won, 6 to 2, Eller going to the box when the Giants started to get rough with Ring. Again the next day the Reds won, Sallee twirling a masterful shutout to beat Benton, 6 to 0. The Giants took the final game, 4 to 0, behind Jess Barnes, but the Reds had taken the series and the advantage was now theirs.

It was a hard-fought series, too. The long-suffering Red fans, having been tormented by McGraw for so many seasons, were violently partisan, booing every umpire's decision that went against their darlings, hissing every futile effort the Giants made to fight back.

But the big test was yet to come. The Reds and Giants were scheduled to meet in three successive double-headers, in as many days, at the hostile Polo Grounds, starting August 13. Feeling between the two clubs ran so high that the Reds took their own bottled drinking water to New York, rather than run the risk of being poisoned.

A six-game series between the first- and second-place clubs in the heat of a pennant race is the ultimate test. And Pat Moran found that a six-man pitching staff is a handy thing to have around.

On the first day—the big day—the Reds won both games by one run, Dutch Ruether beating Artie Nehf, 4 to 3, and Slim Sallee nosing out Shufflin' Phil Douglas, 2 to 1. On the following day it was the Giants' turn, Toney beating Ring, 2 to 1, in a splendid duel in the opener, then Moran gambling with Rube Bressler and losing the contest to Rube Benton, 9 to 3. But on the final day the Reds once more reached the heights. With the series at stake, Hod Eller shined up the ball as he never had before and brushed by Jess Barnes, 4 to 3. And in

138

BILL McKECHNIE

ERNIE LOMBARDI

The Sporting News

JOHNNY VANDER MEER

The Sporting News

the final contest of the six, Ray Fisher wielded the whitewash brush, blanking McGraw's club, 4 to 0, to give the Reds the series, four games to two. That was it! The pennant race was decided then and there. In the other cities of the East, the Reds really romped, taking two out of three games in Brooklyn, three straight in Boston, and five straight in Philadelphia, running the winning streak to ten in a row. By that time there was no doubt that the Reds were going to win, and by September 2 they had increased their first-place margin to seven full games. The shortened schedule made the prospect of the Reds' winning a virtual certainty. The actual clinching of the pennant took place on September 16, when Dutch Ruether beat the Giants and Fred Toney, 4 to 3. The Reds were nine games ahead with only eight to play.

When the curtain fell on the 1919 season, the Reds had won 96 and lost 44, and the Giants were second with a record of 87 and 53.

It was team play more than individual accomplishment that brought the pennant to the Reds. The infield of Daubert, Rath, Kopf, and Groh functioned with a precision that was disheartening to the opposition.

The outfield had been bolstered by the late-season purchase of Pat Duncan from Birmingham, and he displaced Bressler and Magee as the regular guardian of left field.

Edd Roush led the league in batting once more, hitting .321, three points better than a young St. Louis infielder who showed promise of becoming a fine hitter, Rogers Hornsby. Groh hit .310, Daubert .276, Kopf .270.

The two southpaws Slim Sallee and Dutch Ruether turned out to have the best records of any of the pitchers, Sallee winning 21 games while losing 7, and Ruether having a record of 19 and 6. Eller was 19 and 9, Fisher 14 and 5, Ring 10 and 9, and Luque, capable but seldom used during the season's last half, won 10 and lost only 3.

Cincinnati fandom, having a championship team for the first time since 1882 and for the first time ever in the National League, now turned its attention to the World Series against the powerful Chicago White Sox.

☒ 16 ☒

SOX OF ALL SHADES

1

On the evening before the first game of the 1919 World Series, Edd Roush, star center fielder of the Cincinnati Reds, was standing out in front of the Sinton Hotel, breathing in the night air and wondering what the morrow would bring.

A fan slipped up behind him and touched his arm. "Hey, Eddie! Do you know what's going on? The series is fixed. The White Sox are going to throw it!"

Roush turned away without comment, walked into the hotel, and crossed the lobby. "Damned if you don't hear the silliest things at World Series time," he said, half aloud. "The series fixed! You hear that every year. I wonder how those rumors start."

The feelings of the Cincinnati populace on the eve of the series can well be imagined. For the first time in National League history the Reds had succeeded in doing what every fan had hoped for annually for too many years to remember. The town was in a festive mood as throngs milled around the streets, discussing the coming set of games with the formidable Chicago White Sox, champions of the American League. Garry Herrmann, proud as punch, set up an elaborate press headquarters that set the pattern for every series afterward.

There was no question but what the White Sox had a formidable ball club. They had defeated the Giants in the 1917 World Series, four games to two, with practically the same club. Many observers called them the greatest team of all time.

Ray Schalk, the catcher, was one of the most famous receivers in the game, and then was in his prime. The infield of Arnold (Chick) Gandil at first, the great Eddie Collins at second, Charles (Swede) Risberg at short, and George (Buck) Weaver at third was considered baseball's best. "Shoeless Joe" Jackson, probably the greatest natural hitter of all time, was in left field, with Oscar (Hap) Felsch in center and John (Shano) Collins in right. Infielder Fred McMullin and outfielder Harry (Nemo) Leibold were capable reserves. The pitching staff was built around Ed Cicotte and Urban (Red) Faber, right-handers, and Dick Kerr and Claude Williams, southpaws.

The White Sox had led the American League in team batting, Joe Jackson showing the way with a .351 mark. The club was second in team fielding. Cicotte had accumulated an earned-run average of 1.82, a record exceeded only by Washington's great Walter Johnson, and all season long Kerr and Williams had allowed their opponents less than three earned runs per game.

Prior to 1919, all World Series had been on a basis of four out of seven games, but the National Commission had increased it to five out of nine, announcing that the longer series would give more fans an opportunity to witness play.

By any logical analysis, the White Sox should have been the favorites. They had the experience in series play that the Reds lacked; they had in Jackson one of the most fearsome hitters in baseball; they had in William (Kid) Gleason a manager who, though he had just completed his freshman year as a pilot, was recognized as one of the brainiest strategists in the game.

But the gamblers were betting on the Reds. All sorts of strange characters appeared in hotel lobbies and on the streets with plenty of money to offer—on the Reds. It didn't make sense at the time.

Pat Moran chose Dutch Ruether to oppose Ed Cicotte in the first game at Cincinnati, and a throng of 30,511 jammed Redland Field on the warm afternoon of October 1. In the very first inning the loyal Cincinnati rooters had a chance to cheer, as the White Sox failed to score off Ruether, Edd Roush ending the inning by making one of his copyrighted sprints and a one-hand catch to snare a long drive off the bat of Buck Weaver. In the last half of the frame the Reds scored a run when Rath was hit by Cicotte's second pitch, took third when Daubert singled to right, and crossed the plate after Jackson had caught Groh's fly in deep left field.

Kopf put the Reds in the hole in the second inning when he fumbled Jackson's roller and then threw wild to first, Joe taking second. He soon scored the tying run when he was sacrificed to third by Felsch, and Gandil was safe on a Texas Leaguer on which Roush made a spectacular try.

The score was 1 to 1 when the Reds came to bat in the fourth for what was to become one of the most controversial innings of baseball ever played. With one out, Duncan lined a clean single to right. Cicotte then knocked down Kopf's smash and threw to second, forcing Duncan. Neale then popped a little fly in back of short that Risberg did not hold, Kopf pulling up at second. Wingo singled, scoring Kopf, Neale taking third, and Wingo continuing to second on the throw. Ruether, always a dangerous hitter, lined a triple over short that counted both runners, and Rath singled him home. When Daubert followed with another safety that scored Rath, Kid Gleason jumped from the Chicago dugout and waved Roy Wilkinson to the box, Cicotte walking dejectedly off the field.

That five-run salvo was the ball game, and the two runs scored by the Reds in the seventh and one in the eighth, which made the final count 9 to 1, were just superfluous. Ruether breezed in, allowing the mighty White Sox only six hits.

On the next day Moran sent his other southpaw, Slim Sallee, to the box, and put Bill Raridan in the game to catch him. Gleason countered with his left-handed artist, Claude Williams. For three innings the contest was runless, and then the Reds scored a flurry of three in the fourth round on walks to Rath and Groh, a single by Roush, who was later caught in an attempted double steal, and a triple by Duncan. In the

142

sixth, the Reds counted again when Roush drew Williams' fifth pass, was sacrificed to second, and tore home on Neale's one-bagger. That was all Sallee needed, and though he yielded two tallies to the Sox in the seventh, he finished strong and won the tilt, 4 to 2, though yielding ten hits. Oddly enough, the Reds made but four safeties.

The scene then shifted to Chicago, but before it did, peculiar things occurred. The Reds had humbled the mighty White Sox twice in a row. Kid Gleason knew that something very strange was going on. He had heard the rumors, of course, that certain of his players had agreed to let the Reds win. At first he hadn't paid too much attention to them. But certain plays that had come up in the first two games had made him wonder. As far as errors were concerned, the Hose had made only one in each game, a dropped throw by Gandil in the first game, a harmless fumble by Risberg in the second. But the Sox had looked bad on other plays, failing to slide on the bases and handling relays from the outfield with slowness.

The night after the second game, Gleason confided his worst fears to President Charlie Comiskey. After a long talk, they were both convinced that certain Chicago players were not giving their best. Comiskey felt that the matter should be reported immediately to the National Commission, which at that time was composed of Garry Herrmann, John Heydler, president of the National League, and Ban Johnson, president of the American. Comiskey obviously couldn't go to Herrmann with the story, because Garry was also president of the opposing club. And he couldn't go to Johnson, for at that time Comiskey and Ban were not on speaking terms. Heydler was the only one left. So it was that at two o'clock in the morning Commie called on Heydler.

"John," he said, "something most peculiar is going on. Gleason can't exactly put his finger on it, but he feels that his players have let him down. Now, naturally, I can't go with this to Herrmann. And you know how I stand with Ban. So I'm telling you—the president of the National League."

Realizing the grave implications of what he had been told, Heydler dressed immediately and went to see Ban Johnson.

Aroused from a deep sleep, Johnson listened to what Comiskey had told Heydler and replied, "That's the yelp of a beaten cur."

But if Johnson didn't at first place credence in what Gleason and Comisky believed, it gave him food for thought.

But on the next day at Chicago, the matter was forgotten temporarily as the White Sox rallied behind Dickie Kerr, who pitched a masterful three-hitter, blanking the Reds 3 to 0. Gleason made only one change in his line-up, sending Nemo Leibold to right field in place of Shano Collins when Moran pitched Ray Fisher, a right-hander. The change had no connection with any of Gleason's suspicions, but was merely a percentage move, Leibold being a left-handed hitter.

Cicotte went to the box for Gleason again in the fourth game, opposed by Jimmy Ring. Both hurlers worked with proficiency, the Reds making only five hits and the Sox three. The Reds scored twice in the fifth inning, the only runs made in the game by either side, and they obtained the runs in a most peculiar way. With one out, Duncan smashed the ball back to Cicotte, whose throw to Gandil at first was wild, and Duncan reached second on the error. Kopf followed with a short single to left that sent Duncan to third, and when Jackson made his throw to the plate, Cicotte ran over, deflected the ball out of Schalk's reach, Duncan racing home and Kopf reaching second. Neale then doubled over Jackson's head, scoring Kopf. Cicotte had been superb except in that fifth inning, when his two errors cost him the game.

With a 3-to-1 lead in the series, Moran sent Eller after the fifth game, and the "shine ball" artist came through with another shutout, winning 5 to 0. Williams pitched on even terms with Hod until the sixth, when four Cincinnati runs crossed the plate on only three hits. Hap Felsch made one error in the inning and was saved from another when generous scoring credited Roush with a triple on a drive that Hap failed to hold, two runs scoring on the play.

Once more the scene shifted back to Cincinnati for the sixth game, and Dickie Kerr kept the faint White Sox hopes alive when he won a close one, 5 to 4, the contest going ten innings. Ruether started for the Reds and went five stanzas, Ring being touched for the winning run in the tenth when Weaver doubled and Gandil singled. Risberg made two errors and Felsch one for the Sox, but Kerr overcame the disadvantage.

Cicotte made a comeback in the seventh game, beating Sallee, 4 to 1, and the Sox drew within one game of a tie. The White Sox performed creditably as a team for the first time, Cicotte having a 4-to-0 lead before he granted Moran's clan their only run in the sixth.

That game so strengthened Chicago's hopes that followers of the club felt sure the Pale Hose could return to Chicago and snatch the last two games, and attain victory in the long series.

But those hopes were quickly dashed. In the eighth game, on October 9, Claude Williams, pitching for Chicago, was batted soundly for four runs in the first inning. Singles by Daubert and Groh and doubles by Roush and Duncan blasted Williams from the premises. Bill James came in and allowed the final run of the frame on a single by Raridan. Eller, pitching for the Reds, had no trouble winning on the strength of that fat start by his mates. And when the Redlegs picked up another run in the second, one in the fifth, and three in the sixth, it was all over. A saddened Windy City crowd of 32,930 saw their hopefuls blow the contest, 10 to 5, losing the series, five games to three.

2

Almost a year passed before the whole nasty story of what went on in that World Series was made public. And then there was a version to please every fancy.

Fans got the first inkling that something was up in September 1920 when Bill Veeck, president of the Chicago Cubs, startled the baseball world by revealing that he had received an anonymous tip that a game between the Cubs and Phillies, played on August 31, 1920, had been fixed and that Fred Mitchell, manager of the Bruins, had substituted Grover Alexander for Claude Hendrix in the pitcher's box upon learning of it, the Cubs losing, despite the shift, 3 to o. Veeck appointed the Chicago baseball writers to investigate the yarn.

A Chicago grand jury, meeting at the time, decided to investigate every phase of gambling and its relation to baseball. The prosecutor promised his co-operation, and the probe assumed three phases: the 1919 World Series, concerning which there had been many rumors, the alleged fixed game between the Cubs and Phils, and the business of baseball pools. Subpoenas were sent out to officials, players, and others involved, and on September 20 an official inquiry began.

In the year that had passed, baseball's official family had worked tirelessly in an effort to trace down rumors of crookedness. Ban Johnson, at first unimpressed with Comiskey's claim that something abnormal had taken place, made every possible investigation. And to Johnson must go the lion's share of the credit for eventually cracking the case wide-open. He followed every possible clue until he was convinced that he could prove his charges. Comiskey, for his part, had offered $10,000 to anyone who could give him proof that the series had been thrown.

Rube Benton, the pitcher for the New York Giants who had previously been with the Reds, came forth with the claim that there was a ring of gamblers in Pittsburgh that provided money for players who wished to bet on fixed games.

Charlie Comiskey then testified that he had heard rumors of the fix during the series, that he had spoken to John Heydler about it, that he had had Kid Gleason make an investigation, and that he had held up the checks of the eight players he considered probably guilty.

A bombshell was thrown into the investigation when a newspaper, the *Philadelphia North American,* secured from Billy Maharg, a former boxer, a strange story that he (Maharg) and Sleepy Bill Burns, a pitcher who had been with the Reds in 1910, had entered into a deal with Abe Attell, another former boxer and gambler, to fix the series. Maharg claimed that Ed Cicotte, the White Sox pitcher, had asked Burns if he could raise $100,000, saying that he had eight players ready to throw the games for that amount. Burns replied that he'd find out if that much money could be found. Maharg claimed that later he and Burns found the deal was too big to swing, but that they thought perhaps the money could be obtained from Arnold Rothstein, the notorious New York gambler who was later slain. Although Rothstein declined to have anything to do with the deal, Burns wired Maharg that Attell had found a backer. Maharg said he saw Attell and Burns at the Hotel Sinton in Cincinnati, that Attell had the money with him, and that Burns had fixed the players.

However, Maharg claimed, the players got only $10,000 on account, Attell holding back the rest saying that he needed the money for betting purposes. According to the agreement, the players lost the first two games and collected $10,000 more. Maharg said that when Dickie Kerr won the third game for the White Sox despite attempts by the others to lose it, Maharg and Burns lost every dollar they had. Maharg contended that he then quit in disgust and returned broke to Philadelphia, but that Burns had stayed on and arranged a new deal with a group of St. Louis gamblers, and that Attell had cleaned up after double-crossing the White Sox, or, as they were called by this time, Black Sox.

Well, that was Maharg's story. But Burns had disappeared. Attell had gone to Canada. Rothstein denied he was implicated in any way. And Maharg, having delivered himself of so much intimate data to the *Philadelphia North American,* refused to repeat his story to the Chicago grand jury.

On the strength of all it had learned, the grand jury then indicted two Boston gamblers and the following eight Chicago players: first baseman Arnold Gandil, center fielder Hap Felsch, shortstop Swede Risberg, third baseman Buck Weaver, utility infielder Fred McMullin, outfielder Joe Jackson, and pitchers Ed Cicotte and Claude Williams. Gandil had not reported to the White Sox in 1920, and the other seven men were immediately suspended, thus wrecking any chance Chicago might have had for the pennant.

Comiskey then did a very generous thing, giving approximately $1,500 each, the difference between the winning and losing shares of the series, to the Chicago players he considered honest.

Ed Cicotte, with tears in his eyes, then appeared before the grand jury and admitted that he had been given $10,000 for losing the first game, and that the money had been placed under his pillow in his Cincinnati hotel room the night before the contest. Cicotte admitted that in that first game he had lobbed the ball up to the plate so easily a batter could have read the trade-mark on it. Cicotte also said that Maharg's story was true in every respect.

Jackson was the next to testify. His story was that he had received $5,000, which also appeared under his pillow, that Risberg and McMullin were the pay-off men, but that he had received his from Williams. Jackson revealed that each player had been approached individually, but that each knew who the other culprits were. Jackson said Gandil was the leader, and that at first, when the additional money was not forthcoming, the players felt Gandil had double-crossed them, but that they learned later that Abe Attell had never paid Gandil. Jackson admitted that in the series he either struck out or else hit easy balls when runners were in scoring position.

After Cicotte and Jackson had implicated the six others, the next to come forth with confessions were Williams and Felsch. Williams said the deal was made in the living room of a South Side Chicago hotel with two Boston gamblers, Joe (Sport) Sullivan and a gentleman known only as Brown, Williams said he received $10,000 from them, and gave $5,000 to Jackson.

These confessions came about after Cicotte had gone to Kid Gleason and said he had a load on his mind. Gleason sent him to Charlie Comiskey, who listened to the pitcher's tale and replied that the story checked completely with information he had obtained from detectives. Comiskey then called his attorney, A. S. Austrian, and the pitcher was taken to Judge McDonald. The confessions and indictments followed.

First, the grand jury indicted a group of thirteen. The eight Black Sox were reindicted to overcome legal difficulties,

148

and the finger was also pointed at Abe Attell, Joe (Sport) Sullivan, the gentleman named Brown, Hal Chase, and Sleepy Bill Burns. They were all charged with "conspiracy to commit an illegal act," and there were five counts to the indictment. Chase was implicated as the middleman between Burns and Attell.

Three of the indicted players, Risberg, McMullin, and Weaver, gave bonds of $10,000 each and protested their innocence.

Then came various delays and legal manipulations. There was one postponement of the trial date after another and a change in the district attorneyship. Witnesses had disappeared. Before the trial, Hal Chase escaped extradition on a technicality. Attell also escaped extradition by the simple process of claiming he was not the Abe Attell mentioned in the indictment. Then Cicotte, Williams, and Jackson made affidavits denying their confessions. Charlie Comiskey gave each of the eight players his unconditional release.

Still newer indictments were issued on March 18, 1921, which included four new men. They were: Carl Zork, a shirtwaist manufacturer of St. Louis; Ben Franklin, listed as a citizen of St. Louis and presumably no kin to a more famous man who bore the same name; Ben Levi, of Des Moines, Iowa; and David Zeiser, address unknown. These men were alleged to have been responsible for an entirely different plot that originated after Abe Attell had allegedly failed to pay the players in full.

These new indictments contained three counts, and bail was set at $24,000, and since, under the law, the amount can be doubled, it was raised to $48,000.

By April 1921, all had surrendered except Hal Chase, Abe Attell, and Joe (Sport) Sullivan. Attell was in New York, Sullivan was seeing the sights of Canada, and Sleepy Bill Burns (not mentioned in the indictments) was in Mexico.

The trial actually got under way on July 16, 1921, and Bill Burns showed up as a star witness for the state. This was the work of Ban Johnson, the American League president, who spent much time and money ferreting out the pitcher in Mexico.

Burns said that in September 1919 he had met Cicotte in New York, and that Chick Gandil and Billy Maharg were also in the party. According to Burns, Cicotte revealed that the eight players were ready to throw the series, and that they needed $100,000 for the job. Burns said that through Hal Chase he was able to get to Attell. Burns insisted, though, that after the second game the guilty players, not having received their money in full, tried to cross the gamblers and win the series.

The state's case was weak because of failure to bring Attell within jurisdiction of the court or even get a statement from him, and because of inability to introduce the repudiated confessions of Cicotte, Jackson, and Williams.

The jury brought in a verdict of acquittal.

There followed about as disgusting a scene as could be imagined. Chick Gandil, using tact that was worse than his English, rose to his feet and said, "I guess that will learn Ban Johnson that he can't frame an honest bunch of players."

There was cheering and back-slapping, and as if that were not enough, the acquitted players and the jury adjourned to a café and celebrated most of the night.

But out of the messed-up trial rose the magnificent figure of baseball's new commissioner, Judge Kenesaw Mountain Landis. Shaking a bony finger at the world at large, Landis issued this splendid credo of America's great game:

Regardless of the verdicts of juries, no player that throws a game, no player that entertains proposals or promises to throw a game, no player that sits in a conference with a bunch of crooks and gamblers where the ways and means of throwing games are discussed, and does not promptly tell his club about it, will ever play professional baseball. Of course, I do not know that any of these men will apply for reinstatement, but if they do, the above are at least a few of the rules that will be enforced. Just keep in mind that regardless of the verdict of juries, baseball is entirely competent to protect itself against the crooks both inside and outside the game.

By that ukase, Landis barred the eight Chicago players for all time. None has ever been reinstated.

So there were Sox of all shades in the World Series of 1919. Some were white and some were black and some were dirty gray. Some players with guilty knowledge of what was going on quite possibly were never discovered and continued their careers without ever revealing what they knew. It is also possible that, of the eight players who were barred, some were innocent.

Consulting the sheer statistics of the series offers not a clue. Joe Jackson made twelve hits in the series, as many as any player ever made, batted .375, and played errorless ball afield. Buck Weaver hit .324, and also was faultless defensively, accepting twenty-seven chances without a miscue. The Sox made twelve errors in the eight games, but, for that matter, so did the Reds. Whatever the truth is, it is hopelessly buried in confusion.

The sellout left Charlie Comiskey, who had given his life to baseball, a broken, disillusioned man. And poor Garry Herrmann, who had tried to win a world's championship for seventeen long years, suffered the indignity of having one handed to him at last, as casually as a waiter might hand him his beloved sausage.

But baseball recovered, for three reasons. First of all, the public knew that although a combination of circumstances might make it possible for eight out of the eight thousand men who had played the game to turn crooked, the great majority was as honest as the North Star. Secondly, in the person of Judge Landis the game had found a savior of the highest possible type. And third, and most exciting of all, there was a player named Ruth, a magical man named Ruth, who was hitting home runs the like of which had never before been seen.

Baseball had survived its darkest hour. And meanwhile new chapters of the game were being written on the playing field. The Cincinnati Reds moved on with the great game, adding their colorful portion to the fabric that was being woven.

151

⊗ **17** ⊗

A COUPLE OF HOLDOUTS

1

Pat Moran led his world's champions to Miami, Florida, to train in 1920, a more fitting place for monarchs than Waxahachie, Texas. The ball club was the same, but the rules were different. Babe Ruth had hit twenty-nine home runs for the Boston Red Sox in 1919, an unheard-of feat at the time, and the magnates were anxious to give every advantage to the hitter and popularize home runs. Toward this end, the rules committee made a law that no pitcher coming into the majors could use the spitball, which was an unhygienic sort of pitch, and such freak deliveries as Hod Eller's shine ball were banned. Slim Sallee was even given notice to please keep his hands out of his pockets before delivering the ball, the assumption being that Slim was up to some sort of witchcraft and doctoring the pellet in an unknown manner.

All the regulars from 1919 were back, and there weren't any additions except a few youngsters. Sherry Magee, the veteran outfielder, had been let out, but there was no need for him with Edd Roush, Greasy Neale, and Pat Duncan on the job, and Rube Bressler and Charlie See in reserve.

A crowd of almost twenty-five thousand jammed Redland Field on opening day, and saw Dutch Ruether beat Grover Alexander and the Cubs, 7 to 3. On the next two days Jimmy Ring bested Hippo Jim Vaughn, 4 to 3, and Eller, going to the relief of Luque, trounced Elwood Martin, 11 to 6. That swept the series, and indicated that the Reds were as powerful as ever.

Then, after losing three in a row, the club rallied for six straight, and was apparently headed in the right direction. At this stage of the race, Eller, Fisher, Ring, and Ruether were pitching with all their cunning. Sallee was not in good condition, and was seldom used.

But as the season progressed, it became clear that some phases of the Reds' play were not so sharp. The combination at second and short of Morris Rath and Larry Kopf was still functioning with keenness, but Kopf was having trouble at bat. And as the year grew older, Eller, virtually helpless without his shine ball, found it difficult to win. Nor was Fisher having the fine year on the mound that he did when the flag had been won.

Nevertheless, the Reds remained well up in the race. Roush was clubbing with all his cleverness; Daubert, Groh, and Duncan were also getting their share of hits.

Opposition came from an unexpected source. Wilbert Robinson's Brooklyn Dodgers, who had finished fifth twice in succession, showed surprising strength and were fighting for every game. And, of course, the Giants of McGraw, as always, were terrors. In winning the pennant, the Reds had defeated the Giants 12 times in 20 meetings, but now they resumed the old business of blowing game after game with the lads from the Big Town.

Leaving for an eastern trip in late July, the Reds were still fighting for the league lead. When Jimmy Ring beat Rube Benton, 6 to 2, at New York, July 31, the Reds took first place. But on the next day Fred Toney nosed out Luque, 3 to 2, and Moran's club slid back to second. On August 12, at Boston, the team again was within striking distance of first. Pat called a clubhouse meeting and addressed his players in this manner:

"Boys, we can win the pennant if we stick together and do our best. But I am entirely through with the alibi. We have the best club, and if we lose it will be our fault."

Perhaps inspired by Pat's oratory, Dolf Luque took the slab that afternoon and pitched the Reds back into first place with a 6-to-5 triumph over the Braves. But once more the club was unable to follow up the advantage. In Chicago three days later George Tyler shut the Redlegs out, 1 to 0, shoving them back to second again. The Reds simply lacked the ability to go on a prolonged winning streak.

No one had dreamed that Brooklyn would hold up, but by late August the Dodgers were still contesting the Reds and Giants for the league lead. Disaster struck the Reds on August 26, when Larry Kopf broke a thumb and was shelved for the season, his place at short being taken by Sam Crane, the only newcomer on the squad who broke into many box scores. Then, on the next day, a long duel with the Giants was lost to Artie Nehf in the seventeenth inning, 6 to 4. Samuel (Buddy) Napier, a recruit from Texas, was given a starting role at Boston, and he surprised with a handsome 8-to-2 victory that moved the Reds into first place once more. Again the stay at the top was of only twenty-four hours' duration.

The Reds reached the pinnacle for the last time on Labor Day, when Ring and Fisher hurled victories over the Cardinals. But when the team started its last eastern swing and a double-header was split at Boston, the Reds lost the lead and never regained it. Their path thereafter was downward. Brooklyn surged into the lead and went on to win the flag, their first since 1916 and their second in modern times. It was at this time that the Black Sox scandal broke, and that, too, wasn't designed to help the Reds' morale. As the season closed, the Giants also passed the Reds. Moran's club finished third, with 82 wins and 71 setbacks.

2

The events of the 1920 season tended to prove that the Reds, as constituted, were no longer a pennant-winning combination. Garry Herrmann, working closely with Pat Moran, decided to enter the market for new players, preferably young ones.

Eugene (Bubbles) Hargrave, a young catcher who had had a previous trial with the Cubs and who appeared to be a good batter, was purchased from St. Paul for $10,000. Sammy Bohne and Lew Fonseca, a pair of young infielders, were purchased from the Pacific Coast League, and both proved to be valuable additions. Dutch Ruether was shipped to Brooklyn in an even swap for the veteran Rube Marquard.

But the deal that turned out better than any other was one that saw Jimmy Ring and Greasy Neale depart for Philadelphia, with Eppa Rixey, a southpaw of many talents, coming to the Rhineland.

Little more than a year had passed since the Reds had won the flag, but that fine six-man pitching staff of Moran's had been completely shattered. Ring and Ruether had been traded, Sallee had been released, Fisher declined to report in 1921, and only Luque and Eller remained, with Hod being about at the end of the trail.

The case of Ray Fisher had interesting repercussions. A graduate of Middlebury College, Fisher had pitched successfully for the Yankees before coming to Cincinnati. His record in 1920 was 10 and 11, but Garry had counted on his staging a comeback. Instead, he signed as baseball coach for the University of Michigan at Ann Arbor, a job, incidentally, that he still holds. When the college baseball season was nearly over, Fisher decided to join the Reds and applied for reinstatement. There were rumors that he had had offers from an outlaw club at Franklin, Pennsylvania, and to prevent him from joining forces with that team, Garry offered him an advance of $1,000 on his contract. But when the appeal for reinstatement reached the Commissioner's office, Judge Landis made one of his few inexplicable decisions. He made Fisher's ineligibility permanent, and Ray was prevented from joining the Reds not only then but for all time.

The plight of the Reds was intensified when Heinie Groh, the great third baseman, became a determined holdout. Today players are usually able to work out financial arrangements with their employers on an amicable basis. A few hold out, but seldom does a player miss a game because he cannot come to terms with the club. Twenty years or more ago, however, the practice of holding out was widespread. Garry Herrmann had two hard men to sign in Edd Roush and Heinie Groh. And in 1921 Heinie Groh proved very hard to sign indeed. When the season began, Heinie, having missed the entire training period at Cisco, Texas, was still cooped up in his Cincinnati apartment, as adamant as marble.

With Fisher and Groh not even with the club, the Reds got off to a wretched start. Marquard and Rixey proved willing workers, but not steady winners. The new infielders, Bohne and Fonseca, both in action with Morris Rath gone and Groh still holding out, were often erratic in the field. By Decoration Day the team had won 13 and lost 27 and was taking on all the lackluster qualities of Garry's prewar clubs. The situation was really getting desperate.

John McGraw, trying to bolster his Giants, thought he might obtain Groh from Garry, especially when June arrived and Heinie was still sulking in his tent. The Reds' directors, practically frantic over the Groh business by now and hearing of McGraw's feeling, authorized Garry to dispose of the player. Groh, quick to sense the situation and seeing a chance to play with the formidable Giants, announced that he would not sign with the Reds unless it were guaranteed that he would be traded. McGraw then made an offer for the player, the papers saying that he would give up $100,000 and three players.

Commissioner Landis then entered the case, called off any deal that was under way, and ruled that Groh could play with no club but Cincinnati for the balance of the season. That ended the matter for the time being, and Groh signed a Redleg contract.

An event occurred on June 2 that indicates how the game of baseball changes through the years. Pat Duncan, swinging against Marvin Goodwin of the Cardinals, hit a fair ball over the left field fence at Redland Field, his home run helping the team to an 8-to-5 victory. Today, home runs at Crosley Field—the same field—are commonplace, and are hit at a rate of one every two games or so. But Redland Field with the fence that is still in use was opened for play in 1912. Duncan's hit was the first fair ball that had cleared the barrier in a decade. Babe Ruth was an American Leaguer, but his influence was felt as much in Cincinnati as elsewhere. The ball had been made more lively in 1921, no question about it!

The fabulous Ruth made his first appearance in Cincinnati during the 1921 season. After he had increased his home-run output from twenty-nine in 1919 to a tremendous fifty-four in 1920, he was the talk of the nation. National League clubs, unable to show Ruth to their fans in championship games, scrambled for exhibition dates with the Yankees. Ruth made his showing at Cincinnati on July 27. At that time Duncan's hit had been the only fairly batted ball to clear the fence. But Duncan's wallop had been to left field. The center-field wall, 426 feet away, and the right-field bleachers, an even 400 feet from home plate, were virgin territory. Ruth took care of both details. Batting against a youngster named Fritz Coumbe, he propelled one ball over the center-field barrier and another into the bleachers. No one had ever seen anything like it, and the fans responded with a gigantic collective gasp.

At about the same time, Herrmann announced that the Reds had signed a college pitcher, a stalwart young right-hander from Texas Christian University named Pete Donohue. He had been given a $5,500 bonus to ink his signature, rather an excessive amount for those days, but even so, the fans felt that he was just another in the parade of youthful hopefuls who had appeared on the scene, and they thought that he was probably destined to be discarded like so many before him. Pat Moran, however, considered Donohue an exceptional prospect. He let him finish up three losing games before throwing him into a close one, and then Pete got his first decision, a 9-to-5 victory, when he relieved Marquard at Philadelphia on July 18. Heartened by that performance, Moran decided to throw Pete at a tough club in a game of his own. So Donohue started against the Giants on July 23 and was batted out without being credited with a decision, but a week later he faced McGraw's club again and outpitched the canny Artie Nehf in eleven innings, 4 to 3. Young Donohue had never pitched professionally before, and it was obvious that a star was born at the Polo Grounds that afternoon. Here, indeed, was a lad worth tabbing!

But even the fine promise of Pete Donohue and the return to the club of Heinie Groh failed to raise the Reds from the swamplands of the second division. The year of 1921 simply had to be written off. September was merely a repetition of the previous disappointing months. The club slumped to sixth place, and finished with 70 triumphs and 83 reverses. It was the worst showing Pat Moran had yet made.

There were individual bright spots. Edd Roush hit .352, continuing to scintillate in all departments of play. Groh, despite his lack of training, broke into ninety-seven box scores and batted .331. Pat Duncan, Rube Bressler, and Jake Daubert were also over the .300 mark. The new pitchers had done their best, Rixey winning 19 and losing 18, and Marquard taking 17 while dropping 14. Luque lost a number of close games, and his record of 17 and 19 was not a fair estimate of his work. The pitching staff had been rebuilt, and there was hope.

3

The moratorium on the trading of Groh was lifted, and in December 1921 Garry Herrmann shipped the star third baseman to the Giants, receiving in return a package of cash estimated at $100,000 and a thirty-one-year-old outfielder, George Burns. The gaping hole at third base caused by Heinie's departure was believed filled when the club sent the fading Hod Eller, another pitcher named Lynn Brenton, and cash to Oakland of the Pacific Coast League for a young guardian of the hot corner named Ralph (Babe) Pinelli. Another youngster from San Francisco, shortstop Jimmy Caveney, was secured in a deal for pitchers Fritz Coumbe and Bob Geary, and $25,000. With Caveney on hand, shortstop Larry Kopf and pitcher Rube Marquard were peddled to Boston for pitcher Jack Scott. Thus the Reds had developed almost an entire new infield in the two years that had elapsed after the championship. Jake Daubert, at first, was now thirty-seven, but the other infielders were kids—Sammy Bohne was twenty-five, Lew Fonseca twenty-three, Jimmy Caveney twenty-five, and Babe Pinelli twenty-five. All of them had graduated to the Reds from the Pacific Coast, a region that was by now producing ballplayers in profusion.

Another valuable addition to the 1922 team was George Harper, a hard-hitting outfielder bought from Oklahoma City. He was not quite thirty, and had had a previous trial with Detroit.

If Garry Herrmann thought he had a persistent holdout on his hands in 1921 in Heinie Groh, he had not yet experienced the worst in his dealings with Edd Roush. The star center fielder announced his intentions of holding out as bitterly and long as did Groh unless his salary demands were met. And Roush, when roused, was as stubborn as quicksand and just as unyielding.

The season started with George Burns in Roush's familiar center-field position, flanked by Pat Duncan and George Harper. Roush, who had missed the spring training camp at Mineral Wells, Texas, entirely, was still encamped at Oakland City.

Moran's club at the start of the campaign was horrible, winning one game out of the first eleven. Phone calls to Oakland City. Would Roush report? No, thanks.

In later years, Roush, always frank and outspoken, discussed his annual battles over salary. "I didn't hold out because I wanted to," Edd said. "But I never heard of any other method open to a ballplayer for getting the money. In spite of all the knocks I got, I never intended being unreasonable. I placed a valuation on my services that seemed to be fair, and I asked for that valuation. I wasn't surprised that the owners didn't always yield to my suggestions without delay. That was their privilege. I followed the only common-sense, businesslike road there was to follow, and I'd do the same thing again if I were beginning my career. The magnates wanted to give me what they thought was a fair salary. O. K. I had different ideas. And they usually came around."

By Decoration Day the club had climbed up to the .500 mark. It was felt that with Roush in center field the team

159

might win the pennant. More calls to Oakland City. Would Roush report now? No, thanks.

Eppa Rixey, Pete Donohue, and Adolfo Luque gave the Reds a trio of pitchers who guaranteed a well-pitched game almost every day. And a new hurler, Johnny Couch, another acquisition from San Francisco, seemed blessed with one of the nicest attributes a player can have, luck. If Couch allowed no runs, the Reds would make one. If he allowed five, his mates would make six. He won his first five starts, and proved to be a very handy guy to have around.

By the Fourth of July the Reds were still at the .500 mark, and Roush was still at Oakland City. The directors were fuming.

"You know my terms, gentlemen," Edd replied.

Finally, on July 23, when the Reds had won four more games than they had lost, Roush capitulated and came into the fold. Within a few days he was in the line-up.

"I never saw anything like it," Pat Moran said. "All that fellow has to do is wash his hands, adjust his cap, and he's in shape to hit. He's the greatest individualist in the game."

The New York Giants were riding high, breezing to their second successive pennant. Jack Scott, the hurler Moran had obtained in the deal for Kopf, proved worthless to the Reds, and he was released with a lame arm. Scott then signed with the Giants and helped pitch them pennantward.

The Reds couldn't beat out the Giants, but they could finish second. And with Edd Roush batting with all his vigor, they did, winning nine out of their last eleven games, finishing with 86 victories and 68 reverses. Roush had hit .352 in the 49 games he had played, topped only by Lew Fonseca, the reserve infielder, who had a mark of .361. Jake Daubert, at first, had an exceptional year, the veteran batting out 205 hits in 610 trips to the platter, for a .336 mark. George Harper, in his first year with the club, socked .340. Pat Duncan was at .328, Bubbles Hargrave at .316, and Babe Pinelli at .305. Those averages indicate what had happened to the baseball used in the major leagues.

But in spite of the emphasis on hitting, the Reds' pitching

160

in 1922 was extraordinary. Rixey won 25 games and lost only 13. Donohue, now an established star, had a record of 18 and 9. Luque won 13 and lost 23, but those figures failed to reveal the excellence of his work, for the Cuban was always a tough-luck hurler. And Couch, on whom the gods had looked with so much favor, won 16 and lost 9. It had been a great year.

⊗ 18 ⊗

THE LAST OF THE SCANDALS

1

Pat Moran managed the Reds for the fifth time in 1923, a tenure that matched that of Buck Ewing, who had led the club in the last years of the previous century. In many ways the administrations of Ewing and Moran were similar. Buck had never won a pennant for the club as Moran did, but his teams were generally up in the race. Moran's teams were also contenders, with the bitter exception of the 1921 outfit.

A training camp was set up at Orlando, Florida, the home of Joe Tinker, the great shortstop who piloted the 1913 Reds. Tinker, mellowing with the years, had pointed out to Garry what an ideal camp Orlando would make, and it did. The Reds were to make the town their spring home for seven straight years. That was a relief, for Moran had really needed a Baedeker to get the club around in previous springs, jump-ing from Waxahachie to Miami to Cisco to Mineral Wells and now to Florida, where the Reds hadn't conditioned since 1908, when John Ganzel gathered his flock at St. Augustine.

There weren't many newcomers in the 1923 camp, since the influx of rookies the year before had given Pat the nucleus of a good nine. There was a young pitcher named Bill Harris, drafted from Winston-Salem, who bore a distinct facial resemblance to Pete Donohue. There was a reserve infielder named Chester (Boob) Fowler, another product of Texas Christian University. When the Reds had scouted Donohue at Texas Christian, many prowlers for other major-league teams were on his trail. Pete had a battery mate at Texas Christian with the astonishing name of Astyanax Saunders Douglas, and Pete informed Boyd Chambers, the scout for Garry who arranged the signing, that he wouldn't go with the club unless Douglas were also given a trial. So, in order to land Pete, Astyanax was also imported. Now Boob Fowler gave the Reds a third Texas collegian.

But one addition to the Reds of 1923 really caused a tempest in a teapot, and the player was one who had been with the team before, southpaw John Calhoun (Rube) Benton, the South Carolinian who had become a stormy petrel because of what he knew or said he knew about the Black Sox scandal.

Rube Benton, killed in an automobile accident in Alabama in 1937, had pitched professionally for twenty-five years. Bought by the Reds for only $4,000 in 1910, he had remained with the team until 1915, then had pitched for the Giants. Throughout his career, the Rube, like so many others of his era, demonstrated a talent for pleasures of the night. He liked to sit up late in dubious beer emporiums, he liked to wager an occasional buck on the funny nags, and he wasn't too particular about what he said concerning his contemporaries. But the Rube didn't get into any real jam until he had a row with Buck Herzog, the former Redleg manager. Benton and Herzog had clashed in the summer of 1920, Rube stating that Herzog had offered him a bribe to throw a game to Cincinnati in the summer of 1919. Herzog countered with the charge that Benton not only had guilty preseries knowledge of the Black Sox mess, but had cleaned up to the tune of $1,500. Art Wilson and Tony Boeckel, National League players, backed up Herzog by swearing to affidavits that Rube had boasted of winning the $1,500. But later, testifying before the Cook

County grand jury in Chicago, Rube stated that his winnings on the series really amounted to a slightly different sum—$20, to be exact.

As for Rube's charge that Herzog had offered him a bribe, he was never able to back it up. Rube had reported this to Frank Graham, then a sports writer on the *New York Sun* and still one of the most brilliant baseball analysts in the nation. Graham repeated the allegation to his sports editor, Joe Vila, and Vila had gone to John Heydler, president of the National League, with the yarn. As a consequence, Benton was questioned further, and he claimed the bribe was offered in a Chicago saloon. Heydler and Benton then made a trip to Chicago and made the rounds of the saloons (by this time known as speak-easies, since by federal law saloons no longer existed), but Rube was unable to locate the bartender who could verify his story, one of the few occasions in his life when he was unable to find a bartender.

As a result, Benton became *persona non grata* in the National League, and was given the brush-off. Now, John Heydler was one of the finest presidents the National League ever had. He was a man of impeccable veracity and unimpeachable integrity. But his manner of treating the Benton case was distinctly provincial. No charges were brought against Rube. He was allowed to go and pitch in the American Association but could not pitch in the National. This is much like the attitude of a municipal judge who gives a derelict twenty-four hours to leave town, the presumption being that it is perfectly O. K. to be a vagrant in Podunk as long as you stay out of Pueblo.

After Benton had had a fine year with St. Paul in 1922, Garry Herrmann secured him in a deal for cash and pitcher Cliff Markle. Heydler, of course, was furious and advised Herrmann that Benton was "undesirable" and couldn't pitch in the National League. Heydler then carried the case to Judge Landis, asking for a ruling on the question as to whether Benton had guilty knowledge of the Black Sox business.

Much to John Heydler's surprise, Landis ruled that Benton could pitch for the Reds, and in his decision the Judge severely denounced Benton's detractors.

Another great opening-day crowd, 30,338, watched an excellent game, with Pete Donohue beating Lester Sell of the Cardinals, 3 to 2, in eleven innings. But then the Reds lost 11 of the next 17 games, with Frank (Cactus) Keck, a rookie purchased from Springfield, Missouri, dropping his first four starts and Eppa Rixey losing three of his first four.

But on their first eastern trip, the Reds perked up, reaching the .500 mark by mid-May as Rube Benton replaced Keck as a starter.

One odd incident occurred on that first swing around the league, and though the Reds were responsible for it, they weren't there to see what happened. Garry had scheduled an exhibition game for the club at Allentown, Pennsylvania, on May 13, when the Reds had an off day at Philadelphia. In the morning it was raining hard at Philly, so Moran phoned Allentown to say the team would not keep the date, but somehow the message was never delivered to the proper people. At any rate, four thousand fans swarmed around the Allentown park waiting to view the major-leaguers, who never arrived. The Allentown club had unfortunately failed to provide rain checks or even change, and a mob of spectators raided the box office, fans who paid fifty cents to get in making off with twenty-dollar bills in the confusion.

The Reds' play improved as the season aged, and by July 17 Moran's boys had won 50 and lost 30, a pace that wins pennants in some years. But McGraw's Giants, strong as usual, were gunning for their third straight flag.

Five big games with the Giants in Cincinnati in early August gave the Reds a chance to win the flag, but they were not up to the task, losing all five of the contests. Luque, usually a demon when working against the Giants, was batted from the box in the first game, and the New Yorkers continued the attack against Bill Harris and a recruit named Herb McQuaid, winning behind Rosy Ryan by the rather horrible score of 14 to 4. On the next day Hugh McQuillan shut out the Cincinnatians, helpless behind Rixey, 2 to 0.

Then came a twin bill, with Virgil Barnes beating Rube Benton, 4 to 2, and Danny Gearin nosing out Donohue, 5 to 4. Luque started the fifth game, but again was defeated, 6 to 2, with John Watson pitching for McGraw.

The Cincinnati fans were desperately disappointed, and the series had repercussions. A sporting scandal sheet named *Collyer's Eye* alleged that prior to the series Pat Duncan and Sammy Bohne had been approached by gamblers who offered them $15,000 each to toss the important games. Bohne and Duncan, called to John Heydler's office for an investigation, swore that the story was utterly without basis in fact.

Bohne and Duncan, acting under advice, then sued the publication for defamation of character, each filing an action for $50,000. Later the cases were settled out of court, with Bohne and Duncan vindicated. Actually, Collyer hadn't accused them of throwing the games, only with being asked to. But he was never able to produce witnesses to prove any offer was made.

The Giants had been in first place when the five straight were swept from the Reds, but the pennant was practically won in that series. Nevertheless, the Reds hung gamely on, took four out of five from the Giants on their next visit to New York, and rolled up a winning streak that extended to nine games before Pete Donohue bowed to the Braves, 7 to 0, in the second game of a double-header, August 27. In September the Reds continued to shine and stayed right at the Giants' heels. When the season ended on October 7, the Reds were in second place with 91 victories and 63 defeats, four and one-half games behind New York, who won 95 and lost 58.

Once more, in 1923, Cincinnati had maintained its reputation for getting good pitching. Today a club is lucky that has one hurler capable of winning twenty games. The 1923 Reds had three such hurlers. Dolf Luque had a phenomenal year, winning 27 and losing 8. Pete Donohue won 21 and lost 15, and Rixey 20 and 15.

Their styles were vastly different. Eppa Rixey, the only southpaw of the trio, was a towering colossus on the hill, six

165

feet five inches tall. Though he didn't issue many bases on balls, he was frequently behind the hitter, often just missing the plate. Most batters who tried to wait him out, however, found that Big Eppa ended up ahead of them. Rix was a smart hurler and an intelligent man, with a master's degree in chemistry from the University of Virginia. He had been observed in collegiate circles by an umpire on the National League staff, Charlie Rigler, who coached baseball at the university. Under Rigler's coaching, Eppa developed into a fine pitcher, and Rigler tipped off the Phillies, who signed him for a promised $2,000 bonus in June 1912. Rixey never got the bonus, though Rigler thought he had, and their relations were strained until Rigler found out that Eppa hadn't received it. After that, a rule was passed preventing umpires from entering into such deals.

Rixey was an instant success at Philly, pitching under Pat Moran there and breaking into the last game of the 1915 World Series. When Moran later came to the Reds he wanted Rixey with him, and was finally able to swing the deal.

Donohue, more normally proportioned, was a right-hander and a pitching stylist. Looking like a matinee idol, the bronzed Texan did share one experience with Rixey. Each had come to the majors directly from college, making the grade without the usual apprenticeship in the minor leagues. Pete was a curve-ball pitcher, and his change of pace was really a thing of beauty.

Luque, whose 1923 record was the best he ever made, was normally a hard-luck pitcher, losing game after game by close scores. He had a nice fast ball, fielded his position like a bear, and the chief thing about him was his courage. No better competitor ever took the mound. He was as persevering as a bulldog, and just as snarling.

Because of his dark color, the Señor was the target for much jeering when he first hit the National League, and the jibes boiled his hot Spanish blood. Luque often lost his temper and would fight at the drop of a hat. But the barbs never prevented him from pitching with effectiveness. In fact, it was a dangerous pastime to shout abuse at Dolf, as he would just as soon throw at a batter as not.

The Boston Braves had originally signed Luque in 1914, but he appeared in only a few games at the Hub and then started on a tour of the minors, with stops at Jersey City, Toronto, and Louisville. When he won 11 and lost only 2 for the Colonels in 1918, the Reds grabbed him.

Luque's 27 and 8 record not only gave him the best winning percentage of the league's hurlers, a figure of .771, but he also paced the loop in earned-run average, holding all opponents to the parsimonious figure of 1.93 earned runs per nine-inning game. No pitcher had led the league in both departments since Grover Alexander had pulled the stunt in 1916.

The much-discussed Rube Benton rounded out the staff of starters, winning 14 and losing 10. Johnny Couch, whose remarkable luck had made him a winner in 1922, won only 2 out of 9 games and was waived to the Phils.

Edd Roush had another of his numerous good years at bat, hitting .351, and playing almost the full schedule, 138 games, for a change. It is doubtful if any good hitter ever batted with the strange consistency of Roush. For three years his figure varied only by one percentage point, as he hit .352 in 1921, .352 again in 1922, and .351 in 1923.

Bubbles Hargrave was second on the hit parade, with .333, and Pat Duncan socked the horsehide to a .327 tune. Only batting disappointment among the regulars was Sammy Bohne, who slumped to .252. Sammy had one day in 1923 that he has never forgotten, however. Against Brooklyn on June 17 Bohne delivered a single with two out in the ninth that spoiled a no-hitter for Dazzy Vance, the celebrated fireballer of the Dodgers. Vance later got a no-hitter, but against the Reds he had to be satisfied with a 9-to-0 shutout after Bohne's annoying blow.

It can be happily reported that 1923 saw the end of any talk of scandals in Cincinnati. The silly charges against Bohne and Duncan were forgotten, Rube Benton pitched in a way that made him as desirable as any other athlete, and the

167

Black Sox mess had long been forgotten. In all three cases the Cincinnati players involved were completely exonerated of any wrongdoing.

⊗ **19** ⊗

JACK HENDRICKS MAKES HIS BOW

1

Garry Herrmann thought that he might well win the pennant in 1924 with secondary pitching capable of backing up the top trio of Luque, Donohue, and Rixey, and he attempted to bolster the staff by acquiring during the winter two hurlers with similar names, Carl Mays and Frank (Jakie) May.

But if their names were similar, their personalities were not. Carl Mays had been a stormy figure in the American League for years, his sale from the Boston Red Sox to the New York Yankees almost breaking up the American League. Mays also won unpleasant notoriety when a pitch from his hand struck and killed the splendid Cleveland shortstop Ray Chapman. Many players would have been so affected by that tragedy, had it happened to them, that they would have ceased their careers. Not Mays. Carl was about as unsentimental a man as ever played the game. He was a grim figure, a lone wolf, a hurler of great courage, and a man completely devoid of humor. A right-hander, Mays was a devotee of submarine pitching, with a fast curve ball being his best bet. Batters were bothered by his unorthodox delivery.

Jakie May, on the other hand, was a fat, fun-loving southpaw who employed a side-arm delivery. He had originally been brought to the majors by Branch Rickey, who signed him for the Cardinals in 1917. Jakie was with the Redbirds

168

for five seasons, but won only ten games during that time, a rather appalling annual average of two. But he was blessed with a world of stuff, and Rickey kept thinking he was just on the verge of greatness. Finally, Jakie drifted to Vernon of the Pacific Coast League in 1922, where he startled the world by winning 35 and losing only 9. The Yankees were hot on his trail after that banner year, but the quoted price was too high even for the refined taste of Colonel Ruppert, and May was allowed to remain on the Coast. When he had a bad year in 1923, the price went down and Garry Herrmann was able to arrange his purchase for $35,000.

With May and Mays added, it was a hopeful club that gathered at Orlando for spring training. But gloom soon descended over the entourage when manager Pat Moran became seriously ill. Pat had always been a heavy drinker, and during the winter he had become so devoted to the bottle that he passed up numerous opportunities of eating, a way of life that soon resulted in a breakdown. His kidneys and liver were all shot, and he was a dying man when he arrived at the training camp. Removed to the hospital, he passed away on March 7, his death being listed as resulting from Bright's disease, though there were complications.

Pat's death occurred just as he was to launch his sixth season with the team, and four of the five years he was at the helm were extremely successful ones. Moran left a record of 425 victories and 329 defeats for Cincinnati, for a percentage of .564, a figure exceeded by only one other Redleg manager who ran the club for any great length of time, Buck Ewing, whose 394 successes and 297 reverses from 1895 to 1899 gave him a .570 mark.

There is a memorial erected to Moran at Fitchburg, Massachusetts, the home town that loved him when he was alive and revered him in death. A public park there was named Pat Moran Park, with a shaft of Barre granite dedicated to his memory.

To succeed Moran, Herrmann chose Jack Hendricks, who had just been added to the club as a coach.

The selection of Hendricks was almost automatic, and

though strictly fortuitous, it worked out very well. Genial Jack immediately took charge with firmness and demonstrated managerial talents that were unsuspected.

Hendricks, born at Joliet, Illinois, on April 9, 1876, was a graduate of Northwestern University Law School and was admitted to the bar in 1897. For fifteen years he had practiced law in and around Chicago, pursuing his baseball chores on the side. Jack originally went to the major leagues as a left-handed hitting outfielder. But like so many other successful managers, he had not been much of a player. In the minor leagues he started managing clubs in all parts of the country, Springfield, Ohio, Fort Wayne, Denver, and Indianapolis. At Denver he won three Western League championships, and at Indianapolis he copped the American Association flag in 1917. That job earned him a chance to pilot the Cardinals, and he signed a two-year contract with them in 1918, leaving after that abbreviated season to go to France as a secretary for the Knights of Columbus. Returning from the wars, he found that Branch Rickey had himself decided to act as field pilot of the 1918 Cards, so Hendricks was paid off for the year. He then went back to Indianapolis and stayed five seasons, joining the Reds as a coach just in time to benefit by Moran's passing.

Hendricks wasn't a driving manager of the McGraw school, and he assumed his players were intelligent enough to think for themselves. But his teams were aggressive, and Jack had a remarkable memory for small details that often mean the difference between victory and defeat.

The club he inherited from Moran seemed adequate for a first-division berth, with a chance for the flag, providing the fine pitching of the previous year held up.

The Redlegs got off to a fast start, winning seven of their first nine encounters, then slackened that torrid pace. The players were considerably miffed when on three successive days at St. Louis in early May Branch Rickey postponed games because of "threatening weather" though the sun was shining. Rogers Hornsby, the star second baseman of the Cardinals at the time, was suffering from a bad thumb, a circumstance that might have had something to do with Rickey's reluctance to take the field. Jack Ryder, writing in the *Cincinnati Enquirer*, observed, "Three successive games have now been called off due to cold feet. Umpires and not club owners should decide such matters."

Caught off stride by that enforced vacation, the Reds had difficulty in picking up the threads of victory, and by early June they had bogged down to the .500 mark. Their plight was not helped when Lew Fonseca, playing regularly at second base, was injured. But in those days of independent operation, it was possible to buy first-class players from the high-grade minor leagues. Garry Herrmann, seeking a replacement for Fonseca, reached over to Minneapolis and came up with Hugh Critz, a diminutive guardian of the keystone who made an instant hit.

Critz, who pronounces his name Crytz (as in cry), was a graduate of Mississippi A. & M., where his father was a member of the faculty. Hughie talked with the southern drawl that is so familiar in the deep South, and proved to be an exceptional raconteur in addition to a highly skilled infielder. Garry handed Minneapolis $15,000 and the contract of Bill Harris for Hughie's services.

Another deal negotiated that summer saw Hendricks trade outfielder George Harper to the Phils for another gardener, Curt Walker. Though Harper had produced a fine freshman year with the team in 1922, he won a regular berth only because of the prolonged holdout of Edd Roush. And when Edd finally came into the fold, Harper, skilled player though he was, had to be relegated to bench duty. This trade was about as even a one as could have been made. Harper and Walker were of the same general physical proportions, both were left-handed hitters, and both batted with more skill than they fielded.

But although the addition of Critz and Walker was of tremendous long-range value, there was no immediate perking up of the club. The death of Pat Moran that spring had apparently been a bad omen. Jake Daubert, the veteran first baseman and captain, was in and out of the line-up with various injuries, and Dolf Luque, though still effective, was not able to repeat his remarkable won-and-lost record of the previous year.

After being as high as second early in May, the Reds drifted as far south as fifth by August, then braced and climbed back to fourth in September. As the season closed, they were still improving, and landed a strong fourth with 83 wins and 70 defeats.

Edd Roush had another of his good years, hitting .348, though injuries kept him out of thirty-two games. Rube Bressler, subbing at first for Daubert and alternating with George Burns in the outfield, hit .347. Hughie Critz, breaking into 102 games after his purchase, hit a surprising and resounding .322. Babe Pinelli finished at .306 and Bubbles Hargrave at .301.

Not one of the three twenty-game winners of the year before managed to repeat, Donohue winning 16 and losing 9, Rixey 15 and 14, and Luque 10 and 15. But the staff did produce a twenty-game winner, Carl Mays. Showing off his underhanded shots to National League batters for the first time, Carl won 20 and lost 9, proving especially terrifying to the Phils, beating them on six occasions without absorbing defeat at their hands. Jakie May was out most of the year with a sore arm, winning three and losing three, thus accounting for only thirteen victories in six major-league seasons. But on the days when his arm felt strong, he showed flashes of potent promise.

Luque had proved so successful a pitcher that he brought another young Cuban to the Reds in 1924, Pedro Dibut. Handicapped by the inability to speak English, Pedro ate ham and eggs most of the summer because it was the one dish he could pronounce. But his lack of fluency didn't prevent him from winning three games without a loss.

The season that had started so ominously with the passing of the Reds' manager ended with the death of their captain, Jake Daubert. As soon as the season was over, Jake was operated on for appendicitis and gallstones. He had also suffered insomnia ever since being struck on the head by a pitched ball at St. Louis early in the season, though the injury had nothing to do with his death. Following the operations, complications set in, and Jake died on October 9.

2

Replacing Jake Daubert at first base was the biggest problem Jack Hendricks had when the 1925 team was assembled, and the problem remained a thorny one all season. Though Jake had been thirty-nine at the time of his death, he was still a better-than-average performer, and major-league first basemen don't grow on trees. Bressler could play the bag, but if he were used there, another outfielder would have to be obtained.

Most prominent among the new men on the 1925 team were Charles (Chuck) Dressen, a twenty-six-year-old infielder purchased from St. Paul, and Elmer Smith, veteran outfielder who hit a home run with the bases full for Cleveland in the 1920 World Series and who came to the Reds via Louisville, where he had been sent by the Yankees in a deal for outfielder Earl Combs. Dressen was expected to give Pinelli competition for the third-base job, and Smith was protection against the use of Bressler at first base.

The Reds began the season with three straight victories, Donohue, Luque, and Rixey notching successive triumphs over the Cardinals, each going the route in 1923 form. But after that fast start, troubles began to develop.

Edd Roush came up with one of his patented charley horses when the season was only ten days old, and Hendricks told Garry he'd better telephone and get an outfielder. The result of this was the acquisition of Henry (Hi) Myers, a veteran gardener from the Dodgers. The career of Myers with the Reds lasted exactly three afternoons. Still not far enough away from Brooklyn to be rid of eccentricities, Myers cost the Reds one game when he neglected the rather ordinary precaution of taking his sun glasses to the outfield with him, the oversight resulting in Hi's dropping a fly ball because of solar interference.

Myers was a resident of East Liverpool, Ohio, and at one

173

time he had had a rather sad experience there. Always a popular Dodger, Myers was delighted when Brooklyn scheduled an exhibition game in his home town. And his pleasure mounted when Charlie Ebbets, president of the Brooklyn club, offered Hi 25 per cent of the gate receipts. After all expenses had been deducted, Myers received a check for $4.50.

The year of 1925 was a shining one in the National League, as the loop celebrated its golden jubilee. Every park in the circuit staged a celebration of some sort to recall the battles encountered in the fifty-year fight for survival. The National League had survived various wars with rival circuits, first the American Association, then the Union Association, the Brotherhood, the American League, and the Federal. It had survived periods of economic depression and national emergency such as war.

Baseball fans are notoriously sentimental. There is something touching about seeing again the players of yesterday. And when the Reds met New York at the Polo Grounds as the Giants celebrated the golden year on May 14, the pageant that took place at home plate when the old-timers were introduced left scarcely a dry eye. The roster of old-time players, still hale and hearty, who stepped out to receive the accolade of the multitude read like a Who's Who of nineteenth-century baseball. Introduced to the crowd were such celebrated performers as Dan Brouthers, Roger Connor, Amos Rusie, Joe Hornung, Billy Gilbert, George Gore, Bill Dahlen, Art Devlin, Sam Crane, and John Morrill. And the home crowd saw their beloved modern Giants, winners of four consecutive National League flags from 1921 to 1924, win the ball game from the Reds that afternoon, 5 to 4, in twelve innings, with a young curve-baller named Walter Huntzinger triumphing over Dolf Luque, who pitched the route with his customary dignity and cunning.

Later in the trip the Reds stopped at Philadelphia, and after Jakie May proved brutally ineffective in losing the 9-to-1 opener, Pete Donohue not only came through with a fine game the next afternoon, winning 11 to 2, but had about as great a day at bat as any pitcher ever had, making five hits, including a home run, in as many times at bat. Then, on the next day, came trouble.

Among the players on the Phillies was Jimmy Ring, who had pitched for the Reds during the pennant days of 1919. During the 1920 season Jimmy accused Jake Daubert of loafing on a certain play, and the incident led to bad feeling. That winter Ring was traded.

In this particular game, when Ring came to bat for the first time, Ivy Wingo, who was catching, reminded Jimmy of his accusations against Daubert. Ring was perfectly furious, and engaged in a heated verbal dispute with Wingo. Coaching at first base for the Reds that afternoon was Astyanax Douglas, Donohue's Texas Christian acquaintance who had come back to the team for another trial. Later in the game and without warning, Douglas suddenly accosted Ring and hit him in the jaw, and both players were removed from the pastime by the umpires. Ring waited at the clubhouse, Douglas accepted the challenge, and they went at it hammer and tongs again. The third round occurred after the game, when Ring followed the Reds to the North Philadelphia station and punched Astyanax again. Cooler heads then prevailed, and there was no further trouble.

The Reds returned home in June and promptly won seven games in a row. And with the string still intact, Redland Field's Golden Jubilee was scheduled for June 12. Garry Herrmann, always at his best as a host, put on a party that was a dandy, although prohibition agents turned out for the occasion and threw something of a damper on the postgame activities.

In the morning there was a street parade, and before the contest the old-timers were introduced. Old battery mates who hadn't seen each other for years clasped hands, former enemies forgot the old recriminations, and all was joyous and nostalgic along the Rhine. Among the former Reds who visited the park that day were George Pechiney, Heinie Peitz, Bob Ewing, Bobby Mitchell, Kip Selbach, Dummy Hoy, Long John Reilly, Orville Woodruff, Jesse Tannehill, Ollie

Beard, Jack Sutthoff, and Algy McBride—all voices from the distant past.

And as if that were not enough, the Reds of 1925 then stepped out and ran the winning streak to eight by winning the ball game from the Dodgers, a handsome shutout for Rixey, 6 to 0.

Judge Landis was among the spectators that afternoon, lending official dignity to the occasion. And who knows what his thoughts were as he slouched, chin in hand, in a box seat in the very park where queer actions by the Black Sox had made necessary his election as commissioner? Yes, the great National League was fifty years old, and it had survived the Black Sox scandal too.

The finest address of the afternoon was made by John Heydler, president of the National League, who said, in part, "This is a fine tribute to our national game. It shows in what esteem the sport is held by fans young and old. I have been at all the Golden Jubilee celebrations of the National League up to today, but the big turnout in Cincinnati sets them all in the shade."

Heydler wasn't just talking in the manner of a politician, either. He spoke with genuine emotion, and he well knew what an integral part Cincinnati had played in the rich history of his circuit.

The winning streak was shattered at eight the next day when Dazzy Vance hurled Brooklyn to a 12-to-3 verdict. But in the next few weeks the Reds continued to play intelligent, interesting ball, and on their next home stand, in late July, they ran up a winning skein that reached nine before Boston punctured the bubble.

The Reds advanced from fourth to third place on July 27 and held that position until the end of the season, winding up with 80 wins and 73 defeats, three games worse than their pace of the year before, yet one place higher in the standings. A young Pittsburgh manager named Bill McKechnie, the same McKechnie who had come to the Reds as a third baseman with Roush and Mathewson in 1916, was the man who ended John McGraw's monopoly on the pennant. McKechnie

176

brought his Pirates home in front, the Giants finishing second. Cincinnati hadn't done badly at all under Hendricks, despite problems, some of which might have been anticipated. The first-base business was a season-long headache. Bressler started the year at the bag, then in May Herrmann traded Tom Sheehan, a pitcher who had come to the club from St. Paul the year before, to Pittsburgh for Al Niehaus, a native Cincinnatian. Niehaus failed to produce, and was replaced with Walter Holke, a veteran claimed on waivers from Philadelphia.

Pete Donohue ended an unusual record in the latter part of the season. The young hurler with the magnificent change of pace had defeated the Philadelphians twenty consecutive times when he faced them on August 19 at Baker Bowl. But a great hitter named Cy Williams put an end to the string. Like a later Williams, Ted, Cy was a fine left-handed hitter, and strangely enough, as in the case of Ted, the clubs shifted way around to the first-base side of the diamond when he came to bat. With the score tied, 4 to 4, in the ninth, and a Philadelphia runner on base and Donohue's winning streak at stake, the infield and outfield made the shift. Cy crossed them up, rifled a ball into the vast expanse of unoccupied left field, and Donohue was beaten, 5 to 4.

One more celebration remained before the season was packed in moth balls. At this stage of National League history the catcher who had caught the most games had been George Gibson, the famous maskman of the Pirates, who had gone behind the dish on 1,195 occasions. Ivy Wingo, the aging backstop of the Reds, was rapidly approaching Gibson's total. When he passed the mark and established a new record on September 3, friends presented him with a chest of silverware in recognition of his accomplishment. On the same afternoon a concrete chair was dedicated in the press box to the memory of the late Bill Phelon, baseball writer of the *Cincinnati Times-Star* whose genius for writing light verse was exceeded only by his rather perverted sense of humor. Bill had occupied the same perch in the press gallery for fifteen years.

Rube Bressler, alternating between first base and the outfield, batted .348 for the year. Edd Roush had a .339 mark, and Curt Walker, playing the full season in right field, became the darling of the bleacherites when he hit .318.

Donohue and Rixey had fine seasons, Pete winning 21 and losing 14, Eppa having a 21 and 11 year. Carl Mays, however, had been side-lined most of the year with torn ligaments in his back, and he won only 3 games while losing 5, a tremendous drop from his inaugural season as a Red.

⊗ 20 ⊗

THE YEAR THAT BROUGHT
EVERYTHING

1

Of all the jobs in baseball, one of the most difficult is to know what to do to make a pennant-winner of a contending club. It is simple enough to change a tail-ender: all that has to be done is to dismantle the team and obtain a new one. But when you have one of those clubs that just fails to reach the top, and use poor judgment in strengthening it, you are apt to wind up with a loser on your hands.

So Garry Herrmann and Jack Hendricks took inventory. What was needed to enable the Reds to win in 1926? A first baseman, for one thing. That foolish procession of Bressler, Niehaus, and Holke in 1925 had cost many a game. Bressler was a fine player and a really outstanding hitter, but the time had come when he would have to settle down at one position. A shortstop also seemed called for. Jimmy Caveney in 1925 had been erratic in the field and had hit only .249, proving to be just shy of the standards for major-league performance. Ivy Wingo, too, was aging, and Bubbles Hargrave would require more robust aid than Ivy could summon in the backstop department. Those three defects—first base, shortstop, and the second-string catching job—were as glaring as headlights on the highway.

Herrmann and Hendricks did something about it. In January a package of $20,000 was handed the New York Yankees for the services of a veteran first baseman, Wally Pipp, who had become excess baggage in the Bronx because of the presence on the Yankee club of a promising young first baseman named Lou Gehrig. Shortly afterward the second-string receiver was obtained when Val Picinich, another veteran, was secured for the $7,500 waiver price from the Boston Red Sox. Another pitcher was added in Charles (Red) Lucas, who came from Seattle for $10,000. Lucas had had previous trials with the Giants and Braves, and was said also to be a good hitter. Still another acquisition was outfielder Walter (Cookoo) Christensen, a clowning gardener from St. Paul, who cost the Reds $24,000 and the contract of Al Niehaus.

But though Garry and Jack looked high and low, they could not find a shortstop. Scanning the winter waiver lists of the other major-league clubs failed to reveal one. Running through the rosters of the high-grade minor leagues failed to reveal one. Consultations with the club's scout, Bobby Wallace, failed to reveal one. If there was in the wide land a shortstop who could help the Reds, he didn't make his presence or availability known. And you don't obtain major-league players by placing want ads or giving the job to the president's son.

So it was decided that Sammy Bohne would have to play the position, though he was better at second base, with the possible help of Frank Emmer, a veteran recruit purchased from Portland who had had a brief trial with the Reds under Mathewson in 1916. And it was felt that the infield of Pipp, Critz, Bohne, and Pinelli or Dressen was an improvement on the inner works of the preceding year.

If there ever was a time when the Reds knew what they

needed and made every effort to get it, it was in those days of preparation for the season of 1926.

On opening day, the Reds met the Chicago Cubs, who had a new manager, a fellow who had never even played in the big leagues, Joe McCarthy. And McCarthy, who later with the Yankees was to win with tiresome regularity, lost the first ball game with which he was charged in the major leagues. It went ten innings, and the Reds won, 7 to 6, with Jakie May, who followed Donohue and Luque to the mound, receiving credit for the victory. On the following day the Cubs squared the series when a rookie named Charlie Root, making his first National League appearance, bested Carl Mays, 9 to 2, Mays yielding in the late innings to a Redleg recruit, Clyde (Pea Ridge) Day, a strange citizen from Pea Ridge, Arkansas, more famous for calling hogs than for pitching. In the third and final game of the set, Hendricks gambled by starting Red Lucas, the rookie from Seattle, and what Lucas did made the players and fans gasp, as he beat the great Grover Alexander, 2 to 1, winning his own game with a triple.

Pittsburgh came in to Redland Field next, and the Reds took two out of three, Red Lucas winning his second start, 5 to 2, in a duel with the curve-balling Johnny Morrison. Then the club went to Chicago, always a dangerous locality during prohibition, and suffered a terrible shellacking, 18 to 1, that gave the Reds cause to stop and think. A virtual parade of Cincinnati hurlers worked in that encounter, one of them, Rufus Meadows, experiencing his entire National League career that afternoon. Possibly there have been players who lasted less time than Rufus Meadows, though that is doubtful. Rufus pitched to just one man, Cliff Heathcote, who rolled to Pipp, and that was his career with the Reds. Others who saw service during the long afternoon were Carl Mays, Pea Ridge Day, a young man known as Bradford Springer, and, finally, Red Lucas, though why he was sent into such a game is difficult to fathom, unless Hendricks was anxious to get the team safely back to the hotel before dark.

The Reds rebounded from that grim experience the next

day in St. Louis when Red Lucas shut out the Cardinals, 4 to 0, for his third in a row. Cincinnati fans had a new hero by now in the wondrous redhead. Lucas was defeated his next time out, bowing to the Pirates, 3 to 2, but he had already displayed enough talents to establish him in the hearts of the fans. A pitcher who could pitch was always a pleasant article to have around, and when a pitcher could also hit—oh, boy!

On May 15, when the Reds were entertaining the eastern clubs on the fine lawn at Findlay and Western Avenues, Pete Donohue defeated the Giants in an 11-to-6 game that sent the team bounding into first place. And when Dolf Luque repeated the next day, it dawned on the club that it might actually be possible to stay in that exclusive region. So the Reds just roared on, winning with consummate ease almost daily. Their chief opposition came from the Pirates and, oddly enough, from the hitherto helpless St. Louis Cardinals, who had never won a National League pennant, but who had rallied under the fiery leadership of their playing manager, Rogers Hornsby.

Throughout the rest of May and into June, the Reds continued to be on top. Fans actually began to sniff a pennant in the air. But that awful shortstop situation was still the same. It was felt that if the Reds only had a shortstop, they would assume so titanic a lead they could never possibly be surpassed. Sammy Bohne had started the season at the post and was a distinct disappointment. Then Frank Emmer was given a whirl at the job, and he was even worse. In desperation, Hendricks played Babe Pinelli, the third baseman, at short, but Babe, though unusually adaptable, was unable to master the intricacies of the position. Then Emmer was tried again, and he failed wretchedly once more. And, hopelessly, Bohne again took over. All this in the space of two months! Wasn't there anyone that could be bought? How about Joe Boley at Baltimore? Not for sale. Shannon at Indianapolis? No, he'd never make the grade. Peckinpaugh? You'd never get him out of the American League. And so it went. Phone calls, telegrams, letters, tryouts! Won't somebody please play shortstop? But the world was deaf to Garry's cries.

The Reds dropped back to second place on June 9, but for just one day. Again, on June 18, they dropped back again. But once more it was only for one day. Despite the great vacuum that existed between second and third bases, those Reds of 1926 fought on, remaining in first place through the rest of June, and throughout almost all of July.

The Boston Braves came to Cincinnati for a week-end series of games beginning Friday, July 23. When a Beantown recruit named Henry Levi Wertz arose from obscurity to beat Carl Mays, 6 to 2, in the first game, the Reds were a trifle piqued. And when, in the Saturday affair, Larry Benton, a native Cincinnatian, took the hill for the Hub and humiliated his home town, beating Luque, 2 to 1, the Reds dropped back to second place again. During the course of that Saturday game Art Devlin, the old Giant who was now a Brave coach, began hurling insults at Babe Pinelli. This was dangerous business, for not only was Pinelli a temperamental young athlete who liked nothing better than to sock a tormentor on the jaw, but the Reds, seeing first place slipping from their grasp, were in a highly sensitive state. For Devlin to have selected such a time to shriek vile, McGravian names was like lighting a cigarette around gunpowder.

Between halves of the third inning, as Pinelli was going from his third-base position to the bench, he chanced to pass Devlin on the field, and by a strange coincidence, his spikes happened to encounter Devlin's feet. The Boston coach began to howl and started swinging. At this, a horde of Reds belched out from the Cincinnati dugout, with Luque in the front ranks. In some way, Devlin was knocked to the ground, and when he arose, he was badly cut up, but silent. Both Pinelli and Devlin were put out of the game, and the Babe was later fined $100 by the league office, and Devlin was given a thirty-day suspension.

Because of this incident, trouble was expected when the teams met in the final game on Sunday. Pinelli, nursing a bruised hand, had to witness proceedings from the shade of the press box. And the trouble was not long in coming.

The Braves had arranged that they would retaliate for the

slugging of Devlin by giving the works to Val Picinich, the catcher of the Reds. It was agreed that the first man who reached third base safely and had a chance to score would give Picinich a good going-over at the plate. But by an odd circumstance the first man to reach third for Boston was outfielder Jimmy Welsh, as nice a guy as ever played the game and as innocent and harmless as snow. But Jimmy was a good team man, and he tried to do the assigned task, crashing into Picinich like a Notre Dame blocking back. Val got to his feet, placed his big catching glove strategically under the Welsh chin, and delivered a ringing right to Jimmy's nose, knocking the Boston outfielder galley west. At this, players from both teams rushed out on the field and began to engage in a series of free-for-all melees. Police rushed from the grandstand out on the field and became involved in several of the numerous scraps. A Boston outfielder by the name of Frank Wilson had left the bench, swinging at any Red in sight. But unfortunately the first chin he was able to hit was attached to a policeman, and five other officers, witnessing the assault on one of their brethren, subdued the unruly Brave, backed up the police patrol, and shipped him off to jail in his uniform. That seemed to have a narcotic effect on the other battlers, and quiet was gradually attained. When the smoke cleared, umpire Barry McCormick ejected Picinich; Welsh was permitted to remain in the fray. But the angered Reds lost the game, their third in a row to Boston, 8 to 4.

Fights on the field between ballplayers usually aren't worth mentioning. They often consist of a few dirty looks and a few feeble swings that end in a clinch. But there have been occasional brawls on the diamond that were worth watching, and the one between the Reds and Braves on that hot Sabbath afternoon of July 25, 1926, was a lulu! Excitement buzzed until late at night throughout the city's streets. Sure, the Reds lost, but the fight! Why, it was worthy of Kelly's Killers!

2

Three days later, wonder of wonders, the Reds obtained a capable shortstop. His name was Horace Ford, and he was bought from Minneapolis for $25,000 and Frank Emmer. Horace had been up before, and why it hadn't occurred to anyone to buy him earlier couldn't be understood. He was possessed of an unusual sense of rhythm, he had a soft throw to first that was a beautiful thing to see, and he teamed with Hughie Critz as if they had been lifelong associates.

With Horace Ford at short, the Reds braced. Although the team sank to third on August 10, a winning streak that reached nine straight helped them along on the road back. Second place was regained on August 27 when Eppa Rixey shut out Brooklyn, 4 to 0. Another shutout, pitched by Donohue against the Cardinals on September 4, elevated the team to first place again. Now they were back, and with Ford in the line-up they would win!

But, baseball is an uncertain pastime. Events may cast their shadows before them in other walks of life, but not in baseball. At least there was no way of knowing what was to come on Labor Day.

Back in the game's halcyon days, before the double-header mania, holidays were gala affairs. On Decoration Day, Fourth of July, and Labor Day it was customary for a team to indulge in a morning contest, clear the park so the fans could go out for lunch or home brew, and then stage a matinee. No one minded paying two admissions, because the St. Louis Cardinal influence had not yet taught the patrons to expect two contests for the price of one.

And on Labor Day 1926 Redland Field had never looked lovelier. Matty Schwab, who had been superintendent of grounds since 1903 and whose father, John Schwab, had preceded him in that capacity, starting in 1894, had the infield grass so neat you could play 18.1 balk line on it. And the outfield was as green as April woods. The Reds were around first place, the world was lovely, the grandstand was jammed, and out on the hill that exciting morning a duel began between roly-poly Jakie May, who had finally fulfilled his early promise, and Charlie Root, the redoubtable youngster of the Cubs.

In the third inning, Cliff Heathcote, a left-handed hitter

for Chicago, hit the ball on the ground to Wally Pipp at first base. Pipp fielded it, waited, and made the easy toss to Jakie May, racing over to beat Heathcote to the bag. Jakie made the play all right and tagged Heathcote for the out, but in making his turn, Cliff veered the wrong way, and his spikes made a deep gash in the Achilles tendon of the May heel. Down to the ground tumbled Jakie. The fans gasped. A rookie, Roy Meeker, replaced May, and a hushed crowd watched the Cubs score twice and win, 2 to 0. In the afternoon tilt, the Reds atoned for the morning's work when Eppa Rixey tamed the Bruins, 7 to 4.

With May out of the line-up, Jack Hendricks took stock of his pitching for the final drive for the pennant. There were Donohue, Rixey, and Luque, ready and willing, but how able? Luque of late had been ineffective. There was some question also about Mays, who might be brilliant or brooding, according to his mood. And there was Red Lucas for relief. If they were right, the team could still win, even without May.

St. Louis and Cincinnati were virtually tied when the Reds began a long eastern trip, the schedule calling for twenty games, five in Pittsburgh, five in Brooklyn, three in New York, three in Boston, and four in Philadelphia. Then the Reds were to return home on September 26 for a single game with St. Louis that would end the season and might well decide the pennant.

The first three games at Pittsburgh were all lost, but the Reds salvaged the last two, with Lucas, used as a starter again, winning 5 to 2, and Mays taking a 10-to-6 triumph.

The Brooklyn series opened with a double-header on September 12. Donohue threw a shutout at the Dodgers in the first game, blanking the great Vance, 5 to 0, and then rushed to the relief of Luque in the nightcap, saving a 4-to-3 decision for the Cuban. That double victory helped. If Pete could just hold up now! It was a shame that Hendricks had to call on Donohue so often, but there was no other choice.

When Rixey pitched another shutout, beating Burleigh Grimes, 4 to 0, on the next afternoon, the Reds and Cardinals were tied for first place, each with 82 victories and 60 defeats.

Mays came through with a brilliant 5-to-1 effort next, while the Cardinals were idle in the East, putting Hendricks' club a half game up. Rixey then came back, pitching with one day's rest, beat Jesse Petty, 7 to 2, and the Reds had swept the five-game set from the lads from Flatbush. The Cardinals also won that afternoon, but still the Redlegs had that half-game advantage.

New York was next. Pete Donohue had had three full days of rest, enough under the maddening conditions that made it necessary for him to pitch out of turn. Rixey was bigger and stronger than Pete. The strain on Eppa hadn't been too severe. Pitching against Virgil Barnes, Donohue came through with a shutout, the third for the Reds in five days, 3 to 0. But on that same afternoon the Cardinals took two contests from the hapless Phillies, and the teams were tied again, each with 85 victories and 60 defeats.

Then it was Luque's turn again. The Giants hit him hard, and Donohue, though he had pitched the day before, once more rushed into action, holding the Giants at bay. Then Rixey came on, and the struggle was locked up, 4 to 4, as the tenth inning began. With two out in the tenth and the bases empty, Frank Frisch, McGraw's great second baseman, lined a pitch by Rixey high into the beckoning right-field stands for a home run, and the Reds had lost, 5 to 4. With that game went first place, as the Cardinals won and passed them.

It was Carl Mays's turn to pitch the last game in New York on September 18, but Carl said he had a cold in his arm. Hendricks dejectedly looked around the dugout.

"Give me the ball," Pete Donohue said. "Come on, give me the ball."

It was a nice gesture, but Pete didn't have it. He had pitched a complete game on September 12, a shutout over Brooklyn. He had relieved on September 13, pitched another shutout on September 16, and relieved on September 17. To expect him to pitch and win on September 18 was sheer folly. But he did his best, bowing 5 to 4 to Kent Greenfield, a young hurler with a singing fast ball and a beautiful pitch-

186

ing form, a young man as crisp and fresh as the Kentucky bluegrass that spawned him. It was a pathetic sight, with Greenfield and the Giants, having nothing at stake, leisurely beating the Reds. New York had had so many triumphs through the years. And there was Pete Donohue, who was eventually to wear a Giant uniform himself, pitching his heart out under Coogan's Bluff, his right arm aching after each delivery.

The next day was an off day technically. But of all things, the Reds went to New Haven, Connecticut, to play an exhibition game, risking life and limb to enrich by a few hundred dollars the coffers of the club. After all the heartbreak of the previous week, they were asked to strut their stuff before the citizens of New Haven. It would have been worth a hundred times the receipts of that silly expedition to give the Reds a rest. Edd Roush, Curt Walker, Hughie Critz, and Cookoo Christensen were all used in that ball game. And as if to underline the futility of the whole endeavor, Pete Donohue went into the exhibition contest as a pinch hitter!

But they got the game in, and the check was forwarded to Garry, and it no doubt pleased the directors immensely.

Then came Boston. In Boston, it was felt, the Reds might battle their way back into the lead. But Boston had not forgotten the fight with the Reds in July. If there was any club in baseball that the Braves wanted to beat, it was Cincinnati. A double-header was scheduled for September 20, and Eppa Rixey took the mound.

In the second inning of that game, Andy High, a little left-handed hitter who played the infield for the Braves, lined a drive to center field. Edd Roush came tearing in to make one of his famous catches, but he missed the ball completely, and it rolled past him for an inside-the-park home run, the only kind of home run that Andy High could possibly hit.

The Reds fought back and took a 2-to-1 lead. Then, in the sixth inning, Leslie Mann, the Beantown outfielder, raised an easy fly to center field. Roush trotted in, set himself, and then made an appalling muff of the ball, as the tying Boston run crossed the plate.

Rixey went back to work. The Reds again forged ahead, 3 to 2. The game went into the eighth. Andy High came up again. Once more he hit an outfield fly, this one to left field. Bill Zitzmann came racing in and failed to catch it. Two runs scored on that one, which won the game for Boston, 4 to 3.

That was the game that sealed the Redleg fate. After all the bitter pills that Cincinnati fandom had had to swallow through the weeks, the news from Boston seemed doubly depressing. Edd Roush, of all people, missing an easy fly! It was like hearing that Einstein had flunked long division.

Something died that afternoon in Boston. Completely whipped, the Reds dropped the second game also, as Bob Smith, a reformed infielder, beat Luque, 3 to 0. Roush misjudged another ball in that game, Jimmy Welsh getting a home run on the drive when the shoestring catch failed.

That did it. The Reds were two games behind the Cardinals now. Pete Donohue tried to salvage something from the wreckage in the final Boston game, but lost, 4 to 0, to Joe Genewich. The Braves had had their revenge.

The schedule still called for four games in Philadelphia, and there was nothing to do but play them. Rixey started the first one, and it developed into a fifteen-inning tie, halted by darkness. Donohue pitched in that one too. Then, on September 24, when Red Lucas bowed to Claude Willoughby, 9 to 2, the Cardinals clinched the National League flag.

The last game of the season at Redland Field with the Cardinals on September 26 was a meaningless mockery. Donohue, anxious to win an even twenty games for the season, pitched and won it, 2 to 1, from a wild St. Louis rookie southpaw, Bill Hallahan.

St. Louis finished with 89 victories and 65 defeats, two games ahead of the Reds, who had a record of 87 and 67.

The Reds, of course, were surly about losing out at the last moment after waging such a courageous fight all year. The lack of a shortstop for half the season, the spiking of Jakie May on Labor Day, and the strange delinquency of Roush in Boston had all conspired to make the season a tragic one. Errors, of course, are part of the game, and Roush was not blamed. But it did seem ironic that the greatest outfielder in the National League should suddenly go awry at such a time.

Roush didn't even bother to go back to Redland Field for the final game, but went right to his farm at Oakland City. The other players went back with heavy hearts. Curt Walker, maddened by recent events, threatened to strike because he was given an upper berth on the return trip. He would have been foolish to do so, as it would have cost him his second-place money in addition to a suspension.

But when we look back at the events of 1926 from a long-range view, it is probably just as well that the Cardinals won the pennant that season. For, by their victory, they made possible one of the game's most dramatic moments, Grover Alexander's trudging from the bull pen to the mound and striking out Tony Lazzeri to end a threat by the New York Yankees in the seventh inning of the seventh game of the 1926 World Series. The Cardinals were the better team—they won. Rogers Hornsby and his gang were great champions.

But the Reds had provided their full share of drama in the year that brought everything.

3

The individual accomplishments of the Reds of 1926 were on a par with the high quality of the team play. Some of the players produced far beyond their normal stride.

Bubbles Hargrave, the catcher, won the batting championship of the National League, with a .353 mark for 105 games. That was really an extraordinary feat. In the first place, no catcher had led the National League in hitting since King Kelly of the White Stockings in 1886, just forty years previously. In the second place, Rogers Hornsby led the loop in batting for six straight years, starting in 1920, and had come to look upon the feat as routine for him. But the cares of managing the Cardinals in 1926 whittled his average, and a new leader was able to sneak in.

Hargrave was a right-handed batter, thirty-four years of age when he won the award. He had always been a good hitter, but he was slow of foot, and not the type one would think of as a batting leader.

When asked how he accounted for his great season at the plate, Bubbles made a remarkable reply: "It was because I was sick in the spring."

The remark needs amplification. Bubbles had been sick, with an attack of appendicitis. Doctors insisted on operating, as they usually do, but Bubbles refused to permit such an invasion of his anatomy. Instead, he went on a rigid diet, and for some time ate no solid food. Surprisingly, the diet seemed to help his vision, and he also lost fourteen pounds. He felt so much better at the plate that he started the year batting at a .400 clip, and when the inevitable slump came, he was in such good condition that he was still able to achieve his finest season.

Bubbles was so pleased with himself that he continued to diet, and though he liked food, whenever he got hungry he would go off on a buttermilk binge. He had had a long and fine acquaintance with buttermilk, which is frequently found on kitchen tables in the area where he was brought up, around New Haven, Indiana.

For some time during the season, though, there was some question as to whether Hargrave wouldn't be surpassed by a member of his own team, Raymond (Rube) Bressler. Only the National League rule that states that a player must participate in one hundred or more games to receive credit for leading the league kept the Rube from taking the honors, since Rube had a .357 mark, four points more than Bubbles, in the eighty-six games in which he played.

Bressler is an interesting figure in the pastime, and was a much greater athlete than most fans think. His whole life is something on the fantastic side.

For instance, Rube was born in a town that no longer exists. There is a certain permanence to most towns in America, but Raymond Bloom Bressler happened to be born at Coder, Pennsylvania, which was a lumber town. The people who lived there made their living, for the most part, by helping a corporation chop down trees. This interesting pursuit lasted only as long as the trees did, lumber companies being as devoted as they are to conservation, so Rube's family had to move on to another town, Ashtola, which soon disappeared in the same fashion. Having survived two towns before he was in his teens, Rube went to work in a railroad shop at Renova, Pennsylvania, and there learned to play baseball.

Most fans recall the great Philadelphia Athletics of 1914, who were upset by the Boston Braves in the World Series, much to the chagrin of the game's dopesters. And most fans recall that the pitching staff Connie Mack assembled that year included Eddie Plank, Chief Bender, and Jack Coombs, and such fine youngsters as Bullet Joe Bush, Bob Shawkey, and Herb Pennock. Well, Rube Bressler was a pitcher on that club, too. Only nineteen years old, he had been discovered at Renova by Earle Mack, son of Connie, and though not breaking into a game with the A's until midseason, he won 14 and lost 3, and had an earned-run average of 1.76, which was topped in the American League only by George Foster, Dutch Leonard, and Walter Johnson. He then ran into a disappointing season in 1917, and the next year was shipped back to Atlanta. When he won twenty-five tilts there and helped bring the Georgia capital a pennant, the Reds bought him.

When the Reds won the 1919 flag, their great pitching staff refused to move over for Bressler. So he toiled in the bull pen, hoping for his chance.

Jake Daubert suggested one day that Pat Moran try Bressler in the left-field spot that had given the team so much trouble. Pat did. Rube proved to be a fair outfielder and a good hitter, and held the job. When the double-headers started piling up, Rube was needed on the mound once more. But his pitching proved ineffectual. Then it was too late for him to go back to the outfield, since Pat Duncan had been purchased and was filling the bill.

In 1920 a broken ankle handicapped Bressler. He stayed around for the next few years, doing a little pitching, a little work at first base, and more in the outfield. Then, in 1926, he came into his own.

Like Hal Chase, Bressler threw left-handed and batted right-handed. His success as a hitter was due to terrific powers of concentration. He used a peculiar, crouching style at bat and never for a second took his eyes off the opposing pitcher. He was a slashing line-drive hitter, often smacking the ball right back through the box, which, many say, is the test of a good hitter.

Bressler, today, is still around Cincinnati, and he has never lost his love for the game. He was chiefly responsible for the organization of Ball Players of Yesterday, which has done so much to keep intact the communion of former players. Rube is a sentimentalist and a dreamer, and he likes to ponder on such ideas as a home for old ballplayers. He is completely devoted to the game in which he excelled.

Hargrave and Bressler weren't the only .350 hitters on the club. Walter (Cookoo) Christensen, the recruit from St. Paul, a left-handed hitter and thrower, hit exactly .350 in 114 games. Everything Cookoo touched that season turned to gold. He delighted the crowds by his clowning, turning flip-flops in the outfield after he had made sparkling catches, bantering amicably with umpires and opposing players. Christensen played left field that year, sharing the post with Bressler. Roush, in center, finished up with .323, and Walker, in right, the idol of the bleachers, hit .306. Pipp, still dependable despite his long American League service, hit .291, but Critz slumped to .270.

During the 1926 season, the team also signed a prospect for the future, Ethan Allen, a local boy who played the outfield for the University of Cincinnati. Highly thought of by scouts of many major-league clubs, Allen got a bonus of $8,598.43 for signing and made the major-league grade without the usual apprenticeship in the minors, though he spent the first year learning things on the bench. Another mid-season addition was southpaw Roy Meeker, of Lead Mines, Missouri, who was purchased from Portland, Oregon, for $25,000.

With all his overwork in the season's last half, Pete Donohue had only 34 decisions, winning 20 and losing 14. Mays won 19 and lost 12 before his late-season lameness, and Jakie May, preceding his Labor Day spiking, won 13 and lost 9, as many victories as he had recorded in six previous seasons. Rixey won 14 and lost 8, Luque 13 and 16, and Red Lucas, the early-season sensation who went to the bull pen when the staff came around, 8 and 5. A good shortstop for the season's first few months might well have added to the victories of all the team's hurlers.

⊖ **21** ⊖

DECLINE AND FALL

1

Garry Herrmann decided to get rid of Edd Roush. The greatest player who had ever worn the Cincinnati uniform was now no longer wanted. Roush had spent almost eleven years with the team, and for the most part the association had been pleasant. Despite his annual holdouts and his occasional charley horses, Edd had always given his best, which usually proved to be very good indeed. One of baseball's most feared batsmen and most skilled fielders, Roush, nearly thirty-three years of age, was still highly valuable property. Garry made his intention of selling Roush known, waited for the offers, and on February 9, 1927, traded him to the New York Giants for George Kelly, a slugging first baseman, and a wad of cash the denomination of which has never been discovered.

Roush, the individualist, was not so sure he wanted to play in New York. Anticipating that, the Giants offered him a contract for $70,000 for three years. But Edd did not care for John McGraw's methods of browbeating and spying on players.

"We'll hit it off all right," McGraw told him.

"I'm not sure we will," Roush replied. "I don't like to be watched all the time. I don't drink or carouse around or indulge in late hours. Baseball is a serious profession with me. But I would like to go to bed without thinking any minute there'd be a knock on the door and the trainer would like to know if I was in."

But $70,000 can buy a lot of groceries in Oakland City, and Edd eventually entered the Giant fold.

Roush was the most stubborn and independent player to achieve prominence that ever lived. But though his methods might have failed to work for others, they brought him princely rewards. Club owners would have you believe that the most successful players are those who keep on amicable terms with their employers. Roush usually signed on his own terms. Players will tell you that the percentage is against place hitting. Roush almost always tried to place his hits, and ended up with one of the highest batting averages of his era. Students of the game will tell you that although batters can assume a stance in any given place in the batter's box, a firm stand in one place is absolutely imperative. Roush always shifted about in the box, moving both feet, and often changed his stance after the pitcher delivered the ball. He led the league in hitting three times.

The Cincinnati populace read the announcement of Roush's departure with mixed emotions. Some die-hards, not realizing that errors are part of the game, never forgave him for dropping Les Mann's easy fly in Boston. Others, with more vision, regretted Edd's passing, but agreed with Garry that somehow Roush had come to be associated with the last-minute failure of 1926 and realized that his passing, which someday would be inevitable anyway, might as well take place when he still had value.

George Kelly, who came to the Reds in the deal, was a right-handed hitter who stood six feet three inches in height and weighed two hundred pounds. He frequently hit home

194

runs, and he frequently struck out. He was twenty-nine when he came to the Reds, but a veteran of four World Series. A nephew of Bill Lange, one of baseball's greatest outfielders before the turn of the century, Kelly was a good fielder with a remarkably strong throwing arm, and, being four years younger than Wally Pipp, he promised to give the club first-base protection for possibly five or more years.

The good batting of Bressler, Christensen, and Walker in 1926 made Garry and Jack Hendricks feel that Roush would not be missed too much, and Cookoo Christensen was handed the center-field job.

The only other player of notice purchased during the winter was Ray Kolp, a twenty-six-year-old pitcher purchased from St. Paul for $25,000. He had had a previous trial with the St. Louis Browns, and was alleged to possess not only the usual qualifications for hurling but also an acid tongue that spat tart commentaries designed to rile the opposition.

Otherwise, Hendricks stood pat. He felt that the club that just missed the pennant would probably do about as well. There was none of the conscientious seeking out of weaknesses in the team that had occurred during the previous winter and that had done so much to make the Reds a strong contender.

The first sour note came with the holdout of Hughie Critz, who proved just as adamant with a Mississippi drawl as had Roush with an Indiana twang. To replace him, George Kelly was sent to the keystone. His height made him a grotesque figure at the position, but he had filled in there before with the Giants and could do a fair mechanical job. He proved to be a demon at racing into center field and relaying throws for weak-armed gardeners.

The valiant and overworked Pete Donohue was given the opening-day assignment against Pittsburgh, and he bowed to Remy Kremer, 2 to 1, before a throng reported to be 34,758, the largest in the history of Redland Field. That game was the first disappointment in a season that was to bring many.

When Hughie Critz finally signed, Carl Mays, who had been plagued with every sort of complaint after winning twenty contests his first year with the team in 1924, came up with a hernia that rendered him useless. Good news was always tempered with bad.

The saddest blow was the collapse of the proud pitching staff. Donohue, Luque, and Rixey had worked too long and too often in the years before. All had passed their respective peaks, though Rixey, being blessed with tremendous strength, seemed to have more left than the other two. The injury to Mays gave Red Lucas a chance to take his regular turn, and the Nashville Narcissus, as he had come to be called, responded by winning his games at a consistent clip.

Christensen, in center field, was a big disappointment. The young gardener whose clowning antics had amused the galleries in his freshman year found nothing to clown about as a sophomore. His batting fell off to an alarming degree, and he had to be replaced by Ethan Allen, the fine young collegian who had never played an inning in the minors.

During the first half of the year the Reds were the biggest disappointment in the circuit. When they remained in eighth place as the season progressed, the familiar query "What's wrong with the Reds?" was asked again and again, amid the doleful shaking of heads and the clicking of tongues, wherever people gathered. They remained in eighth place until July 16, when Red Lucas, going to the relief of Ray Kolp, pitched a 3-to-2 victory over Boston.

After that, the uphill progress was steady, but the team had started too late to hope for much. Everett (Pid) Purdy, a diminutive left-handed-hitting outfielder, was purchased for $15,000 from Seattle in August, and seemed to breathe a new spirit into the club. The Reds climbed to sixth place and eventually to fifth. A streak of eight triumphs in a row in early September brought them to a position one game shy of the .500 mark. But they couldn't summon the needed drive to finish higher than that. They eventually won 75 and lost 78 and finished fifth, finding themselves in the second division for the first time in seven years and the second time in twelve.

Pittsburgh won the 1927 flag, and the Reds found the

Pirates a constant source of trouble, beating them only 8 times in 22 meetings. The Smoketowners that year rode to success on a pair of brothers named Waner, Paul and Lloyd. Paul had come to the league the season before, and immediately proved to be one of the circuit's best performers. Then, in 1927, came Lloyd, a little bit of a guy who could run like a deer and who was such a tough target for the pitchers that at times they utterly despaired of getting him out.

At Redland Field, on September 4, the Waners accomplished one of the strangest batting feats of all time. In that year home plate was a great deal closer to the grandstand than it is now, and the box seats in right and left fields extended almost to the foul lines. It was possible to bounce a fair ball into the stands 250 feet from home plate for a home run, though such a hit was extraordinary. Dolf Luque was pitching when Lloyd Waner came to bat and sliced a low line drive over third base that skipped down the foul line and hopped into the stands for a homer. Clyde Barnhart, the next to bat, was retired, and then Paul Waner came to the plate and manufactured a drive that was the exact replica of Lloyd's. After watching that exhibition, the fans began to think there was no way on earth to stop the Pirates. And there wasn't. They weren't stopped until they ran smack into the New York Yankees in the World Series, when two gentlemen known as Babe Ruth and Lou Gehrig proved that home runs don't have to be bounced into the seats to count.

2

The announcement of Garry Herrmann's resignation as president of the Reds was made on October 25, 1927. He had held the job for a quarter century, and though he was sixty-eight years old, he probably would have continued to remain at the post had it not been for increasing deafness. An amiable soul and as gregarious as an ant, Garry began to think that life was unpleasant when he could not hear what people were saying. He had listened for so many years, principally to advice about how to run the team from well-meaning misinformants, that he had grown to rely on his aural faculties.

And when he no longer could hear, he knew that the time had come to quit.

Garry was by no means a rich man. He had always done a good job of dispersing the money that passed through his hands, and he spent it lavishly, giving uncounted pleasure to countless people. He was a professional party-thrower, but he also conducted baseball affairs with an astounding soundness. The players, in the main, loved him, and though he of course made a few business enemies, who in business doesn't? He had outlasted twelve of his managers, had seen the team go to spring training in eighteen localities, and had won one pennant and almost another. Thirteen of his twenty-five teams finished in the first division, which certainly is giving the patrons of the game a fair break. Though by necessity a businessman, he was more of a sport, and it broke his heart to leave the sport he loved.

To succeed him, the board of directors selected Campbell Johnson McDiarmid, an able and prominent attorney of the city who had been acting as secretary of the club. McDiarmid, son of a man who served as president of Bethany College in West Virginia, had played baseball at the University of Cincinnati and in the semipro ranks before going into law. A lifelong fan, McDiarmid had purchased a great deal of stock in the St. Louis Browns of the American League in 1907, and had sold his interest in that club in 1919, buying into the Reds. He was not a practical baseball man in the sense that he grew up around ball parks, but his intentions were of the best and he was devoted to the welfare of the club.

C. J. McDiarmid, as he was always known, was responsible for one policy of the Reds that has been continued to this day. He was absolutely sworn to the belief in the desirability of playing games on the days for which they were scheduled. He was against synthetic double-headers, and believed that when rain threatened, every possible effort should be made to play the game. McDiarmid knew that baseball fans are subjected to various disappointments, and that having a game rained out is almost as bad as losing one. What he would have done had he lived to see the baseball schedules assumed by the major leagues in World War II, with their potpourri of night games, twilight games, twilight-night double-headers, afternoon double-headers, and morning games is not difficult to figure out. He would have been properly appalled.

Before night ball, teams relied for patronage principally on those who hired others, and were therefore free to attend games whenever they liked, and on traveling salesmen who hoped their presence at the game would not be discovered by the home office. When C. J. McDiarmid ran the Reds, both bosses and salesmen knew that if the club was at home there would be a game, a single game, and it would start in the middle of the afternoon. And the iceman who delivered all his ice in the morning and the salesman who made all his calls before noon didn't worry if it thundered while they were consuming the blue-plate special at the Elite Café. If the game could be played, it would be played, and they could go out and root for the Reds. In 1928, under McDiarmid, the Reds played fourteen double-headers, only five of them at home. In 1945 they played forty-one of them.

McDiarmid retained Jack Hendricks as manager, and hoped for the best. The country was prosperous, the National League was making money, and in April 1928 the decline of the Reds was thought of as only a temporary development.

Only a few changes were made. Rube Bressler, seeking his release, was sold to Brooklyn. Cookoo Christensen, a bitter disappointment, was shipped back to Columbus. Those outfielders weren't needed with Ethan Allen developing nicely, Curt Walker continuing to play with skill, and Pid Purdy promising so much. Bill Zitzmann was also still around, and there was a new man, Marty Callaghan, a former Cub, purchased for $10,000 by Garry from Seattle just before his retirement.

Pete Donohue was the only holdout. His salary had been slashed following his disappointing season of 6 victories and 16 defeats, and though the splendid Texan didn't know it yet, his pitching days were numbered. Somewhere along the line in that 1926 stretch drive, he had lost the zing in his fast ball.

Pete missed the training trip to Orlando, but came into the fold shortly after the season opened.

Surprisingly enough, the Reds made a good start. Hughie Critz appeared headed for a great year, and he and Horace Ford at short made a team that saved run after run for the pitchers by executing intricate double plays. Ethan Allen came into his own as the successor to Roush in center field, and Chuck Dressen, stationed at third, began to hit at a pace that had hitherto escaped him. When the Reds won the Memorial Day twin bill at Chicago, 6 to 0 and 2 to 1, they headed east in first place, the talk of the league.

It will be recalled that during the pennant drive in 1926, the team foolishly engaged in an exhibition game at New Haven, Connecticut. Escaping injury in that venture, the front office continued to schedule such contests whenever an off day presented the opportunity.

It was at Buffalo, New York, on their way east for the first time in 1928, that one of these games was played. Ethan Allen, one of numerous Reds offered as a counterattraction to Niagara Falls that afternoon, was struck by a pitched ball that fractured his cheekbone. That was the team's first reverse in fortune of the year, and, of course, was completely unnecessary. At about the same time Red Lucas, who had won 8 of his first 10 games, suffered a broken arm when struck by a ball during batting practice. That combination of injuries assured the club's decline.

As June came in, the Reds reached Boston. Emil Fuchs, the president of the Braves, had great hopes for his team that season. He had obtained the great Rogers Hornsby from the Giants to manage the club, and to make Hornsby's batting even more terrifying, Fuchs had installed a jury box of bleacher seats in left field, bringing the home-run area well within the reach of the mighty Rajah's bat. However, this application of geometry to hitting proved to be a dismal failure from the Boston point of view. Though visiting players often hit balls into the jury box for home runs, Hornsby, for some reason, couldn't find the range.

The Reds beat the Braves on June 1, 7 to 6, with Hughie

Critz, Val Picinich, and pitcher Ray Kolp, of all people, hitting home runs into the synthetic seats. But the real fireworks came the next day. Though Lester Bell, the Brave third baseman, hit three round-trippers and a triple, to give him fifteen total bases for the afternoon's work, Pete Donohue hit for the circuit and his mates made enough safeties of other proportions to win the verdict by a grotesque 20-to-12 score. Then, in the third game of the series, Boston managed to win 5 to 3, but Eppa Rixey, never known as a rival of Babe Ruth though a man of various other talents, socked the third home run hit by a Cincinnati pitcher in as many days. That was enough for Fuchs, and the temporary seats were removed.

But the Reds never had another series like that one. Though they stayed above the .500 mark for the remainder of the year, they finished fifth, with 78 victories and 74 defeats, a record three and one-half games better than that of the season before. Of those players who appeared in more than one hundred games, Ethan Allen was the only .300 hitter, compiling a mark of .305.

Defensively, the 1928 team had class, and principally through the efforts of Ford and Critz established a major-league double-play mark, completing 194 twin killings during the season. For the second year in a row the pitching staff failed to include a twenty-game winner, though Rixey won 19 and lost 18.

In August, a young pitcher named Silas Johnson was purchased for $1,500 from Rock Island, and he broke into three games without a decision, though he had not quite reached his twentieth birthday. Also bought, but for later delivery, was Tony Cuccinello, a hard-hitting infielder from Columbus.

3

Catcher Val Picinich became the club's annual holdout in 1929, and rather than continue the argument, C. J. DcDiarmid shipped the receiver to Brooklyn for Johnny Gooch, another catcher, and pitcher Welton (Rube) Ehrhardt. Two outfielders were purchased, Estel Crabtree from Oklahoma

City and Evar Swanson from the Missions club of the Pacific Coast League. Four more players were drafted, outfielder Walter Shaner from Chattanooga, catcher Leo Dixon from Baltimore, third baseman Rube Lutzke from Newark, and pitcher Marvin Gudat from Houston.

The draftees didn't make out so well. Shaner, who had a remarkable facial resemblance to Jack Dempsey, the prize fighter, was used in occasional pinch-hit roles with average success. Dixon won the third-string catching job, which meant that he could spend most afternoons dozing in the bull pen. Gudat stayed around as a batting-practice pitcher, and occasionally was trusted in a game. Lutzke never appeared in a championship contest, as he aroused the ire of Jack Hendricks in spring training when he blistered his hands sliding down a rope, the horseplay putting him on the side lines. He was returned to Newark when he recovered.

The training camp was saddened by the death of southpaw Roy Meeker, who had come to the club in 1926 and had shuttled to and from Columbus ever since. Meeker died in his Tampa hotel room, March 25, 1929, after complaining for several days of pain in his stomach. In those days ball clubs didn't pay much attention to announcing news to the press, and on the day Meeker died, the sports writers covering the club had gone fishing, no exhibition game being scheduled. When Tom Swope, the able scribe of the *Cincinnati Post*, who had covered every Redleg team since 1915, came back to the hotel that night, he asked one of the club officials in a routine way if anything had happened during the day.

"Yes," was the casual reply. "Roy Meeker died."

Wally Pipp, who hit .283 in 1928 but who was definitely on the way out, was given his unconditional release, opening the way for George Kelly to play first base. Having two first basemen of almost equal skill for two seasons had proved to be a luxury, and Pipp was disposed of because he was older. Bubbles Hargrave had also come to the end of the line at thirty-six, and he too passed from the scene via the release route. With Johnny Gooch on hand to do the catching, and Clyde

Sukeforth, a youngster that scout Bobby Wallace had dug up in Maine, coming on nicely, Bubbles wasn't even missed.

Kelly, Critz, Ford, and Dressen made up the 1929 infield, with Allen, Swanson, and Walker in the outfield and Gooch behind the plate. The same pitchers were depended on, Luque, Lucas, May, Mays, Donohue, Rixey, and Kolp.

Broadcasting of games was regularly scheduled for the first time in 1929, with Bob Burdette, sportcaster for WLW, being the first to announce the contests from a shed on the grandstand roof. Although the advisability of broadcasting games was then debated, some feeling that fans would stay at home and listen rather than view the tilts, it was felt that the practice would create many new fans. The latter view proved to be correct, but it was not until Red Barber came to Cincinnati during the administration of Larry MacPhail that radio began to pay off. And then Waite Hoyt, assuming the broadcasting chores in 1942, after completing a remarkable pitching career that spanned two decades, became the most popular baseball announcer in the city's experience.

The Reds had not finished in the league basement for fifteen years, but the 1929 club started so slowly that many fans feared that the cellar would be its abode. The pitching had bogged down, the hitting was sporadic. The team was absolutely last through all of June.

Relief from ennui was supplied in Chicago on the Fourth of July, the Reds and Cubs providing their own peculiar brand of fireworks. Ray Kolp, who always liked to shout insulting remarks from the Cincinnati bench, had a particular victim in Lewis (Hack) Wilson, the hard-hitting and rotund outfielder of Chicago. During the first game of the holiday twin bill, which the Reds eventually won, 9 to 8, Kolp continually heckled Wilson. After Wilson had singled, the abuse became more than he could stand, and he left first base, went over to the Redleg dugout, and planted a right hook to the Kolp jaw, then tried to rip the uniform off of every Red player who tried to act as peacemaker. Umpire Charlie Rigler put both Kolp and Wilson off the field, and quiet was restored. Wilson's anger mounted when Chuck

Dressen, the Red third baseman who always enjoyed making smart plays, put the ball on Wilson in the dugout for the out, as Hack had neglected to call time before inaugurating the pyrotechnics. The Cubs won the second game of the bargain bill, 10 to 5, without anything untoward happening.

But that night as the Reds were standing on the platform of the railroad station, waiting to board their train, Hack Wilson put in an appearance and without warning attacked Pete Donohue. At the time he was struck, the Redleg pitcher was quietly conversing with Dolf Luque and Eppa Rixey. Slight remarks were made about Hack's assault on Kolp, when Hack suddenly turned on Pete as he was walking away and hit him in the jaw. Donohue tripped over his suitcase and fell to the ground, as teammates rushed Wilson away.

The episode was slight, but the Red fans were so in need of excitement that summer that the battle took on all the importance of Gettysburg. Fans rushed for their schedules, noted that the Cubs were next due in Cincinnati for a Sunday double-header August 25, and swarmed to club headquarters to buy tickets. Another brawl such as the one with Boston in 1926 was visualized, but it never took place. When the Reds met the Bruins, both teams were as docile as kittens. But a throng of 35,432, largest crowd in Redland Field history, viewed the peaceful proceedings, some perched on rafters and others sitting on runways, with Red Lucas winning the opener, 6 to 3, and the Windy City boys slaughtering Donohue, 10 to 1, in the afterpiece.

The most fearsome pitcher the Reds had to face that year was Fred Fitzsimmons of the New York Giants. Fitz hurled four consecutive shutouts over the club, but they finally caught up with him on August 29, with Donohue winning a 3-to-2 duel.

The Reds finally crept out of the cellar, but just barely, finishing seventh, ahead of only Boston. The team won 66 and lost 88, and of the pitchers only Red Lucas, who won 19 and lost 12, was over the .500 mark.

A batting surprise was catcher Clyde Sukeforth, who hit .354 in the eighty-four contests in which he appeared. Curt

Walker hit .313 and Evar Swanson an even .300. But Swanson's chief claim to fame was his tremendous speed on the base paths. On September 15 he gave a demonstration of his running ability, circling the bases in 13.3 seconds, a record that has never been surpassed.

As the year drew to its disappointing close, Jack Hendricks announced that he would not return in 1930 as leader of the team. This was a mere formality, as Jack would not have been invited back. He had been at the helm for six years, a longer period of time than any previous Redleg manager had lasted in the town, and his Cincinnati teams won 469 games and lost 450. Hendricks' principal fault was overconfidence in his players once the decline started in 1927. He failed to see that the men he relied on had outlived their usefulness, that what was needed was a general house-cleaning. Hendricks came to Cincinnati with a good ball club. He left one that was dying on the vine. And the worst was yet to come.

☻ 22 ☻

THE GREAT DEPRESSION

1

During the late days of the 1929 season, it was rumored that some unknown person was conducting a whirlwind campaign to buy stock in the Cincinnati Reds. It was finally discovered that the man was Sidney Weil, a businessman of ability and wealth. At this time the principal stockholder in the Reds was Lou Widrig, a druggist from Newport, Kentucky, who held 2,500 of the 6,000 shares, lacking only 700 shares of controlling the club. Weil conducted a clever campaign with no advance notice. First he approached Widrig, but when the latter put an exorbitant price on his holdings, Weil turned to smaller stockholders, buying them out one by one. After he had paid $200 a share for stock that had a par value of $50, his brokers found it necessary to pay even more. Events happened suddenly. On September 18 Weil owned 43 shares of stock. A week later he had his 3,200, and control of the team. He obtained more than a thousand shares when he bought out Walter Friedlander, James P. Orr, and Maurice Pollock, three members of the board of directors who disagreed with Lou Widrig on policy and who got even with him by getting their price from Weil's agents and seeing the club pass into new hands.

Sidney Weil had much to commend him. He had inherited money from his father, who was associated with a firm of horse dealers, had seen active duty in World War I, had made money in the automobile business, invested a great deal in General Motors, and owned real estate. At baseball he was a novice, but a fan of the finest type.

Sidney Weil sat in the stands as owner of the Reds on October 4, 1929, three days before the season closed. He had ideas, big ideas, for the future. When Weil assumed control, C. J. McDiarmid handed in his resignation.

One of the first things Sidney Weil did was to grant liberal salary increases to Red Lucas, Horace Ford, Hughie Critz, and Ethan Allen.

The resignation of Hendricks left the team without a manager, and Weil landed his man at the 1929 World Series, signing Dan Howley, a former catcher and a pilot who had had exceptional success with the St. Louis Browns, finishing third and fourth with ordinary clubs in 1928 and 1929.

Howley was about the most genial and kindly man who ever managed a big-league team. Called "Howling Dan" because of his strong vocal qualities, he was soft-spoken off the field, a natty dresser, and a gentleman of polish. Players swore by him.

Dan had never been a great catcher. Born at East Weymouth, Massachusetts, he was first interested mainly in the sea, and he didn't learn baseball until he attended high school. Then he made rapid progress, played semipro ball, and started the climb through the minors. He reached the majors with the Phillies of 1913, the only year he was in the big time. Before managing the Browns, he had served a term as coach on the Detroit Tigers, under both Hughie Jennings and Ty Cobb.

Weil announced Howley as his manager the day after the World Series, and he revealed at the same time that he had purchased two veteran outfielders from the American League, Harry Heilmann from Detroit and Bob Meusel from the New York Yankees. Thirty-six at the time of his purchase by the Reds, Heilmann had, of course, seen better days. But what days they had been! Harry was one of the few players able to attain a .400 batting average, smacking the ball at a .403 clip in 1923. Strangely, Heilmann always performed better in the odd years. He led the American League in batting in 1921, 1923, 1925, and 1927.

Meusel was not the fine hitter that Heilmann was, but he was a dangerous batter who had an exceptionally high total of runs batted in. The regular left fielder of the Yankees, Meusel had starred on the sterling clubs that contained such sluggers as Babe Ruth, Lou Gehrig, and Tony Lazzeri. Though a fine outfielder, Bob always gave the impression that he was loafing, as he took long, lazy strides. He looked like a much better ballplayer from the field than from the grandstand.

Weil was determined to make other changes. He traded the veteran Dolf Luque to Brooklyn in February 1930 for another pitcher, Doug McWeeney, and though not an important transaction, it was a terrible one. Luque remained in the league as a top relief pitcher for six more years, and McWeeney broke into just eight games for the Reds, winning none and losing two.

Another shift made the same month saw Clarke Pittenger, a reserve infielder, go to the Yankees for a twenty-four-year-old shortstop named Leo Durocher and cash. When Durocher joined the Cincinnati Reds in 1930, he was a brash young shortstop who could do remarkable things when he got his hands on the ball, and he had more brass than a secondhand junk dealer.

Sidney Weil was one of the first executives in baseball to take a fatherly interest in Durocher, who had left the Yankees under unpleasant circumstances. Leo arrived in Cincinnati with a string of debts, which Weil paid and then patiently deducted from the shortstop's salary. His nickname in those days was not "the Lip," but "C Note." Talking out of the side of his mouth in gangster fashion, he always wanted a "C note" when he came to the club's office. He usually settled for a double sawbuck.

When the team trained at Orlando for the last time in 1930, it was almost completely made over. But Weil had to do the job piecemeal, as he had lost heavily in the 1929 stockmarket crash. Buying the ball club as a plaything, he found that it had become his business, and in an attempt to save his stocks he pledged his baseball holdings with the Pearl Market Bank of Cincinnati, of which he was a director. The club had cost him $600,000, though it had been capitalized at only $350,000, and had paid no dividends for several years. In addition, Sid had to buy the real estate on which Redland Field stood for an additional $195,000 before the start of the 1930 season.

Howley thought the team had promise. At the start of the season, George Kelly remained at first, Hughie Critz at second, Leo Durocher at short, and Tony Cuccinello, whose purchase had been announced earlier but who did not report until 1930, at third. Harry Heilmann and Bob Meusel were given regular outfield jobs, along with Curt Walker. Clyde Sukeforth was depended on for most of the catching, with Johnny Gooch in reserve, and regular pitching assignments went to Red Lucas, Ray Kolp, Eppa Rixey, and Benny Frey, a youngster who had come up in the fall of 1929.

Early in the year it became obvious that more pitching was needed, and in an effort to obtain it, Hughie Critz was sacrificed to the Giants for Larry Benton, a hurler who had won twenty-five games for McGraw in 1929, but who had been disappointing thereafter. Benton was thirty-two, and a native Cincinnatian who had first reached the majors with the Boston Braves. Six days after that deal was made, the Reds and Giants concluded another swap, the Reds sending Pete Donohue and Ethan Allen for Pat Crawford, a young left-handed hitter who could play both first and second bases.

So now, with the season a little more than a month old, the infield had to be made over. Pat Crawford was given a shot at Hughie Critz's job at second and he proved to be an ordinary fielder, though a pretty good hitter. Horace Ford was also used at second, with Leo Durocher retaining the shortstop post. A little later in the season George Kelly was given his unconditional release, and the first-base position was handed over to Joe Stripp.

The ball used in the National League was extremely lively, and the Reds did their share of hitting. But the pitching bogged down, and the fans could tell that Sidney Weil's first club was not going to be an improvement on McDiarmid's last one.

Howley proved to be a philosopher, and the Reds took their share of drubbings regularly. During most of June they were in sixth place, and had hopes of finishing there. But as the season grew older, it developed that only the Phils were worse than the Reds.

One feature of the summer's play was the remarkable batting of Harry Heilmann. Though in the sunset of his career, he gave the Cincinnati fans a demonstration of the hitting power that had made him such a fearsome slugger all his life. For a while it was thought that he might lead the league in hitting; and though his work later tapered off, he proved to be a powerhouse, pacing the team's offense. Meusel, on the other hand, was unimpressive.

Tony Cuccinello was another whose play was a pleasant surprise. Appearing in the league for the first time, he had no difficulty in hitting major-league pitching, and his fielding at third base was all that could be desired.

One thing the Reds could do in 1930 was beat the Chicago Cubs. The Bruins were fighting desperately to win their second consecutive pennant, and though they had a formidable lead in August, they eventually lost to the St. Louis Cardinals. And the Reds played no small part in hurrying the Cubs to their demise.

Benny Frey, the young right-hander, proved especially adept at taming the Bruins. The first time he faced them, he beat Charlie Root, 2 to 1, then met them a week later and bested Hal Carlson, 1 to 0. He lost his third attempt, but then beat them twice in one series in early July. One of the games between the Reds and Chicago produced a real oddity. Larry Benton started the contest for Cincinnati, but when the Cubs batted him roundly, Howley sent in Kenneth Ash, a young right-hander from Virginia who had a great curve ball. Ash entered the fray in the fifth with none out and the bases loaded, and the Reds trailing by three runs. Ken's first pitch to Charlie Grimm was hit into a triple play. Then, when the Reds came to bat, a pinch hitter was sent in for Ash and the Reds scored four times and took the lead. Ray Kolp then finished out the contest on the slab. Under the scoring rules, the victory was awarded to Ash, yet he pitched just one ball, and with that one pitch retired three men.

Frey beat the Cubs for the fifth time on Labor Day, and the Reds for the season held the Bruins to a standstill, each club winning eleven times. Had Chicago been able to defeat the Reds in the way a pennant contender is expected to lambaste a second-division club, they would have had no difficulty in repeating as champions.

In August, Weil brought up a young southpaw named Harlan (Biff) Wysong from Columbus. Wysong came from a little town forty miles north of Cincinnati, Clarksville, and when it was announced that Biff was going to start a contest on the day he reported, almost the entire population of his hamlet turned out for the occasion. The hurler was called to home plate and "honored" by his fellow townsmen, and then received his National League baptism. What happened was plenty! The Reds were playing the Phillies that afternoon, and in opposition to Biff was a veteran right-hander, Claude Willoughby, who hadn't won a game all season long. Since the Phils were tail-enders and Willoughby was considered such a soft touch, it was thought that the proper spot for Wysong's debut had been selected. But sloppy fielding by Heilmann and Meusel put the kid on the spot in the first inning, and when the Phils started hitting solidly in the second round, Biff had to be removed from the game, in spite of his appreciative audience. To dispense with the game as briefly as possible, it is enough to say that the final score was 18 to 0 in favor of Philadelphia. It is not likely that any player ever made a less pleasant entrance into the league than Wysong.

But the Reds stayed ahead of the Phils and finished seventh, with 59 victories and 95 defeats for a percentage of .383, the lowest reached by the club since 1901, when Bid McPhee managed the outfit.

Heilmann finished the year with a .333 average and a nice collection of extra base hits, forty-three doubles, six triples, and nineteen home runs, more circuit clouts than any Redleg had ever made in the expansive geography of Redland Field. Tony Cuccinello hit .312, and Evar Swanson .309. Curt Walker, at .307, and Joe Stripp, at .306, completed the list of those who had respectable averages.

2

After eight years of training at Orlando, the Reds moved their spring base to Tampa in 1931, and the team has trained there ever since, except for the confused years of World War II, when they were forced to remain in the North.

Sid Weil knew by this time that running a ball club, especially during a time of depression, wasn't the world's most pleasant pastime. The Reds not only had lost all contact with the first division, but they showed alarming symptoms of developing a chronic case of tailenditis.

Howley did the best he could with the material at hand, and Weil tried to obtain more help from other clubs. A young first baseman, Mickey Heath, purchased from the American Association, was expected to win the first-base job. He appeared in just seven games before breaking his arm. Nick

Cullop, a mighty minor-league slugger, had been bought from Minneapolis. Nick had failed in previous big-league trials, and was thought to be suffering from a mental complex that kept him from showing his best form in the majors. He had been bought conditionally, and in order to bolster his confidence, Sid told him that the deal had been completed and that Cullop had only to keep playing his best.

"I'll never make it up here," Cullop said. And he didn't. There were times when Cullop hit the ball so far it seemed to explode. But he also struck out frequently, and the fans rode him hard.

The team dropped its first five games, finally won one with Red Lucas in the box, and then lost the next seven. After a victory by Kolp, five more were kicked away, and the Reds had a record of 2 victories and 17 defeats. By this time it was apparent the cellar was to be reached.

Weil tried desperately to obtain help. Harvey Hendrick, a hard-hitting first baseman, was purchased from Brooklyn as a replacement for Heath.

One of the more interesting transactions of the season was the return to Cincinnati of Edd Roush. After being traded for George Kelly, Roush played three seasons for the Giants and then, as might be expected, staged a holdout. In his days with the Reds, Roush had reported as late as July, but in 1930 he established a new record, remaining at Oakland City for the entire year. Though thirty-seven years of age and offered a contract for $15,000, Edd had decided to ask for more. People called him all kinds of fool, and he didn't mind in the least.

After obtaining permission to deal with the player, Weil called Roush on the phone. Would he be interested in signing with Cincinnati?

"No," Edd said succinctly. "I'm through with the game."

A week later Weil called him again, and asked if he wouldn't come to Cincinnati and talk things over.

"It won't do any good to talk things over," Roush said. "But if you insist, I'm willing to talk."

Finally Roush agreed to sign. "I think you're making a

mistake in giving me my figure," he said. "I'm thirty-eight years old and may not be able to play good ball for you. I'm a definite risk."

He signed. And he played good ball.

With Roush and Hendrick in the line-up, the team began to play with more skill, but the start had been so wretched that there was little hope of getting out of eighth place. Weil found a willing dealer in Branch Rickey of the Cardinals, and Branch unloaded a bit of his surplus talent on the Reds, sending outfielders Wally Roettger and Taylor Douthit to the team. Douthit was a greyhound in center field, one of the best chasers of a fly ball who ever played. He had starred on the Cardinals' 1926 and 1928 pennant-winners, and proved to be a great lead-off man in the batting order, as well as a superlative fielder. But the deal that sent him to Cincinnati broke his heart, and he never played in a Redleg uniform with any spirit.

There was a young catcher on the team named Bob Asbjornson, who came from Concord, Massachusetts. When the Reds visited Boston one afternoon, his fellow townsmen decided to give him a "day." Remembering the experience of Biff Wysong the year before, the Reds wondered what would be in store for Asbjornson. As it turned out, his "day" was even more fantastic than Wysong's. Bob did his part, hitting the only home run of his National League career that afternoon. But something had apparently gone wrong with the plans of the committee of people from Concord. Bob was called to home plate and given a substantial check, but after the game he noted that no one had bothered to sign it. Then a party was scheduled for a Boston hotel after the contest, and when Asbjornson went there, he found that none of the guests showed up. So, if anything, he suffered more on the day he was to be honored than did Wysong, though he was not stung with an 18-to-0 defeat.

The ridiculous outcome of the Asbjornson ceremony seemed to emphasize the team's hard luck. No one likes a cellar club, the home fans, the manager, or even the league umpires.

Sidney Weil had to be blessed with the patience of Job to smile during those days. It seemed as if everything conspired to hurt the Reds. Not only were valuable players injured, but even the weather treated Weil less kindly than the other league magnates, several lucrative dates being washed away by the elements.

And so, in an atmosphere of Stygian gloom, the season slowly closed. One loss was piled upon another like poker chips in a stack, the pitchers regularly bowing to defeat. Only Red Lucas kept his head above the current, and with that miserable club managed to win 14 games while losing 13.

Leo Durocher, at shortstop, was another bright spot. His flashiness was uncanny, even though wasted on the cellar air. During one stage of the season Leo accepted 251 consecutive chances without a bobble, going from May 15 to August 5 without a miscue, then fumbling a little roller hit by Hazen (Kiki) Cuyler of the Cubs. Teaming with Tony Cuccinello, Durocher proved extremely agile at making the double play, and the team tied its 1928 record of 194 twin killings.

For some time it was feared that the Reds might lose one hundred games, something the team had never done before. But they managed to split their last six contests, and finished 1931 with 58 wins and 96 defeats. In eighth place, of course.

⊖ **23** ⊖

ABSOLUTE BOTTOM

1

One of the nicest things about Sidney Weil was his willing-ness to make deals he thought would help the club. There aren't as many big transactions made in baseball today as in the old days, and many of the magnates seem afraid to trade their players. Weil loved big deals, and he proved to be a shrewd trader.

The team was in training at Tampa, preparing for the 1932 season, when he announced one of his biggest coups. Catcher Clyde Sukeforth, second baseman Tony Cuccinello, and third baseman Joe Stripp were sent to Brooklyn for infielder Wally Gilbert, outfielder Floyd (Babe) Herman, and a young catcher, Ernie Lombardi. Herman was the biggest name of the six players involved. A tremendous hitter, though a man who was apt to do almost anything afield, Babe had been the central figure in the bizarre aggregation of Dodgers gathered together by manager Wilbert Robinson. The Babe was said to be so awkward in the outfield that he was apt to be struck on the skull by a fly ball, but all was forgiven when he went to bat. Lombardi was a young giant of a catcher, patterned along the lines of Larry McLean, who had been with the Reds in the early days of the century. Gilbert was the weakest player of the trio, but it was thought that he could man the third-base post.

In another deal, the Reds sent pitcher Benny Frey, first baseman Harvey Hendrick, and cash to St. Louis for out-fielder Chick Hafey, one of the league's finest players when he was in top form. Hafey had come up to the Cardinals in 1924 and developed into one of the circuit's stars. He was a skillful fielder, had a magnificent arm, and was a long-distance hitter. But he was often plagued with sinus trouble.

Weil found it easy to deal with Branch Rickey, the Cardinal executive, whose vast farm chain had developed a great surplus of talent. Rickey was and is a positive genius at knowing when to dispose of a player. Throughout the years he has made numerous deals that looked bad for him at first blush. But he almost always came out on the long end of the bargain. The Hafey transaction was such a deal.

Howley's 1932 club started with a great rush, and for the first six weeks of the season it appeared that the Reds were destined for a higher rung on the league ladder. They gave an example of their courage in the opening game of the season, when they trailed the Cubs, 4 to 1, going into the ninth inning, then scored four times in a frenzied outburst that included a pinch triple by Red Lucas and a payoff single by Taylor Douthit, to win, 5 to 4.

Tremendous clouting by Chick Hafey, Babe Herman, and Ernie Lombardi gave the fans more entertainment than they had had since 1926.

As late as June 1, the Reds were at the .500 mark. But then a losing streak of ten straight pricked the balloon, and the club began a decline. The pitching bogged down badly, with Red Lucas being the only hurler to hold up his end. Larry Benton, Owen Carroll, and Si Johnson failed to win with any degree of consistency. Benton had apparently pitched himself out under McGraw in the heat of the 1928 pennant race; Donohue had had a similar experience under Hendricks in 1926. Carroll, considered a whale of a prospect in his Holy Cross days and as a rookie with the Detroit Tigers, proved just shy of major-league requirements. And Johnson, though a willing worker, always seemed to lose.

In an effort to make a stronger showing, Weil managed to induce Rickey to return Benny Frey and Harvey Hendrick, the players who had gone in the deal for Hafey. Hendrick's

216

return helped strengthen the club at first base, and for a time the Reds rallied.

But with such poor pitching, another cellar finish was inevitable. Despite the fact that the club scored a lot of runs, the last half of the season was a long parade of misery. The Reds' hurlers were by far too weak to compete with the rest of the league.

Though plagued by illness, Chick Hafey batted .344 in the eighty-three games in which he appeared. Babe Herman hit .326 and made his 188 hits good for a total of 312 bases. The young giant Ernie Lombardi socked the ball at a .303 clip, giving promise of inaugurating a long career. Harvey Hendrick also made the charmed circle with a .302 mark. But even with four regulars over the .300 figure, the team won only 60 and lost 94 games, finishing last.

Sidney Weil, his patience somewhat taxed and his bank roll dwindling, nevertheless worked hard to rebuild the team for the 1933 season. Howley's three-year contract expired, and Genial Dan, unable to lead the Reds from the wilderness, was let out. He was replaced by Donie Bush, former shortstop with the Detroit Tigers in the days when Ty Cobb was at his peak and a veteran manager of the Pirates and White Sox.

Donie had piloted Minneapolis to an American Association pennant in 1932, and it was hoped that he would be able to preserve his winning habit in the majors. Like Howley, Bush was a favorite with the players, but he was more aggressive than Dan, and he had an acid tongue when riled.

Sid Weil, finding himself in need of money to continue operation, parted with Babe Herman, sending the slugger to the Cubs for $80,000 and four players—pitcher Bob Smith, outfielders Johnny Moore and Lance Richbourg, and catcher Rollie Hemsley.

The fans were sorry to see Herman leave, as he had lived up to all his clippings in the one season he spent with the club. The butt of many a joke and the inspiration of many a wild yarn, the Babe was never so strange as he was painted. Though usually thought of as being slightly lacking in wisdom, the Babe always won his winter battle for more salary, and when he finally quit playing the game he retired to a beautiful home in Glendale, California, with an eighteen-acre farm, eight hundred fruit trees, and five thousand turkeys for each season's market. His reputation for dumbness only added to his color and made him more of a gate attraction.

Of the players received in the deal with Chicago, Richbourg never played an inning, but Moore was given a regular outfield berth in 1933, flanked by Chick Hafey in left, and Harry Rice, a former American Leaguer purchased from Minneapolis, in right.

Sid Weil was not yet through dealing with Rickey. Jim Bottomley, the veteran first baseman of the Cardinals, was obtained, with the Reds transferring the contracts of Owen Carroll and eleven minor-league players to St. Louis farms in the exchange. Bottomley, then, started the 1933 season as the Reds' first baseman, with Joe Morrissey, purchased from St. Paul, at second, Leo Durocher at short, and Andy High at third.

Donie Bush, the new manager, developed an infected foot during the training season and had to leave the team before it returned home. He turned over the reins to his coach, Jewel Ens, a veteran infielder who had been associated with Bush at Pittsburgh. The infected foot was only the beginning of a bad year for Donie, who later developed bronchial pneumonia and pleurisy, and he never did get to spend much time with his team.

The club split its first sixteen games against the tough western teams when Sidney Weil announced another important transaction. Leo Durocher, the shortstop whose sparkling fielding had featured the team's play for three years but for whom a base hit was an event, was traded to the Cardinals, along with pitchers Jack Ogden and Dutch Henry, for pitcher Paul Derringer, third baseman Earl (Sparky) Adams, and pitcher Allyn Stout.

This deal is one of the best examples in baseball history of a transaction that proved of benefit to both clubs involved. In Derringer, who was only twenty-six when he came to the team, the Reds obtained an anchor man for a new pitching staff, and Paul remained for a decade. Durocher, on the other hand, supplied the spark for a Cardinal pennant in 1934, becoming one of the key men on the Gashouse Gang, filling a gap at shortstop at St. Louis that had existed ever since Charlie Gelbert severely injured his leg in a hunting accident in the fall of 1932.

Paul Derringer had joined the Cardinals in 1931. A product of their vast farm chain, he was a sensation as a freshman, winning 18 and losing 8, and then being given the honor of starting the first game of that year's World Series against the Philadelphia Athletics. In 1932 his work tapered off somewhat, and he had an 11-14 record.

The Reds of 1933 lost too many close ones. May 7, the day the deal for Derringer was announced, was an example. Bob Smith, pitching against Carl Hubbell and the Giants at the Polo Grounds, really had it, turning back the New Yorkers inning after inning, and at one stage striking out five batters in order. But a heartbreaking home run by Sam Leslie beat him, 1 to 0.

Derringer started taking his turn on the hill as soon as he reported, and his work was a notable demonstration of the fact that pitching averages are often deceiving. Though he pitched excellent baseball, finishing most of his starts, a disheartening succession of one-run losses came his way. The difference between major-league teams is extremely slight. But if one club is just a shade worse than its opponents, winning becomes extremely difficult.

Another player who joined the Reds in midseason was Jack Quinn, one of the most controversial players of all time because of his age. No one ever did find out how old Jack Quinn was. He originally said that he was born at Hazleton, Pennsylvania, on July 5, 1885. Later he altered the birthplace to Pottsville, Pennsylvania, and the date to 1888. It is known, though, that he pitched professionally at Connellsville, Pennsylvania, in 1903, and he made his first appearance in the majors in 1909 with the New York Highlanders. An advocate of the spitball, Quinn pitched in the American League throughout most of his career, then put in two seasons with

Brooklyn before joining the Reds as a free agent. Bluffing the spitter on every pitch but seldom throwing it, Jack was still a capable relief hurler for an inning or two. He was of Welsh descent and had a rugged constitution that was further hardened by spending his youth as a worker in the anthracite fields. If the original date of birth he issued was correct, he was forty-eight when he was still pitching in the majors with the Reds.

2

The season proceeded with Donie Bush absent on account of illness most of the time. When Jewel Ens was suspended briefly for a run-in with the umpires, Andy High, the veteran third baseman, managed the club for two days.

In his struggle to hold an even keel financially, Weil was having hard going. The depression was at its worst in 1933, and so were the affairs of the Reds. As an economy measure, Sid sold Bob Smith to Boston for the waiver price in July.

The departure of Durocher had left the Reds without an experienced shortstop. A rookie named Otto Bluege, whose older brother, Ossie, had been a famous American League player for years, tried to fill the gap, and although his play in the field was adequate, he was even more of a failure at bat than Durocher. In 108 games that season, he made only 62 hits.

The team was even further crippled when second baseman George Grantham, after playing slightly more than half the schedule, broke a leg and was forced out for the season. There was no money to buy adequate replacements, so the team signed a local amateur, Eddie Hunter, for use in case of emergency.

Eddie Hunter probably had as short a career in major-league baseball as any player of history. He broke into one game at third base, without having a fielding chance and without going to bat. That was his entire career in the National League.

If there was any doubt that the Reds would finish last for the third time in succession, it was eliminated when the team lost ten in a row in late July and early August, won three out of four, and then dropped another ten straight.

Through it all Red Lucas, spending his eighth year with the team, took his regular turn on the mound, and won as often as was humanly possible. On days when he didn't pitch, he was frequently used as a pinch hitter for his faltering mates.

To appreciate the Cincinnati work of Red Lucas properly, it must be understood that the team finished last during three of the eight years, seventh twice, fifth twice, and second once. But despite hurling for seven second-division teams in eight seasons, Lucas won 109 games while losing 99, and pitched 158 complete games.

Red was a throwback to the early days of the game when players really loved to work. As a farm boy in Tennessee, he often walked five miles or more to get a chance to pitch amateur ball, improving his control en route by throwing rocks at trees, birds, and various other rural objectives.

Lucas was purchased by John McGraw for the Giants following the 1922 season, when he won twenty games for Nashville. McGraw thought the redhead was too small to make a major-league pitcher, and he shipped him to San Antonio. Then came another trial with the Boston Braves and a sojourn at Seattle before he joined the Reds.

From the grandstand it didn't appear that Lucas had a great deal of stuff, and he never was very fast. But he was what the trade calls "sneaky" and a great pitcher to spots. His control was superb.

The Reds struggled on to the season's end, and finished with 58 victories and 94 defeats. The cellar was beginning to seem like home.

After the season, Sidney Weil decided to abandon the fight, which had begun to appear hopeless. After four seasons of battling, he had grown weary with the repetition of disaster. In November 1933 he stepped aside as president and resigned as a director, turning the club over to the Central Trust Co., which had held his stock for three years. Charles W. Dupuis, president of the bank, which had been dictating what Weil could and could not do, announced his resignation from the club, and said that two officers of the bank, Thomas M. Conroy and David C. Jones, would serve on the team's board of directors.

But what the bank really needed was a practical baseball man to serve as the team's general manager and breathe new life into the franchise.

The appointment of just such a man was announced on November 7. His name was Larry MacPhail.

⊖ **24** ⊖

LOUD LARRY MACPHAIL

1

Leland Stanford MacPhail, a superb actor who has assumed many roles in his brilliant and erratic career, was cast in the part of Moses when he came to Cincinnati to take over the affairs of the Reds. The wilderness out of which he was expected to lead the club included an eighth-place team, a franchise with limited resources, held by a bank, a park that was in need of repairs, and a following of fans who had completely given up. It was the sort of situation that Larry loved; a challenge to his vivid imagination.

MacPhail is the living demonstration that Euclidean geometry is wrong. The shortest distance between two points may be a straight line, but not one that Larry has ever taken. Throughout his life he has zigzagged from one interesting pursuit to another.

He made his first public noise as a freckle-faced rogue playing a church organ in Detroit. Then, upon graduating from high school, he received an appointment to Annapolis, but he went instead to Beloit College, then to the University of Michigan, and finally to George Washington University, where he graduated with a law degree and began to practice the profession in Chicago.

One of his legal clients was a large corporation, and as time passed, MacPhail found himself doing more and more work for the corporation and less practicing of law. One of the creditors of the firm was a Nashville dry-goods store, and Larry went to Nashville to run that business.

Then came World War I. He enlisted on the day war was declared, saw action at the front, and was gassed. It was after the Armistice that he took part in the fantastic plot to kidnap the Kaiser. On New Year's Eve, 1918, MacPhail and seven other men, including Luke Lea, the youngest man except Henry Clay ever to sit in the United States Senate, determined to raid the castle of the German Emperor at Amerongen, Holland. By January 6 they reached the drawing room after disarming a guard, but two hundred escaped German soldiers arrived at the castle and frustrated the kidnaping. MacPhail escaped with the Kaiser's ash tray as a souvenir of the expedition.

After the war he continued to move around. He ran a glass factory, sold automobiles, played a lot of golf, and refereed football games. Finally he found baseball and purchased an option on the Columbus team of the American Association, which he sold to the St. Louis Cardinals. Remaining as president of the Columbus club, he finished sixth the first year, fourth the second, second the third, and first the fourth. Prior to MacPhail, Columbus had finished in the second division for fifteen straight seasons.

Success palls on Larry. It is the chase that is exciting, the building up that quickens his pulse. His baseball career, at Columbus, at Cincinnati, at Brooklyn, and at New York, has always followed the same pattern. He has always taken over a team that has known despair, built it into a spectacular winner, and then quit—or has been fired. It is often difficult to tell which.

223

He was fired at Columbus, despite putting the club on its feet and building a fine new park for the team. He had an agreement with the Cardinals that they could not raid his team in midseason, and when St. Louis sought second baseman Burgess Whitehead, Larry demanded five players in exchange. Columbus got the players and won the pennant by fifteen games, but Larry was out of a job.

When he came to Cincinnati he was forty-three years old, dressed immaculately in various shades of tan and gray, and crowned by a hat with the brim invariably turned down.

He reported to the Reds' office in the Keith Building on November 7, 1933. His first occupation was to look at the club's roster, a revolting experience, and he immediately asked waivers on every player on the club as a feeler for possible deals.

Ten days later he attended the minor-league meeting at Galveston, traded second baseman George Grantham to the Giants for pitcher Glenn Spencer, and surprised Cincinnati fans by shipping Red Lucas to Pittsburgh for second baseman Tony Piet and outfielder Adam Comorosky. Gordon Slade, a shortstop, was purchased from the Cardinals in a straight cash deal.

Then Larry flew to California for a personal chat with outfielder Chick Hafey. Did Chick want to play with the Reds again in 1934? He did? O. K.

Back to Cincinnati. Another deal. Shortstop Otto Bluege and infielder Irvine Jeffries to the Phils for infielder Mark Koenig. Then Glenn Spencer was sent to the Cardinals for pitcher Sylvester Johnson and catcher Bob O'Farrell. In O'Farrell he found a manager.

A famous catcher on the pennant-winning Cardinals of 1926 and manager of the team in the following year as a result of his fine play, O'Farrell was not Larry MacPhail's first choice for the Cincinnati managerial job. Jimmy Wilson, also a catcher, was the man Larry wanted but could not get. O'Farrell was the compromise selection.

But the team still needed money. Banks are notoriously conservative, and Larry knew that his situation would not be really happy unless he induced some wealthy citizen to invest in the club and furnish capital for the rebuilding job.

One of the men MacPhail called upon was Powel Crosley, Jr., an extremely able businessman who had made a fortune in the radio business. Crosley had been approached before about purchasing the Reds, but had shown little interest in the proposal. But he had never before encountered a salesman with the persuasive powers of Larry MacPhail.

The appointment was arranged by Reamy Field, an associate of Crosley's, who got Powel to agree to have lunch with Larry.

Between courses, MacPhail sold Crosley the ball club. His approach was to the civic spirit of the magnate, and Larry pointed out that if Crosley did not buy the club it might be necessary to transfer the team to some other city. Crosley hated to think of Cincinnati, the birthplace of the professional game, not being represented in the major leagues, and he told MacPhail that he would make a decision one way or the other in a few days.

On February 4, 1934, it was announced that Crosley had purchased a controlling interest in the team. Actually, he bought $175,000 worth of preferred stock, and took an option on 80 per cent of the common stock, of which he later bought 51 per cent. In addition, he notified MacPhail that he would advance money for the purchase of players.

Crosley did not buy the Reds to make money, but he hoped to lose as little as possible in the venture. It has paid him handsomely. He has proved an able and sensible owner, allowing men trained in baseball to conduct the actual operation. And he grew to love the game, which had absorbed him as a youngster before he abandoned playing for more lucrative pursuits.

Now, blessed with an angel, MacPhail was all set. He immediately continued preparing for the 1934 season, the first step in raising the Reds from the abyss.

MacPhail knew that no modern team could possibly succeed without a farm system. This method of operation, first used by Branch Rickey with the Cardinals, had spread to other clubs. Originally the system was a form of self-defense, for the Cardinals, unable to compete with wealthy clubs in the open market, were forced to develop their own talent. The Cards were so successful with the chain idea that it was rapidly copied.

Larry hired as an assistant Frank Lane, a Cincinnatian who had long been a popular sports figure and one of the foremost football and basketball officials in the country. Though limited in baseball experience, Lane proved to be a terrific worker and an aggressive baseball salesman. He climbed rapidly in the baseball world and is now president of the American Association.

MacPhail and Lane made a good pair. They had much in common. Both were hard-working and highly strung, and each tried to outshout the other. MacPhail furnished the ideas and Lane carried them out. Somewhere along the line an organization was built.

Milton Stock, a former infielder in the National League, also joined the club as a scout and director of tryout camps for players. Almost immediately the team began to add satellite clubs. Before the season got under way the Reds had either bought outright or had arranged working agreements with Toronto of the International League, Wilmington, North Carolina, of the Piedmont, Beckley, West Virginia, of the Middle Atlantic, Bartlesville, Oklahoma, of the Western Association, Mt. Airy, North Carolina, of the Bi-State, and Jeanette of the Pennsylvania State Association.

The fans knew that dawn had arrived.

O'Farrell selected as coach Burt Shotton, a former outfielder of the Browns and a lifelong associate of Rickey's. Burt used to manage Rickey's teams for him on Sunday when Branch's keenly developed moral sense kept him from entering the park on the Sabbath. A few weeks later another coach, Val Picinich, who caught for the Reds in 1926, joined the ranks.

MacPhail was not through dealing, either. He picked up Dazzy Vance, the once-feared fireballer of the Dodgers, on waivers from the Cardinals. Les Mallon, a second baseman, was purchased from Toronto. Fred (Sheriff) Blake, another veteran National League pitcher, was added. Fans began to wonder what Larry was going to do with all his new players.

One of the players on the Reds who talked to MacPhail about the team's plans was Eppa Rixey, the veteran hurler who had been with the club since 1921. In recent years Rixey had done little pitching, being used principally against Pittsburgh, a team that found him a nemesis.

"I can still pitch," Rixey assured MacPhail. "I've been in the league for twenty-two years, but I can still pitch and not only against Pittsburgh," he asserted. "If O'Farrell doesn't want to use me against other clubs, I'm going to quit."

"I can't guarantee how O'Farrell will use you," MacPhail replied. "He's the manager, and you'll pitch according to his instructions."

So, rather than face another summer of pining away on the bench, Rixey announced his retirement. He left the team after thirteen seasons of performance that showed a total record of 179 victories and 161 defeats, with 180 complete games in 356 starts. Three times he had been a twenty-game winner and in two other years he just missed the magic total by one triumph. Only Will White, who performed in the seventies and eighties, when a pitcher worked every day, was able to win more games in a Cincinnati uniform. And the team has long been celebrated for its cunning hurlers.

From the team's training camp at Tampa came word of a tremendous renaissance. The Reds were on the rise again! They had the backing of Crosley, the genius of MacPhail, and the biggest horde of players ever assembled.

2

The Reds made their National League getaway on a chilly April 17. MacPhail had painted the park, he had dolled up the ushers and installed cigarette girls so cute they made the customers want to smoke themselves to death. But he couldn't do much to the Reds, who were held to one hit by Lonnie Warneke of the Cubs, thereby blowing the opener, 6 to 0. It was a sad start for the resurgent Reds, but of course Larry knew that the rebuilding job would take time. Things weren't much better the next day when Dazzy Vance, making the first start of his highly publicized comeback attempt, bowed to the Bruins, 8 to 4. And on the third day Paul Derringer met defeat, 4 to 1.

MacPhail waited only a few weeks to make more changes. When the team launched a losing streak that reached eight on May 7, he got into action. Outfielder Johnny Moore and pitcher Sylvester Johnson were shipped to Philadelphia for outfielder Wes Schulmerich and pitcher Ted Kleinhans. Schulmerich was blessed with the rugged constitution of a piano mover and was something of a comedian, and it was also hoped that he could play the outfield. Larry then purchased a southpaw pitcher, Tony Freitas, from St. Paul, and an outfielder, Harlin Pool, from Sacramento.

Although the club changed from day to day, here is how the team lined up:

Jim Bottomley was a fixture at first base, with Tony Piet at second, Gordon Slade at short, and Mark Koenig at third. Ernie Lombardi did the catching, and the outfield was composed of Adam Comorosky, Chick Hafey, and Wes Schulmerich. The season began with Ivy Shiver, a former star football player, in right field. MacPhail, with all the confidence of a side-show barker, informed the writers who followed the team that Shiver would "out-Ruth Ruth and out-Gehrig Gehrig." He did neither, and was optioned to St. Paul after hitting .203 in nineteen games. Another outfielder, Lincoln Blakely, had an early whirl in left field. Blakely was originally intended for one of the Red farm clubs and was paid a salary as modest as his assignment. When he had two good days at the plate, he took the advice of a Cincinnati newsboy, staged a one-man sit-down strike for more money, and wound up at Toronto. He never again appeared in the majors.

Dazzy Vance's comeback was an utter failure. He appeared in only two games, lost them both, and moved on. The regular hurlers were Paul Derringer, Benny Frey, Si Johnson, and Tony Freitas.

Freitas was a Portuguese and about as tiny a southpaw as ever made the grade. And he soon became a favorite with the fans.

In spite of the numerous changes, the team couldn't win. Outside of Ernie Lombardi, who could always hit, the only player on the club who showed a fondness for slugging was Harlin Pool, the new outfielder from Sacramento. A chunky left-handed hitter, Pool began raining base hits all over the place, but he played the outfield as if his feet were tied. All the stories that were told about Babe Herman's fielding could have been applied with more justice to Harlin Pool.

A famous game with the Cardinals took place on July 1. A double-header had been scheduled, and the first contest developed into a heated struggle between St. Louis's great Dizzy Dean and the Reds' pocket edition of a pitcher, Tony Freitas. Inning after inning was reeled off, and finally in the seventeenth Joe Medwick, the nonpareil slugger of the Redbirds, connected for a home run. But the Reds came back in their half to score a run and tie the score again. In the eighteenth the Cardinals scored three times. Once more the Reds came back. With one run in and runners in scoring position, Jim Bottomley, side-lined with an ailing elbow and now used as a pinch hitter, lined what appeared to be a hit down the left field foul stripe, but Medwick came racing over, made a circus catch, and the Cardinals won, 8 to 6. That battle consumed most of the afternoon, and the teams had time only to travel to a 2-to-2 tie in the five-inning nightcap. The games were important, for Freitas, though inspired that afternoon, was weakened by going the route against the much stronger Dean. Never afterward did he exhibit the same form.

The Reds were winning about half as many tilts as they lost, a rate of victory that could assure only another finish in the cellar. Larry wanted desperately to avoid that, but he saw that he could not hope in one year to accomplish a miracle. He knew that the farm chain he was building up contained players who would someday make a better showing. But they were two or three years away. Meanwhile, he was stuck with a chronic loser.

He began to feel that part of the blame should go to Bob O'Farrell, who was not an aggressive leader, and who seemed to take defeat in stride. This was curious, because as a player, O'Farrell had learned the game under the tutelage of real fighters, Fred Mitchell, Rogers Hornsby, and John McGraw. But O'Farrell seemed complacent. Often when MacPhail would go to the clubhouse after a bitter defeat, he would find O'Farrell, his golf clubs slung under his arm, leaving the park and perhaps wondering if he could get in nine holes before it got dark.

MacPhail decided to get a new manager. And he proposed to get one right away, not wait until the end of the season. With the co-operation of the Bell Telephone Company and various air lines, he got busy. At Nashville he found his man, Charlie Dressen. O'Farrell was let out on July 28, when the team had won 31 and lost 60.

Dressen had been only an average player for the Reds in the seven years he had played, starting in 1925, but he always had been recognized as a smart performer. He paid a great deal of attention to small details and was enamored of what he called "inside baseball." He had landed the managerial job at Nashville through a bit of daring.

After his release by the Reds, Dressen found himself at the end of his career without a job and without money in the midst of the nation's worst depression. He was contemplating joining the police force at Decatur, Illinois, when he learned that Nashville was considering a change in managers. Borrowing money for the journey to the Tennessee city, he applied to Fay Murray, owner of the Nashville club, for the job.

Murray made it clear that he was interested primarily in winning and how did smart young Mr. Dressen propose to win? Charlie said that he would take over the team then and there, and if he didn't win more games than he lost during the remainder of the 1932 campaign, Murray wouldn't have to pay him a cent in salary. That rather strange proposal was accepted. Dressen took the job and had a record of thirty-eight victories and as many defeats when the last day of the season came around. Nashville won the final encounter, 12 to 8, thereby earning Chuck's salary, and although Murray later told Dressen that he would have paid him off anyway, he would not have gone along with him as a manager unless he had shown a winning record.

Then, in 1933, the Giants, crippled by an injury to Johnny Vergez, their third baseman, needed infield insurance for the World Series against Washington. Dressen, still active as a player at Nashville, was selected. He sat on the bench in the autumn classic, but achieved a bit of immortality in the eleventh inning of the fourth game, at Washington. The Giants had the lead, 2 to 1, but the Senators had three on base and only one out. At this stage, Cliff Bolton, a reserve catcher whom Dressen knew from Southern Association play, was sent in to bat for Monte Weaver, the Washington pitcher. The Giant infield went into a huddle, speculating whether to play in and cut off the run at the plate or drop back for the double play. Dressen, acting under impulse, for he hadn't been consulted, rushed from the bench out on the field and told manager Bill Terry, "Set the infield back. I know Bolton. He's slow, and if the infield is back you can get two."

"O.K.," Terry agreed. "Play for two, boys."

Bolton did hit into the double play, Ryan to Critz to Terry. It ended the game, the Giants winning, 2 to 1.

That was an example of Dressen's attention to details, but it was rather spectacular, and Larry MacPhail, sitting in the grandstand that afternoon, made a mental note that Chuck Dressen might be worth consideration as a manager.

Dressen had gone back to Nashville in 1934, and after he won the first half of the league season by a seven-game margin, MacPhail gave serious consideration to him as the successor to O'Farrell. A flying visit to Nashville clinched the deal.

Dressen reported to Cincinnati on July 29, when the team was at home for a double-header with Chicago. At the same time, Alex Kampouris, an infielder purchased from Sacramento, arrived and was installed at second base.

The inspired work of the team under Dressen was instantly apparent. The players were on their toes. Dressen liked to bunt a lot, he liked to hit and run, and he used the squeeze.

His baseball wasn't cut and dried. Pat Malone of the Cubs beat Si Johnson, 7 to 5, as Chuck made his debut as a pilot, but the Reds took the second game, 4 to 2, behind Tony Freitas.

There was not much left to salvage in 1934, but Dressen came to know his players, and that helped him in determining which ones to keep.

MacPhail certainly provided him with enough so that he had plenty of men from which to choose. As September dawned, and league rules permitted the use of forty athletes instead of the twenty-five allowed during most of the summer, the cream of the first farm crop was liberally poured on Redland Field, now known as Crosley Field in honor of the new president. Among those who made their first appearances in Cincinnati uniforms at the tag end of the year were: Frank McCormick, an awkward young first baseman; Lee Grissom, an eccentric southpaw pitching rookie; Beryl Richmond, another southpaw who had had a previous trial with the Cubs; Junie Barnes, a third left-hander and a real pitching rarity, a submarine port-sider; Bill Marshall, a second baseman; and Ted Petoskey, an outfielder.

With these and other rookies heavily loading the line-up, the Reds finished the year, ending in the cellar for the fourth straight time, with 52 victories and 99 defeats.

That was the year that Dizzy Dean and the Cardinal Gashouse Gang were riding high. The Reds closed the schedule in St. Louis, and Dizzy was anxious to win thirty games for the season. He lacked two of that total as the series began, then quickly picked up one when he beat Benny Frey, 4 to 0. On the last day of the season he started after number thirty, pitching with only one day's rest. He had a 9-to-0 lead, and in a late inning Dressen sent young Ted Petoskey in as a pinch hitter.

Frankie Frisch, the manager of the Cardinals, left his second-base position and went over to the mound. "Now, be careful on this fellow," he warned Dean. "You don't know anything about him. Be careful how you pitch to him."

"Go back to your position, Frank," Diz said. "Who is this guy, anyway? What's his name?"

"Petoskey," Frisch said.

Dean snorted. "Popupski, is it? Well, nobody by the name of Popupski is going to get a hit off old Diz."

And he didn't.

⊛ **25** ⊛

LET THERE BE LIGHT

1

Investigation into the origin of any subject invariably leads back to antiquity. That there is nothing new under the sun is axiomatic. And night baseball, though not anything under the sun, is likewise shrouded in mystery and doubt. If the time ever comes when scholars search for the origin of evening play, it will unquestionably be demonstrated that Cain and Abel were accustomed to indulge in a game of One Old Cat with Adam acting as umpire.

One of the first written references to night baseball that can be found is a story on page one of the March 30, 1887, issue of *The Sporting Life,* a weekly forerunner and one-time competitor of baseball's bible, J. G. Taylor Spink's *Sporting News.* The article was capped with this one-column head:

SOLVED AT LAST

PLAY BY ELECTRIC LIGHT
POSSIBLE

The Scheme to Be Again Tried
at Staten Island—Diffi-
culties Overcome

The story went on to describe a scheme of installing electric lights at the St. George grounds on Staten Island. The idea belonged to a Mr. Johnson, first name unknown, president of the Edison Electric Light Company. Johnson explained that previous failures to make night baseball successful were due to placing the lights too high up, throwing rays on the field that either blinded the players or cast shadows. Johnson proposed to line the foul stripes with electric lights placed beneath the ground and projected by means of reflectors, sending the rays upward through covering plates of corrugated glass.

"Undoubtedly, baseball people and others will be inclined to pronounce this scheme impossible," Johnson said, "but in the light of the annihilation of 'impossibilities' in our century, and calling to memory those wonders of modern times—the phonograph, the telephone, the electric railway—it would be no more than the part of wisdom to withhold the expression of a positive opinion at the present time."

It is known that night baseball was played even before this. What is believed to have been the first nocturnal contest of all time took place at Fort Wayne, Indiana, on June 2, 1883. A team of players known as the M. E. College nine competed against professionals from Quincy, with the latter winning the seven-inning game, 19 to 11. The Jenney Electric Light Company surrounded the park with 17 lights of 4,000 candle power each, an amount of light equal to 4,857 gas burners. That game was described in the *Fort Wayne Daily Gazette* as follows:

Last night was the occurrence of the long looked-for event that was to make Fort Wayne historic and cause her name to be mentioned wherever civilization extends.

Baseball is the American national game but it was reserved for the city of Fort Wayne to be the first in the world to play it at night and by the rays of artificial sun. The degree of illumination was such that the game was well played, although an alarming number of strikes were called by Umpire Morrissey.

The crowd was very large and although the turnstiles registered 1,675 admissions, there were at least 2,000 present.

And so on.

Numerous games were staged at night at various cities throughout the nation as years passed, including the one that took place at Redland Field when Clark Griffith managed the Reds in 1909.

But it was not until the great depression that night baseball obtained a foothold in organized ball. The first league game that was played at night by a member of the National Association took place at Independence, Kansas, April 18, 1930, between the Independence and Muskogee clubs of the Western Association. Within a few weeks owners of other minor-league clubs begged manufacturers of floodlights to install equipment at their parks. Baseball attendance had declined tremendously at the onset of the depression, and the magnates were frightened. Games played during the day could depend for attendance only on the unemployed. And although this number included millions, people out of work are frequently also out of coin of the realm. Those fortunates who still had jobs stuck close to them rather than risk dismissal by watching baseball games.

Obviously, baseball at night, enabling people employed during the day to witness the doings, was the answer. This was understood thoroughly by minor-league officials, but the haughty major-league moguls, with the exception of Larry MacPhail and that often misrepresented official of the Cardinals, Sam Breadon, couldn't see the game at all.

After the Independence experiment, night baseball spread like wildfire. Even minor-league clubs of AA classification, such as Jersey City, installed arcs. The lights played a large part in saving baseball for America during that period of economic chaos.

Among those baseball magnates who knew what the night game could do was Larry MacPhail, who had put in arcs at Columbus, and who knew that attendance at Cincinnati could be stimulated by electric juice. In his first talk with Powel Crosley at luncheon, MacPhail described the remarkable therapeutic powers of night baseball and expressed the hope that he could persuade the conservative major-league tycoons to let him play nocturnally along the banks of the Ohio.

When MacPhail did propose that Cincinnati try night ball, the reaction was violent. The horse-and-buggy witch doctors who ran the game the way it had been run before the turn of the century and whose ideas of public relations included locking the front office doors in the face of standing-room fans who clamored for refunds couldn't see it at all. Night baseball? Ridiculous!

Because Cincinnati was in such perilous financial condition, MacPhail was granted the privilege (*sic*) of playing seven games at night during the 1935 season. But the magnates shook their heads sadly. What would happen to the great game?

What happened was that night baseball proved so popular that within thirteen years every major-league park but one was equipped with lights. Baseball recorded attendance figures that were fabulous, a horde of new fans was created, and the game reached a degree of popularity that was undreamed of.

But in 1935 Larry MacPhail was looked upon as something of a charlatan, trying to breathe fresh life into the corpse of the Cincinnati franchise with the methods of a quack. Let us quote Mr. Clark Griffith, the Old Fox of the Washington club, who enjoys a comfortable old age, largely because of the fact that the lights at Griffith Stadium blaze away nightly. Here is one of Griffith's quoted statements:

"There is no chance of night baseball ever becoming popular in the bigger cities. People there are educated to see the best there is and will stand for only the best. High-class baseball cannot be played at night under artificial light. Furthermore, the benefits derived from attending the game are largely due to fresh air and sunshine. Night air and electric lights are a poor substitute."

The first night game in major-league history was scheduled for May 23, 1935, but had to be postponed twenty-four hours because of rain. Then it took place. Franklin D. Roosevelt, seated in the White House, pressed a button that, by some long-distance legerdemain, lit the 632 lamps that illuminated Crosley Field. Philadelphia was the visiting club that night, and Ford C. Frick, president of the National League, threw out the first ball. A crowd of 20,422 watched Paul Derringer outduel Joe Bowman, bringing victory to the Reds, 2 to 1. The attendance was fully ten times greater than it would have been for an afternoon contest with the Phils. A new era had been ushered in. Cincinnati, birthplace of professional baseball, was now the birthplace of postprandial baseball in the majors. And Larry MacPhail, whose greatest contribution to the game has been his grandiose vision of the glory that lies ahead, proudly and properly was beaming as only Larry could beam.

As far as Cincinnati is concerned, Larry MacPhail was a savior of the game at a time when all seemed lost. His effect on the city was as electric as the 632 lamps that still shine down in tribute to his acumen. The fans of Cincinnati are not included among the detractors of MacPhail, most of whom cannot see beyond their collective nose. The little guy who lays his $1.20 on the line knows who it was that made baseball colorful in Cincinnati.

2

Though the installation of lights at Crosley Field was the greatest achievement of the 1935 season, it was by no means the whole of the club's activity. MacPhail knew that a repetition of the business of finishing in the cellar simply couldn't take place. Even by night a last-place team is not much to look at.

During the winter MacPhail had patiently doctored the weak spots, and by spring a large coterie of worth-while rookies made their debuts. Five of the new men became regulars—pitchers Gene Schott and Al Hollingsworth, shortstop Billy Myers, third baseman Lew Riggs, and outfielder Ival Goodman. Schott and Hollingsworth represent the first fruit of the farm system. Schott, a native Cincinnatian, was a right-hander, and Hollingsworth, a St. Louis resident, was a southpaw. Both had prepped at the Toronto plantation in 1934.

Myers, Riggs, and Goodman were all chattels of the St. Louis Cardinals. MacPhail realized that while he was waiting for the farm system to develop players, he must purchase interim replacements from the surplus of other systems. Myers had been bought during the winter by the New York Giants, and MacPhail then acquired him for infielder Mark Koenig. Goodman and Riggs represented cash transactions with the Cardinals. Sammy Byrd, an outfielder, was also acquired from the New York Yankees. Byrd had come to be known as "Babe Ruth's legs" because he had so often filled in for the Bambino in late innings, while the aging Ruth rested.

Charlie Dressen felt sure the club was on the way up. He started the year with that hardy perennial, Ernie Lombardi, in bloom behind the bat, Jim Bottomley, Alex Kampouris, Billy Myers, and Lew Riggs at the infield posts, and Chick Hafey, Sammy Byrd, and Ival Goodman in the outfield. The pitching staff was constructed around the massive form of Paul Derringer, with Si Johnson, Tony Freitas, and Benny Frey still around, and the new men Hollingsworth and Schott. There was also on hand an ace relief pitcher, Don Brennan, a Gargantuan figure of a man from the state of Maine who liked to come out of the bull pen in late innings and cool off enemy bats. A conservative estimate of Brennan's weight was 220 pounds, and in the flaming-red pants that MacPhail had the boys wear at night games he resembled a department-store Santa Claus. For a few innings he was practically unhittable.

The National League schedule for 1935 called for the Reds to open the season at Pittsburgh. This was sacrilege! Since 1877 the Reds had opened at home, and for them to inaugurate hostilities on the road was pure heresy. MacPhail immediately got the telephone lines sizzling, and the Reds were given special permission to open with Pittsburgh at home a day early, on April 16, then go to Smoketown on the following day. Tony Freitas pitched the opener, and lost it, 12 to 6, to the Pirates, bowing to Waite Hoyt, the skilled American League veteran who had come to spread his magic before hitters in the senior circuit. But after that bad start the Reds found themselves, and before the passing of many weeks it was evident the cellar days were over, and the fresh upper air beckoned.

But the progress was slow. The pitching was still uncertain, with Derringer the only real dependable. By the end of May the team had won sixteen and lost the same number of games, but then began to slump slightly. Chick Hafey deserted the club in early June, leaving only a note for his roommate, Jim Bottomley, saying that he was ill. When Chick was in the proper frame of mind, he was a masterful player, but he never lived up to expectations with the Reds because of his frequent absences from the line-up. When he was able to perform, he showed flashes of his former greatness.

Hafey's self-imposed exile was made up for when the team reacquired Babe Herman for a fraction of the price he had originally cost. Herman had not panned out in Chicago, and had drifted to Pittsburgh before the Reds were able to lasso him again. A few weeks later another famed gardener, Hazen (Kiki) Cuyler, was secured from the Cubs. So Hafey wasn't missed too much.

After the staging of the first night game in late May, the fans looked forward eagerly to the remaining six nocturnal battles. One was staged with the Pirates on May 31, the Reds losing to Bill Swift, 4 to 1. The third saw the Cubs beat Gene Schott, 8 to 4, and in the fourth the Reds slaughtered Brooklyn, 15 to 2. In the fifth contest the Reds beat the Braves, 5 to 4.

But the event of the season was the sixth night game on July 31, with the Reds meeting the St. Louis Cardinals. Interest in the team had spread to the hinterlands, and when night games were scheduled, MacPhail made a deal with railroad companies to run excursion trains into the city from communities all through the Ohio valley. The club these fans wanted to see above all was the Gashouse Gang Cardinals, the world champions of 1934 who boasted such stars as the brothers Dean, Joe Medwick, and Pepper Martin. It was evident that the July 31 affair would be a sellout.

So many reserved seats were sold to customers from out of

town that the general-admission patrons who stormed the gates that night found no place to sit. Still there were those empty reserved seats, protected by ropes, and waiting for the occupants who were to come in by train from West Virginia, Kentucky, and Indiana. As the excursion trains were delayed, play started with patrons milling all over the place. Groups of fans, many of them swilling beer just as their forefathers had in the days of rooters' row before the country was dried up by legislation, broke through the ropes and sat in the reserved seats, in defiance of Larry MacPhail's colorful but callow ushers, many of whom had not yet experienced the adult privilege of shaving. Then, when the trains began to unload the outlanders, a condition resulted that can be described only by the rather overworked word pandemonium.

On the field a pitching battle was in progress between Tony Freitas and Paul Dean, but it was nothing compared with the battle in the grandstand. Finally the overflow of the crowd seeped onto the playing field, and as the game progressed, fans actually were sitting within a few feet of the foul lines.

MacPhail, confronted with such delightful chaos, simply threw up his hands, departed for parts unknown, and left the office in the hands of Frances Levy, the capable secretary who has served every Cincinnati general manager since Sidney Weil. Frances Levy, though a woman of rare talents, was unable to compete with the shouting hordes of people who screamed for their money back. She barricaded herself in the office, locked the door, and peered at the indignant populace through a sliding panel reminiscent of the speak-easy, refunding cash to all.

No one will ever know how many people were in the park that night, for many spectators did not pay to get in but simply hurdled the turnstiles in the confusion. Crosley Field has had larger crowds, but none so turbulent or so badly handled. Judge Landis was there, and he had to watch the contest by standing on tiptoes and peering over the broad German backs of Cincinnatians.

One episode took place that might be thought possible only at a church picnic contest between the fats and the leans.

240

A young girl by the name of Kitty Burke actually grabbed a bat from the hands of bewildered Babe Herman and went up to the plate to hit against Paul Dean.

But the game was finished somehow, and what's more, the Reds won when Billy Sullivan, a reserve infielder, slashed a single into right field in the tenth inning, winning the contest, 4 to 3. Ah, but that was a night worthy of Kelly's Killers!

MacPhail, a veteran of tiffs with public officials, blamed the chief of police for not sending a riot squad to the park. The chief, in turn, blamed Larry for selling more tickets than he had seats.

The fact that it was possible to have more customers than seats at a game demonstrates better than anything else what MacPhail had done for the city.

The Reds finished sixth in 1935. They had climbed two positions in the league race, but so much else was happening, it seemed almost secondary.

3

MacPhail, the man of big and wonderful ideas, gave a hemispheric touch to the Reds in 1936 by scheduling a training session at Puerto Rico before launching the main camp at Tampa. Questionnaires were sent to the players by Gene Karst, the team's publicity man, asking if they would prefer to fly or go by boat to the island.

"If it's all the same to the management, I'll drive," replied one rookie.

Making his last training trip with the Reds that year, although he didn't know it, was Frederick Bushnell (Jack) Ryder, the veteran scribe of the *Cincinnati Enquirer* who was to die of a heart attack in June. Ryder had been on the job since 1904, and his prolific pen had brought more enjoyment to the fans than could be measured.

Baseball writers in Cincinnati have always been on the job for long periods of time. For instance, of the three men who cover the affairs of the club today, Tom Swope of the *Post* has been with the team since 1915, Frank Grayson of the *Times-Star* replaced Bill Phelon upon the latter's death in

1926, and Lou Smith of the *Enquirer* succeeded Ryder in 1936. Veteran fans still recall the other writers of the past who helped describe the game of baseball to the multitude, such legendary bards as Macon McCormick, O. P. Caylor, Ren Mulford, Harry Weldon, Ban Johnson, Frank Rostock, and Bob Newhall.

But Ryder was the king. In the first place, he wrote for a morning paper in those happy days when breakfast was accompanied by news that was often good. Editorial writers and columnists then weren't consistently angry, and especially in the isolationist cocoon of the Midwest, reading pleasant aspects of local affairs was still possible. Breakfast wasn't ten minutes on a drugstore stool and a dash to punch the time clock. America had not yet become so efficient. Breakfast in Cincinnati was plump sausage and barnyard-fresh eggs, strong, fragrant coffee, and Jack Ryder's column.

Ryder loved the Reds and he wrote interminably about them, column after column. His story of the previous day's game, which people consumed avidly, because it was their only source of news about the team, would occupy perhaps two and one-half columns, and there would be two more columns of notes.

Jack had attended Phillips Exeter Academy and Williams College, and he wrote in a classic form that showed familiarity with Greek and Latin. He wrote about the team as if he were describing the gallant battle of titans, but still gave the impression that his tongue was in his cheek. He was a man of extremely strong prejudices, which poured into his copy and vastly amused the reader. Sometimes he even seemed to be poking fun at his audience.

Ryder symbolized fandom with all its hopes and fears. He was the disciple of "Wait till next year" and "Now watch our noble athletes destroy the enemy."

A typical Jack Ryder note would read somewhat as follows:

"Second contest between our noble athletes and McGraw's hated Giants this afternoon at the yard. Rube Benton will start for the Reds if he puts in an appearance by game time,

242

PAUL DERRINGER and BUCKY WALTERS

1940 WORLD CHAMPIONS

and McGraw says that he will rely on Kent Greenfield, the sterling pitcher who comes from the vast Methodist wilderness of Guthrie, Kentucky."

Jack seldom replied to mail, but he would use his column of notes in which to answer his correspondents. Back in 1909 Ryder referred to many of the players by nicknames, but he always called pitcher Harry Gaspar "Mr. Gaspar." This practice puzzled a reader who signed himself "Curious Fan," and Ryder replied in his column as follows:

"Curious Fan—Pitcher Gaspar is referred to by the title of Mr. because of his dignity as a merchant prince at his home in Kingsley, Iowa. It seems proper to refer to the ordinary player by some nickname, such as Old Wapak, Long Bob, Big Jeff, French Johnny, etc., but in speaking of a man who owns the largest store in his county, and is recognized as a leader in the financial world of his section, the respectful title of Mr. is naturally applied."

"Curious Fan" probably read that and wondered who was ribbing whom.

The Reds of 1936 were an improvement on the aggregation of the year before, though they started the season in the same fashion, losing to Waite Hoyt of Pittsburgh, 8 to 6. Bottomley had faded, and the Reds started the season with a rookie, George McQuinn, at first base. The quest for a successor to Bottomley had begun in 1935 when MacPhail acquired Johnny Mize from the Cardinal chain "on a look." Mize showed promise of becoming a mighty slugger, but he had a knee condition that required an operation if he were ever to play regularly. The Cards wanted $55,000 for him, and MacPhail listened to the advice of physicians who said the operation would involve considerable risk. Mize was passed up. The Cardinals had the operation performed, and he has been a star ever since.

So now it was McQuinn, a recruit from the Yankee chain, who was given a shot at Bottomley's old job. But he was unable to hit National League pitching, and eventually Les Scarsella, a product of the Red farm chain, took over at the base. Scarsella had been found in California by Professor Charles Chapman, an instructor at the University of California who dabbled in scouting on the side. Les began to hit, and the problem was solved and Mize forgotten.

Otherwise, the team was intact. Kampouris, Myers, and Riggs all made the major-league grade, and outfielder Ival Goodman proved to be a worthy left-handed hitter.

One memorable game occurred against Pittsburgh on May 23. Bill Swift, always a hard man for the Reds to beat, had them trounced, 3 to 0, going into the last half of the ninth, when Dressen rallied his gang and the Redlegs filled the bases. At this stage Cy Blanton, a sensational young fireballer, was waved in to replace Swift. Sammy Byrd clouted his first pitch far over the left-field fence for the four runs that brought victory.

The team stayed around the .500 mark most of the summer, and that pace was pleasant for the fans after the succession of tail-enders. Cincinnatians weren't accustomed to pennants, and all they asked was a good contest. Ernie Lombardi, Les Scarsella, Hazen Cuyler, and Ival Goodman sprayed enough hits around the premises so that even if the visiting club was ahead, the spectators had reason to believe that the team might rally and win. Sometimes this happened, and the Reds climbed to fifth place, ending with 74 victories and 80 defeats.

As the season was about to close, however, the fans received a jolt. On September 18 it was announced that Larry Mac-Phail had resigned, and would leave the club November 1. On the next day it was announced that his successor had been chosen, Warren Giles, who had headed the Rochester club of the International League. There was no explanation.

Larry MacPhail left the Reds of his own free will. In three years he hadn't accomplished all that he had hoped for, but the early difficulties had been overcome, and the club was paying off its debts to the banks and was shooting upward in the race. MacPhail, once he had seen that his team had hurdled the biggest obstacles, had tired of the sport for the time being. An explosive man, always working under tension, he was ready for a rest. He was to know greater glory with the Dodgers and Yankees, both of which teams won pennants for him. The artificial respiration that he administered at Cincinnati was a profound success.

⊗ **26** ⊗

THE ROUGHHOUSE REDS

1

If Sam Crawford was the hardest-hitting barber ever to come out of Wahoo, Nebraska, and Larry MacPhail was the loudest product in the history of Cass City, Michigan, then Warren Crandall Giles, who succeeded MacPhail as general manager of the Cincinnati Reds, was by all odds the most successful major-league magnate to hail from Tiskilwa, Illinois.

Giles didn't remain long at Tiskilwa. As a youth he attended Staunton Military Academy and spent one year at Washington and Lee University. Then came World War I, and he served as a lieutenant in France.

It was an extremely fortuitous event that led him to take up baseball management as a career. After the war he was home at Moline, Illinois, and paid a visit to a high school football coach to see if he could borrow some football uniforms for a group of children in his neighborhood. The coach agreed to lend them to him on the condition that Giles would attend a meeting of the baseball fans' association to be held that night. This all took place in the autumn of 1919.

Moline at the time had a franchise in the Three-I League, and things were going badly. At the meeting of fans, ways and means to elevate the team were discussed and Giles didn't hesitate to speak his mind, his opinions often being at variance with club policy. The directors finally became so tired of hearing him pop off that one of them said, "Young man, why don't you run the club for a season and see if you can do any better?"

"All right," Warren said, "I will. And if I can't do any better, I won't want to stay for more than one season."

Giles knew next to nothing about baseball law, didn't have a manager for the team, and had few players of worth on the roster. But in the manner of a true Horatio Alger hero, he studied baseball procedure until he was well versed in it, and acquired a manager by signing Earle Mack, son of Connie. Giles read in *The Sporting News* that Mack had just been released by another club, and he properly figured that by hiring a son of Connie, he would receive help from the Philadelphia Athletics. Moline finished fourth in 1920, and won the pennant the following season.

By this time, Warren had established quite a few acquaintances in the game, and in 1923 he left Moline and became business manager of the St. Joseph team of the Western League.

One of the players who later joined St. Joe was Taylor Douthit, the flashy outfielder who was destined to star for the Cardinals. But he might have starred first with another club had not Giles intervened in a most unusual way. Douthit was such a flash at St. Joe that scouts for many major-league clubs came to look him over, but the Cardinals had an option to select him before a certain date. Through some oversight, Douthit was not claimed. This enabled Giles to sell the young gardener's contract to the highest bidder, but instead of doing that he phoned Branch Rickey and said the Cardinals could still claim him.

Rickey, of course, was overwhelmed at such a display of executive honesty, decided that Giles was just the sort of person he needed in his organization, and made him president of the Syracuse team of the International League.

When the Syracuse franchise was transferred to Rochester

in December 1927, Giles went along with it, and it was at Rochester that he had his greatest success, winning four straight pennants.

Powel Crosley first met Warren Giles at a dinner that was held in connection with the All-Star game at Cleveland in 1935. They sat together, and Crosley was charmed by the suave, astute, urbane way in which the Rochester official discussed baseball.

Later, when Crosley was scouting about for a successor to MacPhail, Giles immediately came to mind. Powel said to Tom Conroy, the team's treasurer, "I've got just the man we're looking for."

"Wait a minute," Conroy replied. "I've got a man too. Don't tell me the name of your candidate." He wrote a name on a piece of paper, folded it up, and handed it to Crosley, then said, "Now, tell me the name of your man."

"Warren Giles," Crosley said.

"Look at the paper now," Conroy urged.

The name of Warren Giles was written on it.

Like MacPhail, Giles is a product of the Cardinal farm chain. Like MacPhail, he came from a small Midwestern town. And like MacPhail, he has been a football official. There all similarity ceases. Tactful where MacPhail is apt to be explosive, cautious where Larry is likely to be prodigal, Giles is nevertheless a good promoter with a sharp sense of what constitutes good public relations.

The Cincinnati fans, uninformed of why any change was made, accepted Warren Giles as a replacement for MacPhail without excitement. The thing they liked most about Giles, knowing little about him, was his Rochester record as a winner.

Giles retained Frank Lane, who had been MacPhail's assistant, but brought to Cincinnati with him Gabriel Paul, a personable young man who had been around ball clubs almost from the cradle, starting as a bat boy for the Rochester club when George Stallings, famed as the leader of the Miracle Braves of 1914, managed the team. Young Gabe's first duties for Stallings included freezing the baseballs that were to be used each day, a bit of strategy frequently employed back in the days when teams played for one run. The frozen balls, of course, were put into the game only when the opposition was at bat.

Gabe was the correspondent for *The Sporting News* from Rochester when he was just entering his teens, and when Giles moved to that city, one of his first acts was to call in the various newspapermen. He had met them all except the correspondent for *The Sporting News,* and when he saw Gabe and noticed how young he was, he was vastly amused, and offered him a job. Gabe has stuck with him ever since, occupying the role of a man Friday, a Colonel House, a Harry Hopkins. They have made an admirably efficient pair, and Gabe Paul, who wields much more power than the traveling secretaries or promotion managers of most ball clubs, is regarded as one of the brightest young executives in the game.

Although the coming of Giles to Cincinnati meant little to most people who were not concerned in the matter, it certainly must have meant a great deal to Jack Rothrock, an outfielder who today is one of the successful managers in the minor leagues. Rothrock had played right field for the Gashouse Gang Cardinals of 1934, and the following year he had been shipped to Rochester. Convinced that he was still a major-league player, he went about his work in the International League in a way that left much to be desired. Finally, just before the 1936 season closed, he got another chance in the big time when Larry MacPhail bought him for the Reds.

Giles called Rothrock to his office and said, "Look, Jack, I know that you haven't been too happy here this season, but now you're going back to the majors. Why don't you just write off 1936 as a bad year and give the game everything you've got next season?"

"Listen," Rothrock replied. "When I need your advice I'll ask for it."

A few days later Rothrock must have had confused emotions when he read that Warren Giles was to head the Cincinnati Reds. Nothing could have been more ironic. Rothrock never played for the Reds.

Giles retained Charlie Dressen as manager of the Reds for 1937, though Dressen wasn't the man he visualized for the job. In the back of his mind, Warren was thinking about Bill McKechnie, who had managed for him with so much skill at Rochester. Oddly enough, when Giles started his baseball career with Moline, his first official act was to sell the contract of Charlie Dressen to St. Paul. Baseball careers have a strange way of overlapping, as Jack Rothrock will attest.

MacPhail had left the nucleus of a good club, although there were definite weak spots. Larry had also left a farm system that was just beginning to function. Not that all of MacPhail's dealings were astute. As a matter of fact, his mishandling of the contract of second baseman Lee Handley and catcher Johnny Peacock had caused Judge Landis to make free agents of those two fine prospects. And there were other Cincinnati players whose status was in doubt.

So Warren Giles inherited a bit of an empire that had its bright facets, but there were also aspects of the situation that were not pleasing. Being a skilled, methodical, orderly executive, he went to work, intent on bettering the team's position.

Charlie Dressen, working with his team at Tampa, announced that the Reds were to be aggressive, which is the annual preseason boast of every major-league pilot. This is one of the pastime's greatest clichés. Annually, at every city where there is a team, the manager will rise to his feet at a preseason banquet, thoughtfully wipe his chin with the napkin, and say to the cheering audience, "I can't tell you where we're going to finish in the race, but I'll promise you one thing. My club is going to hustle every minute, from the time the boys step out for batting practice until the last one has had his shower."

In the case of Charlie Dressen, he meant every word he said about those 1937 Reds. They were aggressive, and they fought for every inch. Dressen had played with the Reds when they were really rough, and his style of managing called for bitter fighting. But it isn't every player who reacts kindly to such a style. Many of Dressen's players began muttering behind his back. The really top-notch managers, such as Bill McKechnie, know that each player must be treated as an individual case. It is not good psychology to try to make toreadors out of peaceful citizens.

As if to illustrate what sort of fate awaited the opponents of the 1937 Reds, the team signed a catcher known as Gus Brittain, who had never been known to play ball with any degree of competence, but who had been in one fight after another during his career on the diamond. Built along the general proportions of a bull, Brittain was to sit ominously in the Reds' bull pen just in case of trouble—like a hotel house detective at a high school fraternity dance.

2

Sports writers were impressed by the hustling team, and began calling the 1937 aggregation the "Roughhouse Reds." The name caught on, and to read the press accounts, one would think that the Baltimore Orioles had suddenly swooped down on the modern game.

The idea was perhaps excellent, but the execution was inferior. When the season started and the Reds began to lose one game after another, the roughhouse tactics became something of a joke. During the time that he was employed by the Cincinnati Baseball Club Company, Gus Brittain engaged in only one pugilistic endeavor, and that was with his teammate Paul Derringer, an altercation that ended when Derringer hit the receiver over the head with a mask. The fight had started when Derringer was warming up before the game, and several of his curve balls broke low and hit Brittain in the legs.

"If you'd use that much stuff in a game, maybe you could get somebody out," Brittain said. And Derringer, thinking Gus was just joking, merely laughed. When he saw that Brittain was serious, they went at it. Accounts vary as to who got the better of the brawl, but the opinion is unanimous that the affair ended with Paul striking Gus with the mask.

There were new names to remember that year. Baxter Jordan came from Boston to play first base, and though his name suggests a stagecoach driver out of Dickens, he went about his chores with so much skill that Dressen experimented with Les Scarsella in the outfield. Kampouris, the little Greek god, was still at second, Billy Myers at short, and Jimmy Outlaw at third. Kampouris, incidentally, developed into a long-distance hitter that spring and peppered three home runs in a single game against the Phils.

Outlaw, at third base, was another farm product. Jimmy made three hits in the opening game, a contest lost to the great Dizzy Dean in ten innings, 2 to 0, and the fans thought they were seeing another Heinie Groh. Ray (Peaches) Davis, a lantern-jawed right-hander MacPhail had brought from Fort Worth, pitched that game and might have won it had not Phil Weintraub, another recent acquisition, been hit by a batted ball, preventing a run from scoring for Cincinnati.

For the first month of the season it appeared that Outlaw had taken Lew Riggs's job at third, but then came a game that changed the situation overnight. In the first night game of the season the Reds tangled bats with the Boston Braves, and Dressen started a young southpaw named Johnny Vander Meer, who was said to have terrific stuff. Vander Meer fanned 11 men that night, making the audience gasp with delight, but Outlaw, at third, made three errors, enabling Boston to win, behind Lou Fette, 3 to 1. Errors are part of the game and players soon forget them. But the fans never let Outlaw forget that one bad performance. He was roundly booed after that, and the sensitive young man drifted back to the minors, later regaining the top as an outfielder with the Detroit Tigers. Lew Riggs went back to third.

The outfield caused considerable trouble. Scarsella lost his batting touch after shifting to the gardens, and Cuyler failed to repeat his good year of 1936. In an effort to bolster the attack, Giles induced Chick Hafey to leave his farm at Walnut Creek, California, and report to the club again, sinus trouble and all, much as Sidney Weil had prevailed upon Eddie Roush to come out of retirement reluctantly six seasons before.

The pitching was spotty, but brilliant in the good spots. The brightest jewel of the hurling corps was Lee Grissom, a gigantic southpaw who had first come out of the hills near Los Molinos, California, when MacPhail beckoned in 1934. Grissom had what scouts like to call "a world of stuff." He was extremely fast. Pie Traynor, the greatest third baseman in National League history and later a manager of the Pirates, was once quoted as saying that in all his career there was only one pitcher he was afraid to have his team hit against at night, and that flinger was Lee Grissom.

Combining some of the best features of Rube Waddell and various Ring Lardner characters, Grissom first received national publicity when he came to Cincinnati during the great flood of 1937. Crosley Field, like various other structures of the neighborhood, was hopelessly inundated, the water being 21 feet deep at home plate, much to the despair of Matty Schwab, the superintendent of grounds, who is the master of almost every situation that involves harm for his terrain. Grissom and another Red pitcher, Gene Schott, were photographed as they rowed a boat over the center-field fence, and the picture was widely circulated.

But Lee Grissom soon learned that the best way to receive publicity was by his pitching. He lost his first start to Pittsburgh, 3 to 2, but got going when he whitewashed the Giants at the Polo Grounds early in May, defeating another towering port-sider, Cliff Melton, 4 to 0. After that, he started winning with regularity, and was chosen as a pitcher for the National League in the all-star game in July.

But as the season progressed it was apparent that the Reds had not yet found the right combination. Ernie Lombardi, the old dependable, was the only .300 hitter on the club. Paul Derringer was having a bad year on the mound. And the two young hurlers who had been counted on, Johnny Vander Meer and Lloyd (Whitey) Moore, were not quite ready for the majors and were optioned to Syracuse. Grissom was the pitching staff and was called upon by Dressen in and out of turn.

As September came around, Charlie Dressen wondered how he figured in Warren Giles's plans for the future. And he decided to ask, which was a mistake. For Giles had to tell him that he had other plans for a manager of 1938, and since Dressen now knew that he would not be back, it would be better for all concerned if he were to leave immediately. It wouldn't be a healthy situation to have a man managing a team when he knew he was on borrowed time.

Dressen departed on September 14, along with his coaches, George Kelly and Tom Sheehan. Giles put Bobby Wallace, the great old shortstop, and scout for the Reds since the days of Jack Hendricks, in charge, making it clear that the appointment was only for the balance of the season.

At the time Dressen left, the Reds had won 51 and lost 78. Under Wallace they failed to hustle, figuring the year was over, and won only 5 of the remaining 25 games, losing the last 14 in a row. But despite that sorry finish, there was much to hope for. A bumper crop from the farms was deposited at Crosley Field, including such players as outfielder Harry Craft, first baseman Frank McCormick, and pitchers Johnny Vander Meer, Whitey Moore, and Red Barrett.

The team finished last again, but somehow it was different. The fans sensed that the team was better than that, that there was plenty of plastic clay available for molding, if Warren Giles could only find the proper sculptor. He did find him in the person of Bill McKechnie.

☻ **27** ☻

THE DUTCH MASTER

1

Three important events occurred in the winter between the 1937 and 1938 seasons that were to make the Reds a pennant contender. They were: the hiring of Bill McKechnie as manager of the club, the calling off of a player deal at the last minute, and a change made in the geography of Crosley Field that pushed home plate out twenty feet, bringing the fence in left and center and the bleachers in right in range of the batters.

Moving out of home plate was an idea submitted by a fan in an open letter to Warren Giles that appeared in Nixson Denton's column in the *Cincinnati Times-Star*. Powel Crosley saw the letter that suggested the change, thought the idea was sound, and asked Giles to move home plate. For years the Reds had been handicapped by the great size of the park. Babe Ruth had made home runs popular, and since players could not be made into Ruths, ball parks had to have smaller dimensions to give the fans enough home runs to suit their fancy. The Reds, because of their large park, hit fewer home runs than any team in the majors. Mel Ott, who hit 511 National League home runs from 1927 to 1946, more than any player in the loop's history, was in the circuit for ten years before he connected for one at Cincinnati.

The fences were still a respectable distance from home plate after the shift, but the Reds hit 110 home runs in 1938, more than in any other year of their history. Ival Goodman increased his total from twelve in 1937 to thirty. Ernie Lombardi went from nine to nineteen, Billy Myers from seven to twelve. Harry Craft, a newcomer, hit fifteen, and Wally Berger sixteen.

The deal that wasn't made was with Chicago. During the winter meetings at the Congress Hotel at Chicago, Gabe Paul, the Reds' publicity man, called the newspapermen together and said, "We've just traded Ernie Lombardi to the Cubs, or at least Bill McKechnie thinks he has. He's waiting now for confirmation."

Fortunately, the confirmation never came. P. K. Wrigley, president of the Cubs, never O.K.'d the deal, which had been swung by his manager, Charlie Grimm, and scout Clarence Rowland. Lombardi then led the National League in hitting. It must be understood, however, that the players the Reds would have acquired from Chicago might have done just as well. In the years that Warren Giles has been in Cincinnati, he has not made a single trade that turned out badly for the team.

But by far the most important of the three events was the signing of Bill McKechnie, one of the game's greatest characters. Baseball has produced a host of unique individuals, but none quite like William Boyd McKechnie, the son of Scotch emigrants and the only man in history to win pennants in three major-league cities.

McKechnie is a great family man, and his family respects him with a reverential awe that would have done credit to Massachusetts in the seventeenth century. For twenty years he sang in a Methodist choir, and brought up his children with the fear of God in their hearts. Bill's ideas of religion and respect for the Sabbath are completely sincere. There is an air about him that makes others want to appear at their best. He is the sort of man that other decent men would want their sons to play for. For that reason alone, McKechnie's clubs have acquired players who otherwise might have gone elsewhere.

He is a great sportsman in the best sense of the term, a man who likes to hunt pheasant when the baseball season is over, and fish for trout, and take long walks in the country.

And yet, this man who has such a respect for physical condition and makes such a rigid, almost stoical fetish of proper conduct has an amazing tolerance for the frailties of others. In his long career as a major-league manager he has been forced to handle some of the most errant performers of all time, a gallery that would include Grover Alexander, Flint Rhem, Walter (Rabbit) Maranville, and Moses Yellowhorse.

It was the combination of Maranville and Yellowhorse, an Indian pitcher, that drove Bill almost frantic with the Pirates. McKechnie decided that the best way to handle the two players was to room with them. All went well until one night McKechnie, in a deep sleep, dreamed that he was hanging over a precipice, while vultures pecked away at him. He awoke to find that Yellowhorse was braced against the frame of the open window on the top floor of the hotel, holding the midget Maranville at arm's length out the window. And the Rabbit was busily catching pigeons as they landed on the roof and handing them to Yellowhorse, who added them to the aviary that the room had become.

Once on the ball field, Bill is an entirely different character. He barks at umpires with all the ferocity that a good manager should assume, and at training-camp sessions he can signal to all parts of the field with his shrill whistle. Nothing escapes him on the field. He knows which players to flatter and which ones to etch with his acid tongue. He is a master of psychology without having ever entered a college classroom. He is proud of his teams, and will defend them at all times, and in the clubhouse he has even played nursemaid to his boys, pouring coffee for them after workouts.

Though he is cautious in the company of people he does not know or does not care for, when he is relaxed with friends, his views on baseball are alarmingly frank and eminently reasonable. He is at his best among old friends like Charlie Grimm and Casey Stengel, both National League managers at one time or another.

The only players who ever criticized Bill McKechnie were those who had to be let out because they were inferior performers or for other reasons. Bill keeps a wallet full of crisp

bank notes, just in case he runs into old acquaintances who
are hard up.

Bill wasn't much of a player. He couldn't hit, and his skill
was mostly defensive. And yet when he was a member of the
New York Yankees, manager Frank Chance chose him as his
intimate companion, explaining, "McKechnie has more sense
than the rest of the team put together."

His sagacity was always recognized, and in the Federal
League he managed Newark before becoming a pilot with
Pittsburgh in 1922. He won the pennant for the Pirates in
1925 and followed it up with a victory over Washington in
the World Series. There was dissension on the Pittsburgh
nine in 1926, and Bill was let out by his boss, Barney Dreyfuss, at the end of the year. He then signed to manage the
Cardinals, and won the flag with them in 1928, being dismissed after losing four straight to the New York Yankees in
the World Series.

Sam Breadon, the St. Louis president, always regretted letting Bill go, and he brought him back in midseason of 1929.
That winter he ran for tax collector at Wilkinsburg, Pennsylvania, and would have retired from the game had he been
elected. Instead, he managed the Boston Braves for the next
eight seasons, and though he never brought a flag to the Hub,
many observers feel he did the best work of his career at Boston, finishing fourth and fifth consistently with teams that
seemed destined for the cellar.

It was a fortunate day for the fans of Cincinnati when
Warren Giles brought Bill McKechnie to manage the Reds.
And to Giles must go full credit for the choice.

2

"We don't have a bad team, Warren," McKechnie told his
boss during the first week of spring training. "I think we
might fool some people. That big Frank McCormick can play
first base. I'm going to put him right in there. And Harry
Craft will be all right in center field. I don't know about the
pitching. We could use another pitcher. But we're going to
be all right, mark what I say."

The Reds were all right. The season started with Ival Goodman hitting the ball into the bleachers with regularity. Harry Craft, stationed in center, proved the best guardian of that sector the team had had since the palmy days of Edd Roush. Allan (Dusty) Cooke, a former Yankee purchased from Minneapolis, was sent to left. Frank McCormick took over at first as if he were Jake Daubert, and formed a big target for Alex Kampouris, Billy Myers, and Lew Riggs to shoot at. Early in the season, Kampouris was traded to the New York Giants for Wally Berger, an outfield slugger McKechnie had had at Boston. Lonny Frey, who had been obtained during the winter from the Cubs for slightly more than the waiver price, replaced Kampy at second and Berger shoved Cooke to the bench.

The club had been going along at a clip slightly better than .500 in early June when McKechnie made a morning call to the team's downtown office.

"Warren," he said, "we need one more pitcher. If we get one, I think we might have a chance for the pennant."

"Do you know where there is one?" Giles asked.

"Yes, I think I do. Philadelphia has two of them—Claude Passeau and Bucky Walters. Of the two, I'd rather have Walters."

Giles immediately phoned Gerald Nugent, the president of the Phils. Nugent's club had had rough financial going, and almost every year they were able to show a slight profit by disposing of one or more players.

"Walters can be had," Nugent said, "but I'll have to have a lot of money and some players."

"Would you put a price on him?" Giles asked.

"Well, I couldn't do that. But I'll call you back." Nugent apparently had to get in touch with his bank.

Giles meanwhile called Crosley and said he had a chance to make a deal for a good pitcher, but that it was a big deal and would require a large sum of money.

"Does McKechnie feel Walters will help us?" Crosley asked.

"Yes, he does," Giles said. "And so do I."

258

"How much money will you need?"

"About fifty thousand dollars."

"Can you raise it there?" Crosley asked.

"I think we can."

"Then go ahead. Make the deal."

The Reds obtained Walters for approximately $50,000 plus the contracts of catcher Spud Davis and pitcher Al Hollingsworth. But the arrival of the new pitcher was obscured by the most tremendous excitement the baseball fans of the city had ever known.

On the afternoon of June 11, Johnny Vander Meer, the talented young southpaw who had begun to flash the realization of his early promise, shut out the Boston Braves without a hit, winning 3 to 0. He walked three, but faced only twenty-eight men, and no Brave reached second base. It was the seventh no-hitter in Cincinnati history and the first since Hod Eller had tossed one in 1919.

Four days later it was Vandy's turn to pitch again, and the setting couldn't have been more exciting, for the Reds were scheduled to play the first night game in the history of Ebbets Field, Brooklyn, where Larry MacPhail, by now general manager of the Dodgers, had arranged for Flatbush to become the second nocturnal town in the majors.

Vander Meer began the game by mowing the Dodgers down in order, and the capacity crowd sensed real drama in the making. Could it be possible that a man could pitch two no-hit games in a row? It was an unheard-of feat, never accomplished in all the years of major-league history.

Though the crowd was hostile at the game's start, as the young southpaw of the Reds continued to pitch flawless ball, Brooklyn fans, for one exciting night, began rooting for a rival pitcher.

John was wild. His mother and father as well as five hundred neighbors from Midland Park, New Jersey, were in the stands, and the pressure was terrific. But Vandy just kept pumping, kept pitching, and kept retiring Dodgers. He was much faster than in his outing against Boston, but also much wilder. Still, in eight innings he hadn't allowed a hit.

Buddy Hassett, a left-handed-hitting first baseman, was the first to bat in the last of the ninth. Vander Meer pitched three straight balls, then retired Buddy on a soft roller to McCormick at first. Vandy then became the victim of a mad streak of wildness and filled the bases with passes, walking Babe Phelps, Cookie Lavagetto, and Dolf Camilli on only eighteen pitches. Bill McKechnie called time and went out to the mound. "Relax, John," he said. "Just take it easy."

When play was resumed, the crowd of 38,748 was standing up and shrieking with excitement. The Reds had six runs and would certainly win, but a hit now would prevent the greatest pitching achievement, or at least the most sensational, of all time.

Vandy went back to work. He faced Ernie Koy, a dangerous right-handed hitter, who smashed the ball on the ground to Riggs at third, and Lew threw to the plate to force Goodie Rosen, running for Phelps, for the second out. But the bases were still loaded, and John was one out away from immortality.

Leo Durocher then came to the plate and raised a fly to short center field. Harry Craft came tearing in, waited, and made the catch.

The spectators surged on the field, and Paul Derringer and Jim Weaver, the biggest men on the team, rushed to the mound to protect Vandy. Then, in the stands, other fans discovered Johnny's parents, and they had to have police protection to leave their seats.

The scene in the Redleg clubhouse after the game is hardly describable. Vander Meer staggered in and flopped down onto a bench, grinning and too excited to say anything. Ernie Lombardi went over to him and planted a big kiss on his ear. Bill McKechnie, who previously thought that he had witnessed every possible baseball situation, calmly walked over, congratulated Vander Meer first, and then Lombardi. Wally Berger, perhaps the happiest player of all, threw his hat in the air and said, "Whew! At last I'm with a real ball club!"

In his second successive no-hitter, Vandy walked eight men,

but only five balls were hit out of the infield. He fanned seven. Big Ernie Lombardi had called the pitches wisely.

Johnny stayed in the clubhouse as late as possible, hoping the crowd would disperse, and then sneaked to the modest home of his parents at Midland Park. The Reds were off the next day, and John got up at five in the morning and went fishing.

Back in Cincinnati, the fans were simply agog. There had never been anything like this! Vander Meer was swamped with so many offers of every description that Warren Giles was forced to become his business manager to handle the details.

Interest in the Reds was at fever pitch. Farmers in the Ohio valley, who had to wait for the rural mailman for news of the Reds back in 1919, now had radios on their tractors so they could listen to the play-by-play description of the games. A woman from Durham, North Carolina, phoned the Reds' office and asked that she be given forty-eight hours' notice every time Vander Meer was scheduled to pitch.

Two days after the second no-hit game, the *Cincinnati Enquirer* commented editorially, "It's only fair to warn Adolf Hitler that if he does march in Czechoslovakia one of these fine hot days, he won't have the headlines in these parts if the Reds are playing—and particularly if Johnny Vander Meer is in the box."

Vandy was born at Prospect Park, New Jersey, November 2, 1914, the son of a Dutch stonecutter who came to the United States from Holland. When he was four, the family moved to Midland Park, where the father took a job as a foreman in the engineering department of a silk dye works. John grew up and, like most American boys, grew to love baseball. He never reached high school, but played semipro ball around Paterson, where he was spotted by scouts.

By a strange coincidence, Boston and Brooklyn, the teams against which Vander Meer reached the pinnacle of fame, had both owned his contract before the Reds acquired it. Brooklyn lost it through front-office bungling and the Braves sold him to Nashville in 1936.

261

Nashville offered Vander Meer to the Red Sox for $25,000, but was turned down. Bill Terry of the Giants offered $15,000 for him, but that was also refused. Larry MacPhail obtained Vandy for the Reds for $15,000 and a player. He spent most of the 1936 season at Durham, where he flashed into headlines by striking out 295 men during the season. And the Reds knew they had acquired a gem.

After the double no-hit stuff, even a pennant would have seemed an anticlimax to the followers of the Reds. And a pennant wasn't quite within reach. Bucky Walters proved a valuable addition to the mound staff, but even with Vander Meer, Paul Derringer, and Walters in form, a fourth pitcher was needed. Lee Grissom should have been the fourth, but after recovering from a sore arm in August, he sprained an ankle in a foolish attempt to steal second and was out for the season.

Pittsburgh and Chicago battled down to the wire, with the Cubs finally winning out when Gabby Hartnett hit his famous homer in the dark. The Reds ran fourth, winning 82 and losing 68, and were only six games behind the Bruins. Writers tabbed the Reds as the team of the future.

Ernie Lombardi, who had delighted the fans with his numerous base hits ever since joining the club in 1932, won the league's batting championship in 1938, hitting .342. More important, he had become the most popular player in the history of the club, even more of a hero than Edd Roush had been.

If you did not know that Rostand had written *Cyrano de Bergerac* long before Ernie Lombardi visited this planet, you would have sworn that the hero was patterned after the big Italian from Oakland, California. For Lom was constructed on an epic pattern, a tremendous man but a shy one, a man who looked as if his appetite might rival that of William Jennings Bryan but yet a moderate eater, a man whose voice could make the earth shake if he shouted, but who seldom spoke; and he brought to baseball a nose so lavish in its geography that the more famous schnozzola of Jimmy Durante's seems picayunish by comparison.

Ernesto Natali Lombardi was born at Oakland, April 6, 1908, the son of a grocer who had come to America from Piedmont, in the northern part of Italy. As a youth in the San Francisco Bay district he was known not for his nose but for his gigantic hands, which he was to wrap around a baseball bat with so much effectiveness. He became proficient at a game called "Bocci," a street game loved by Italians, and he is known to his intimates as "Bocci" Lombardi to this day. It is his favorite nickname.

Lombardi graduated from the Pacific Coast League to the Brooklyn Dodgers in 1931, and he fitted right into the fantastic Flatbush follies. Manager Wilbert Robinson, whose abilities at remembering names were akin to Sam Goldwyn's struggles with rhetoric, called the giant catcher Joe Schnapps, which was apparently the closest he could come to saying Ernie Lombardi. Lom caught the opening game for Brooklyn and appropriately made three hits, but for some mysterious reason he was put on the bench.

After six weeks of inactivity, Lombardi went to Robbie and said, "When are you going to let me catch again?"

Robinson looked at Lom and said, "Why, Joe Schnapps! I'd forgotten you were on our club." That winter came the deal that sent Lombardi to the Reds, and he was to stay for a decade.

There have been greater batsmen than Lombardi, though you could name them on two hands. Handicapped by his lack of speed, Ernie went to the plate facing seven outfielders. He used an interlocking grip on the bat, and when he hit the ball on the ground directly at a fielder, it was an almost certain double play. There was absolutely no way to pitch him. If the ball was inside, he would hit to left. It it was outside, he would plaster it down the right field line. On one occasion with the Reds he hit four straight doubles in four consecutive innings off four different pitchers.

Lombardi had a terrific following among the women of Cincinnati. Flocking to the park on ladies' days and learning to come to the lot between the bargain attractions, the ladies shrieked with joy at every move the big catcher made. There was a Sinatra-like adulation of Lom that affected women of all ages, not just bobby-soxers, and after each game they would gather at the entrance to the stairway that led to the Redleg clubhouse, waiting to see their hero emerge in street clothes. This terrified Ernie to such an extent that he customarily stayed in the dressing room for hours, talking to his bosom friends Dr. Richard Rohde, the Reds' trainer, and his assistant, Larry McManus. With that pair of good fellows, Ernie felt at home; and the sight of him, nearly nude, draining a bottle of beer with Gargantuan gusto, would have moved a painter or sculptor to a masterpiece of massive realism.

So, in the summer of 1938, when the ominous clouds of war were growing ever darker, the people of Cincinnati, one slice of the isolationist Midwest of America, were cheering the names of Johnny Vander Meer and Ernie Lombardi, the sons, respectively, of a Dutch stonecutter and an Italian grocer, living testimony as to the value of the melting-pot tradition and the glory of a game.

⊗ **28** ⊗

JACKPOT AND THE FALLEN GIANT

1

One night in March 1939 Bill McKechnie returned to his hotel in Tampa following a dinner at one of the city's celebrated Spanish restaurants and found a special-delivery letter from the patriarchal Connie Mack, asking if the Reds would be interested in obtaining one of Philadelphia's holdouts, third baseman Bill Werber. McKechnie could hardly wait to get to the telephone to complete the deal.

To win the pennant the Reds needed a third baseman, for Lew Riggs was just lacking in the talents required for daily play on a contender for the flag. Werber's acquisition, an enormous stroke of good fortune, was exactly what the situation required.

Werber reported wearing a specially constructed shoe, explaining that he had needed the protection ever since breaking a toe after kicking a water bucket in the dugout during a game at Boston. Werber had kicked the bucket after popping up with the bases loaded. It was a practice indulged in by Lefty Grove, the great southpaw who was then finishing his career with the Red Sox, and who always expressed his disgust with events dramatically. What Werber did not know was that Grove always kicked the bucket with the side of his foot, and in emulating the ace without knowledge of the proper technique, Bill seriously damaged his career.

Bill Werber is an amazing character in many ways. A Phi Beta Kappa from Duke University, he scorned the pursuits that many players follow off the field and went about his work with a sort of hauteur. He seemed to have a low opinion of many of his fellows, and he was frank to a point where it was a handicap. However, no player ever lived who hustled more while on the field, and if he gave the impression that he didn't like the game, it certainly showed more in his conversation than in his work. He was possessed of tremendous confidence in his ability. One day at the Polo Grounds when the Reds were battling in extra innings as darkness approached, Werber went up to the plate, turned to umpire George Magerkurth, and said, "Let's put an end to this contest, George. Do you want to watch Werber put a home run in the stands?" He then socked the first pitch for the game-winning wallop.

Always in the best of physical condition, and a thorough gentleman with imposing intelligence, Bill Werber would have made an excellent magnate had he chosen to remain in the game. Instead, he entered the insurance business and became a big leaguer in that field almost immediately, with the proper financial rewards. There aren't many players who are wasting their time financially by playing big-league baseball. Bill Werber was one of them.

The opportunity to have Bucky Walters pitching for the full season and the addition of Werber to the infield just about made the Reds as a pennant contender. The baseball writers from all over the nation who watched the Redlegs perform at Tampa recognized the trend, and in a national poll picked Cincinnati to win the National League pennant.

Ponderous Ernie Lombardi was set for another year behind the plate, aided by Willard Hershberger, a product of the Yankee chain who had come to Cincinnati the year before. Paul Derringer, Bucky Walters, Johnny Vander Meer, Lee Grissom, and Lloyd (Whitey) Moore were expected to do the bulk of the pitching. However, Vander Meer was slow in showing his proper form and Bill McKechnie surprised one and all by announcing that Gene Thompson, a lad who had pitched only in a circuit of B classification and who came to the team from the Columbia, South Carolina, farm, would be retained by the club. Always a wizard with pitchers, the good Deacon had spotted something in the work of Thompson that told him the lad would go far.

The infield was a thing of beauty and a joy, if not forever, at least for the next few years. Frank McCormick, at first base, had reached stardom in his first full year in 1938, making 209 hits and batting .326. Lonny Frey, at second, had proved much more valuable than Alex Kampouris, the man he replaced at the bag. Billy Myers, at short, though somewhat handicapped by erraticness, showed flashes of sheer genius at short and was a whale of a play-maker. And Bill Werber, at third, added a dash of calm superiority that made the inner works magnificent.

Two of the outfield spots were sealed by Ival Goodman and Harry Craft, but there was something of a problem in left field because Wally Berger, whose bat had boomed the year before, was becoming slightly shopworn. Other outfield candidates included Lee Gamble, Nino Bongiovanni, and Stanley (Frenchy) Bordagaray, an *émigré* from the Gashouse Gang of the Cardinals.

266

Johnny Vander Meer, no-hit hero of the season before, was given the honor of starting the opening game, but he was not equal to the task, and was batted out, though the defeat against the Pirates was charged to Bucky Walters, who relieved him, the Bucs winning, 7 to 5. But then the Reds started rolling, and before many weeks they were the most talked-about club in the league.

Starting on May 16, the team inaugurated a winning streak of twelve in a row. The first ten triumphs were recorded at home against the eastern clubs, and then the Reds went to St. Louis to meet the first-place Cardinals. Bucky Walters beat Lonnie Warneke, 7 to 5, in the first meeting, and on the strength of it, the Reds went ahead of St. Louis into first place. On the next day Lee Grissom added the twelfth straight, a 3-to-2 victory over Morton Cooper, stopped after eight innings because of wet grounds. And the string was ended at twelve when Vander Meer bowed, 6 to 5, to Curt Davis on the day after that.

But the Reds were first, and they began to win with a regularity that bespoke their intentions of staying there. Walters and Derringer were almost unbeatable, and though unrelated by blood, they became as famous a pitching pair as Jerome and Paul Dean of the Gashouse Cardinals of five years before.

"Oh, how I hate to come to Cincinnati!" said Garry Schumacher, then a New York sports writer and now aide to Horace Stoneham of the Giants. "One day you look at Walters. The next day it's Derringer. On the third day you think you're going to win, and Frank McCormick or Ival Goodman beats your brains out. Then it's time to face Walters and Derringer again."

The National League seldom produces lopsided races, and the Reds were prevented from making a runaway of the 1939 chase only because the pitching staff was not fully rounded. Lee Grissom was not the pitcher he had been in 1937. Whitey Moore was in and out, and Vander Meer had lost his touch. Gene Thompson proved to be a bearcat in relief, an unusual accomplishment for a kid, and on the days when Walters or

Derringer was not pitching, he was frequently called upon.

But the Reds remained in first place. There was no team in the league that could stop them. The Cardinals tried hard, and were a constant threat, but the issue was decided in the last series between the clubs in Cincinnati, starting September 26. The clubs were slated to tangle in four games, and when the set started, the Reds were in first place by three and one-half games.

On the first day of the series, Gene Thompson, by now a starting pitcher, shaded Curt Davis, the Cardinal ace, 3 to 1, in the first game of a double-header, with shortstop Billy Myers socking a homer to account for the Cincinnati scores. The nightcap saw the Cardinals turn the tables when Mort Cooper blanked the Reds on four hits, 6 to 0, Lee Grissom losing the tilt. On the following day Fiddlin' Bill McGee of St. Louis poured the whitewash, and the Reds were blanked, 4 to 0, behind Walters.

The fourth game was it. The Reds were two and one-half contests ahead and could lose the pennant if they lost the final game. But if they won, they could clinch the gonfalon. Veteran fans, bitterly recalling 1926, when the same two clubs engaged in a death struggle with victory going to the Mound City, looked on and hoped and sighed. It was up to Paul Derringer.

The Cardinals, those apostles of late-season heroics, were out for blood. With Joe Medwick and Johnny Mize swinging for the fences, they were a potent threat.

The bare statistics of the game do not tell the story of the drama that was involved. The Reds won, 5 to 3, and took the pennant with that victory, and it was one of the most exciting contests ever played in the long horse-hide history of the Queen City.

Derringer didn't have a thing as the game started. He escaped unscathed in the first, but the bench eyed him knowingly as he returned there.

Ray Blades, the manager of the Cardinals, started Max Lanier, a young southpaw, against Derringer, and he was wilder than a Papuan. The Reds had one run in and the bases filled, when Curt Davis rushed in and forced in another run with a pass, the Reds jumping to a 2-to-0 lead.

In the second inning the Cards tied the score with a two-run homer by Terry Moore, and Bill McKechnie paced nervously in front of the bench. "The big fellow doesn't have it," he kept repeating.

"Who have you got that's any better?" asked coach Jimmy Wilson. "Leave him in there. Maybe he'll settle down."

Settle down he did, but the players on both sides were highly nervous because of the pressure. Billy Myers made three errors at shortstop, and Gutteridge and Mize each contributed boots for the Redbirds.

The Cardinal half of the seventh inning was out of the world. With the score tied, 3 to 3, Joe Medwick led off with a double that caromed off the score board. The ball got away from Craft, but Goodman came racing over behind him, a play that had been rehearsed all year in case it ever came up, and threw to Werber at third, who tagged Medwick sliding in, trying to stretch the drive into a triple.

The Reds broke the tie with a run in the seventh, but in the eighth Johnny Hopp hit a pinch-hit double for the Cards. Ernie Lombardi then made a remarkable throw in a dangerous situation that caught Hopp off second, and Derringer was out of the inning.

Again in the eighth the Reds scored, making it 5 to 3, but Big Paul had one more inning to go. Could he make it?

Derringer took the hill, and Bill Werber walked slowly over from third and said, "All right, Paul. Let's cut loose. You throw that ball as hard as you can and we'll all go to the clubhouse."

Derringer never in his life threw harder than in that ninth inning, and he wound up by fanning Medwick and Mize. The Reds had their first pennant in twenty years.

2

Between them, Derringer and Walters won 52 games in 1939. Bucky won 27 and dropped 11, Paul 25 and 7. Each had the greatest season of his career.

Currently it is a favorite hot stove league question in the Queen City to ask, "Now, who was better in his prime, Derringer or Walters?" The problem is as puzzling as "How Old Is Ann?" or "Who Threw the Overalls in Mrs. Murphy's Chowder?" Apparently there is no answer.

Paul Derringer and Bucky Walters are as unlike temperamentally as they could possibly be. Derringer was inclined toward outbursts of temper, was highly emotional, and at times careless. He seldom pitched low-hit games, going about his work in the manner of Christy Mathewson, allowing numerous hits but turning on the heat when the chips were down. Walters was and is cool, calm, and quiet, more spectacular at the plate or on the bases than on the mound, and one of the best fielders of his position that ever took the hill.

Bucky had been a third baseman, a very average third baseman, and he became a pitcher only under pressure from Jimmy Wilson, his manager at Philadelphia. Bucky didn't like the idea of pitching, because he was such a good competitor he wanted to be in every game, but when it was pointed out that he might well become a great pitcher but would always be an ordinary infielder, he made the change to the mound.

Derringer, a Kentuckian, started out as a catcher in high school, but once he took over as a pitcher, he knew he had found his proper position. With the Reds, he had always been handicapped by bad clubs, but when the team got good in 1938, Derringer became sensational.

Of course, there were other factors in the Reds' success besides pitching. Frank McCormick batted .332 and socked 128 runs across the plate. Ival Goodman's home-run total declined because he was hitting the ball to left field more often, but he compiled a .323 batting average. Bill Werber, leading off, scored 115 runs and hit .289. Lombardi suffered one of his few poor seasons—poor for him, that is—hitting .287.

It is often debated in Cincinnati whether Warren Giles or Larry MacPhail built the club that won for Cincinnati its first pennant in two decades. Although a good case can be built up for MacPhail on the surface, it was actually Giles who produced the pennant.

First of all, it was Giles who selected McKechnie, and that was the master stroke. Perhaps managers aren't as important as some people think as tacticians, but their work only starts when the day's game is over. McKechnie was a master handler of men. He infused the team with the morale that was necessary for winning. Some managers will never learn to handle personalities as long as they live. McKechnie in that department was without a peer. And he was the choice of Warren Giles.

It was also Giles who concluded the trade for Walters and the purchase of Werber, and without those key men a pennant would have been utterly impossible.

MacPhail put in the lights. He gave the city an electric shot in the arm in other ways besides. But he did not bring Cincinnati a pennant. He pulled them from the ruck, yes, but many a first-division club struggles for years before copping a flag, as numerous residents of Pittsburgh and Cleveland are well aware.

Paul Derringer and Ernie Lombardi were in Redleg uniforms when Giles came to Cincinnati, but they were brought there, not by MacPhail, but by Sidney Weil in the dismal swampland period of the early thirties.

The only regulars of the 1939 Reds that Larry MacPhail could justly claim as his were Frank McCormick, Billy Myers, Ival Goodman, and Harry Craft. Of these, only Myers and Goodman were regulars with the Reds when MacPhail left Cincinnati. McCormick and Craft were MacPhail's boys, but they hadn't arrived when Giles came to town.

There is no intention of underestimating the job that MacPhail did with the Reds. But it was a different job than winning the pennant. It was a job of raising capital, reviving interest in the team, and getting out of the cellar. Had he remained, he might have won a pennant too.

When Warren Giles arrived to take over the Reds, he was called upon to make a speech at a luncheon club. He thrust his arm into the air dramatically and said, "It is my hope that we can bring Cincinnati a first-place team."

Others had tried for seventeen years without success. Warren did it within three years. And he's the man who deserves the curtain call.

3

When a National League team wins a pennant, it is called upon to meet the champions of the American League, and in the late thirties that was usually unfortunate. For in 1939 the New York Yankees won their fourth straight flag, and the tales the Reds had heard about them were rather terrifying.

The Yanks, managed by the unusually skillful Joe McCarthy, and boasting a line-up that included such formidable names as Joe DiMaggio, Charlie Keller, Joe Gordon, Bill Dickey, and George Selkirk, had won the previous three World Series. To them the annual classic was pleasant October exercise, but hardly a strain.

Yet Bill McKechnie thought the Reds actually might beat them. The series opened at Yankee Stadium on October 4, with Paul Derringer pitted against the ace of the Bombers, Charles (Red) Ruffing.

Big Paul was in superb form, retiring the first eight men before yielding a single to his opposing pitcher. But the Reds were equally helpless against Ruffing until the fourth, when Goodman scored the first run of the contest by walking, stealing second, and scoring on Frank McCormick's second hit, a single. In the fifth, however, the Bombers tied the score when Lonny Frey made a mental error on a cut-off play that had been rehearsed all season, though the fans thought Wally Berger, not Frey, was in error. Joe Gordon had singled when Ellsworth Dahlgren, successor to the great Lou Gehrig, ripped a double down the left field line. Berger retrieved the ball and threw properly to second base, but Frey was out of position and unable to head off Gordon at the plate.

Paul and Red pitched on even terms throughout the rest of the game. But in the last of the ninth Charlie Keller, batting with one out, hit a long fly near the right-center-field bleachers, which should have been caught by Goodman. Ival, unfamiliar with the shadows at the Stadium, a condition that frequently has bothered National League players in the series, let the ball drop for a triple. So the Yanks had the winning run on third with one man out.

DiMaggio, Dickey, and Selkirk were the next three hitters. McKechnie could order Derringer to pass the first two and pitch to Selkirk, or pass DiMaggio and pitch to Dickey, or pitch to DiMaggio.

He chose to have Derringer put DiMaggio on, play the infield halfway in so that a double play could be made by way of second, or a throw could be made to the plate. Dickey isn't fast and he sometimes hits double-play balls. On this occasion he singled and the game was over, the Yanks winning as usual, 2 to 1.

There was some criticism of McKechnie for not passing Dickey too, but it was unjustified. For when you fill the bases and try to make the batter hit the ball on the ground, it is necessary to pitch the ball low. To pitch low to George Selkirk was probable suicide. To take a chance on Dickey was sounder baseball. McKechnie played percentage baseball and lost.

On the next afternoon, Monte Pearson, one of the strangest personalities in the game's annals because he spent most of each season complaining of various aches and pains only to rise to the heights in series play, shut out the Reds and Bucky Walters, 4 to 0, giving up only two hits, a single by Lombardi with one out in the eighth and a harmless one-baser by Werber with two out in the ninth. That game was Pearson's without question.

The teams moved to Cincinnati for the third contest. Vernon (Goofy) Gomez, who had never lost to the National League, was McCarthy's choice, and McKechnie countered with Gene Thompson. Gomez had nothing at all, and the Reds disposed of him after one inning in which they scored once on singles by Goodman, McCormick, and Lombardi. But Bump Hadley went to Goofy's relief and proved a puzzle to the Reds throughout the afternoon. Meanwhile, the

Bombers found the geography of Crosley Field most accommodating. Charlie Keller hit two home runs, Joe DiMaggio and Bill Dickey one each. The Rhineland witnessed a devastating example of Yankee superiority that afternoon. Final score: New York, 7; Cincinnati, 3.

The fourth game began with Derringer back in action again in opposition to Oral Hildebrand. For the first portion of the game Big Paul pitched as he had never done before. For six innings the game was scoreless, but in the seventh, Keller and Dickey connected for home runs. Then the Reds scored three times to take the lead, with Steve Sundra and Grandma Murphy going to the aid of Hildebrand. The Reds tallied again in the eighth, and appeared to be on their way to their first victory when disaster struck in the ninth.

Derringer had retired for a pinch hitter and Walters was on the slab when the Reds tried to preserve their 4-to-2 lead. But Keller singled through the box and DiMaggio lined a one-bagger to left. Then Dickey hit a perfect double-play ball to Frey, whose high throw to second was credited as an error by Myers by the official scorers. That was the break the Bombers required, and when Gordon hit a scorcher to Werber, Bill's throw to the plate was too late to head off DiMaggio with the tying run.

The Reds failed to score in the ninth, and then came the terrible tenth. Frankie Crosetti drew a base on balls, and after a sacrifice by Red Rolfe, Myers fumbled Keller's roller for an error. That set the stage for one of the strangest plays of all time. DiMaggio hit safely to right field, scoring Crosetti, and when Goodman allowed the ball to go through him, Keller also tore around the bases toward the plate. In scoring, Charlie crashed into Lombardi, who lay prostrate on the ground as DiMaggio completed the circuit of the bases, bringing the victory to the Yankees, 7 to 4, and enabling them to sweep the series.

That play has gone down in history as the act of the dying swan, and the sports writers, who always seem to feel each World Series must have a hero and a goat, have long remem-

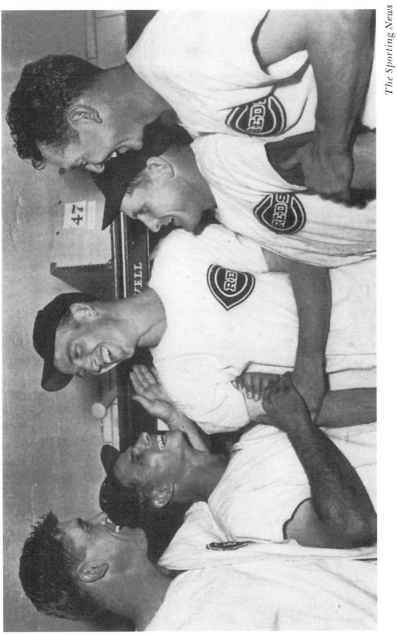

TEAMMATES CONGRATULATE BLACKWELL
AFTER NO-HITTER

Cincinnati Reds

WARREN GILES, JOHNNY NEUN, and
POWEL CROSLEY, JR.

bered Ernie Lombardi as the man who swooned at home plate, while Yankees scampered all over him.

It so happens that when Keller crashed into Lombardi, he accidentally kicked him in the groin with such force that Lom was knocked unconscious and was utterly unaware that DiMaggio was racing across. Perhaps if Lombardi were blessed with the ingenuity that his critics must possess, he would have found a way to retrieve the ball and tag DiMaggio out. If he had, the score would have been 6 to 4, New York, if that would have made any difference.

The fourth game of the 1939 World Series was not lost by Ernie, and it is typical of the big fellow that he never once found it necessary to alibi.

Of course, there is something grotesque about a fallen giant such as Ernie, especially at the windup of such a World Series. Lying there, he seemed to typify the inequality of the struggle. And lying there, he seemed to symbolize the pathetic effort the National League had made against the Yankees for four straight seasons.

The dying swan is part of baseball lore by now. Lombardi was no more a goat than was Fred Merkle, the lad who didn't touch second in 1908, but the myth is no more dangerous than the one that credits Abner Doubleday with inventing the game at Cooperstown exactly a century before.

⊜ **29** ⊜

CHAMPIONS OF THE WORLD

1

Warren Giles took a wise course in preparing for the 1940 season. He knew that the club, in spite of winning the pennant, had developed flaws, and the disappointment of losing four straight to the Yankees in the World Series was too recent to encourage a stand-pat policy. Giles has always been adroit at making deals that appear to be unimportant but that eventually prove of unsuspected benefit. It was in just this way that he traded pitcher Lee Grissom to the Yankees for another hurler, Joe Beggs, and sent first basemen Les Scarsella, so much excess baggage with Frank McCormick alive, to the Braves for pitcher Jim Turner.

In Beggs the Reds obtained a Croatian javelin-thrower from Geneva University and Aliquippa, Pennsylvania, a man who speaks five or more languages with facility, and, more important, a capable pitcher. Bill McKechnie tabbed him for bull-pen duty, and Joe developed into a fireman who would have made a proud record in Chicago during the days of Mrs. O'Leary's cow.

Turner had won twenty games for McKechnie as a belated freshman at Boston at the age of thirty in 1937, and Bill knew what he could do. Jim hadn't fared so well with the Braves in 1938 and 1939, thanks chiefly to stopping a line drive from the bat of Ival Goodman with his nose. The Reds lost nothing in disposing of Grissom and Scarsella, and the two pitchers they received assured the club of winning the close ones if the attack should fall off. That's the way Giles planned it, and it was exactly the way it worked out.

A new center fielder also joined the cast. Myron (Mike) McCormick, born at Angel's Camp, California, where the discovery of gold led to the rush in 1849, took over in center field, though he also could play left when McKechnie chose to use Craft in center. The latter was a distinct disappointment. When Craft took over the center-field job in 1938, he showed all sorts of promise. His fielding was the best that pasture had seen since Edd Roush departed, and it was felt that if only his stick work would improve, he would surely reach stardom. Instead, Harry's work at bat seemed to grow less and less impressive.

The Reds won the first two games of the season by one run, a tip-off of what was to come. Derringer, Thompson, and Walters did most of the early-season pitching, with Jim Turner rounding into form as the fourth starter. Fifteen out of the first nineteen games were won, and it appeared that the Redlegs would be harder to stop than in the year before. The outfield, however, was still uncertain. Wally Berger, definitely through, was allowed to pass on to the Phils, and the left-field berth, which always seemed to be changing tenants, had its usual number of them. Johnny Rizzo, a former Pirate, played there briefly, and after a row with a spectator that displeased Bill McKechnie, was allowed to pass on. Morris Arnovich, a former Phil, then took over in the left pasture.

One of the surprises of the summer was the optional assignment of Johnny Vander Meer to Indianapolis. Southpaws are traditionally erratic, and John had never regained the touch after the 1938 no-hitters. He had been sick a large part of 1939, winning 5 and losing 9 games, and when he failed to show improvement in 1940, Giles and McKechnie talked to him about going to Indianapolis to regain his confidence. Vandy agreed it was a good idea and departed, showing how rapidly a fall from the pinnacle can be accomplished.

For the first time in several seasons the pennant bee was buzzing in Brooklyn, and during the first half of the campaign the Reds had to wrest first place from the Dodgers seven times.

Finally, on July 7, the Reds managed to take the lead and start moving ahead. There were individual achievements: Paul Derringer, having another masterful year, pitched two one-hitters; Harry Craft hit for the cycle, making a single, double, triple, and homer in a single game as the Reds walloped the Dodgers, 23 to 2. Frank McCormick continued to appear in every championship game for the third straight season and to lead the league in hits for the third successive time. But mostly the Reds forged ahead because of team play: stout pitching almost every day, a tight infield, and enough punch to keep the club ahead.

In late July the Reds went east in first place, and the trip was expected to be a jaunt. But on the evening of July 31 a game was lost in New York that should have been won. Bucky Walters had a 4-to-1 lead going into the ninth inning, and before anyone knew what was happening, Hank Danning, the Giant catcher, socked a four-hundred-foot homer that gave the Polo Grounders a 5-to-4 victory. Little Willard Hershberger, the Reds' second-string catcher, seemed to take the defeat a trifle harder than his mates. "I called for the wrong pitch to Danning," he insisted. "It was all my fault." "Forget it," he was told. "We're a cinch to win the flag. What's one ball game?" But Hershy continued to brood.

The Reds had two off days before a twin bill in Boston, and when Hershberger caught the second game that day, he was still in the throes of despair. The Reds lost both games, traveling twelve innings in the nightcap before bowing, 4 to 3, and Hershy went hitless in five trips, an unusual performance for him. On one occasion a Boston batter hit a bunt only about fifteen feet from home plate, and Hershberger didn't make an effort to field it, Whitey Moore, the surprised Red pitcher, coming in to make the play.

Bill McKechnie rushed out from the dugout. "Is something wrong, Hershy?" he asked.

"You bet there's something wrong," the catcher replied, his eyes flashing. "I'll tell you about it after the ball game."

When the contest was completed, the Deacon, who had encountered almost every vagary of the human personality during his long years in baseball, took Hershberger to dinner in his hotel suite. The catcher startled his manager with the announcement that he was contemplating suicide. Such a statement is always difficult to reply to, but McKechnie, seeing that the boy was sorely troubled, talked to him far into the night, and finally succeeded in restoring his good humor. When they shook hands and said good night, Bill was certain that Hershy was over his period of depression.

The Reds had another twin bill scheduled for the next day, and Hershberger got up and had breakfast, eating with Lou Smith, the writer for the *Enquirer* who always travels with the club. The catcher appeared to be more reticent than usual, but apparently in good spirits.

When the Reds were taking hitting practice, McKechnie noted that Hershy had not put in an appearance, and he asked Gabe Paul, the traveling secretary, to phone his hotel room and find out what the trouble was.

Gabe got Hershy on the phone and said, "Bill's worried about you. Aren't you coming out to the game?"

"I can't come out," was the reply. "I'm sick."

"Oh, that's all right," said the always tactful Gabe. "You don't have to get in uniform. Just come on out and sit in the stands and watch the games. Bill will feel better if you do."

"O.K.," Hershy said. "I'll be right out."

When he hadn't arrived by the time the first contest was almost over, McKechnie dispatched Dan Cohen, a Cincinnati fan who was making the trip with the team, to go back to the hotel and find out what the trouble was. It was Cohen who found Hershberger's lifeless body sprawled in the bathroom. He had cut his throat with a safety-razor blade.

Suicides are not rare, and through the years the Reds had had their share of them. Cannonball Crane, who pitched for the team in 1891, ended his life by drinking chloral. Danny Mahoney, a few years later, destroyed himself by swallowing carbolic. Pea Ridge Day, with the club briefly in 1926, was found dead with a loaded shotgun by his side. And Benny Frey, pitcher for the Reds under Howley, Bush, O'Farrell, and Dressen, was found in the garage of his Jackson, Michigan, home, a victim of carbon monoxide.

But all of the previous cases had happened in the off season. Willard Hershberger took his life when on the road with a first-place club that was headed for its second pennant in a row. It was extremely puzzling. There was no more popular player on the team. He had come to the club in 1938, and had always been a sensational substitute for Ernie Lombardi. Physically the antithesis of Lom, he delighted the fans with his hustling style of play and his timely batting. He hit .345 in 1939 and was batting .309 in 1940 when he chose to depart. A man of good habits and a genial personality, he had seemed unusual only in the fact that he always seemed anxious about his health, not a rare complaint among ballplayers. He was the butt of various harmless little jokes performed by his mates, and took them all in good spirit. If anyone with intimate knowledge of the players on the team were told that one of them had killed himself and were asked to guess which one, Hershberger would have been one of the last names mentioned.

2

Naturally, the Hershberger tragedy threw a pall over the team. They came home and played listlessly before righting themselves. The fans seemed to understand and reacted quietly. And the Reds did stay in first place.

Johnny Vander Meer was recalled from Indianapolis to aid in the pennant drive, after demonstrating that he was himself again. And slowly, exhibiting all the class it demonstrated early in the season, the team straightened out its affairs.

Early in September the Reds went east for the last time, and appeared a cinch to win the flag. Brooklyn's bid had been premature; St. Louis was not nearly so effective as in the year before.

In Brooklyn on September 15, Ernie Lombardi suffered a badly sprained ankle, putting him out for the season. Following Hershberger's suicide, this put the catching staff in a very bad way. The only players available were two rookies,

Bill Baker and Dick West. But Jimmy Wilson, the courageous Red coach who had caught in the National League since 1923, donned the mask and pad and went behind the plate again, despite being forty years old.

Three days after Lombardi was injured, the Reds had a mathematical chance to cinch the pennant if they could win that afternoon. And the honor of pitching the game was given to Johnny Vander Meer, who was hot on the comeback trail. Vandy was opposed by Hugh Mulcahy, a fine moundsman, and the contest developed into a hot struggle. At the end of nine innings, each team had two runs, and each added another marker in the tenth. Finally, in the thirteenth frame, Vander Meer himself hit a double, was bunted to third, and scored after Goodman had flied to right field. McKechnie, realizing how much running John had done, wisely removed him from the box, and Joe Beggs, who had become a terrific relief pitcher, got the Phils in order in their half.

That was it, and the rest of the season was merely exercise. The Reds ended with 100 victories and 53 defeats, three and one-half games ahead of their 1939 pace, and twelve full contests ahead of the second-place Dodgers.

One of the players who helped the Reds tremendously in the flag drive was Jimmy Ripple, a former Giant and Dodger outfielder, who was picked up in midseason and installed in left field. Ripple, a slashing left-handed hitter, gave the Reds the added hitting that they required to make the race a rout.

After cinching the pennant for the second straight year, the sixteenth time in National League history that a club had won two in a row, the Reds had only to await the outcome of the American League race for a chance to avenge the previous World Series.

But there was still difficulty on the club. During the last week of the campaign, the Reds were in St. Louis when Gabe Paul placed a midnight phone call to his boss, Warren Giles, at the latter's suburban Cincinnati home.

"Billy Myers is jumping the club," he said.

"What for?"

"I don't know," Gabe replied. "I tried to talk him out of it. McKechnie knows about it too."

All the next day Giles tried in vain to get in touch with the errant shortstop and finally reached him by phone at Columbus, Ohio.

"If you don't come back and play in the World Series," Giles said, "I'll fine you what salary you have coming and see that you aren't cut into the series, and you'll never play another game."

"I don't care," Myers said. "I have personal problems and I don't care if I ever play again. And I don't want any money."

Twice more before the evening passed, Giles talked to him, and finally saw that he was weakening. The press had been told that Myers had gone to Columbus on personal business with the club's permission, and when Myers was assured that he could come back and act as if nothing had happened, he finally agreed to.

Myers came back to Cincinnati and met Paul Derringer, who escorted him to the clubhouse. Big Paul, in addition to his pitching duties, always seemed to inherit extracurricular affairs. And he made a good custodian for the wandering infielder.

Billy Myers is a much-discussed player in Cincinnati, and most fans do not realize how much talent the fellow had. When he reported to the team in 1935, manager Chuck Dressen made him captain of the team. When the umpires called decisions against the Reds, it was the captain's duty to protest. And when the team went badly, the patrons of the game got tired of seeing the freshman shortstop engaged in countless arguments with the arbiters. They began to ride him, and Billy was the sort of personality who was sensitive to taunts from the grandstand.

Myers made numerous errors, mostly on comparatively easy chances, but he came up with plays frequently that were simply uncanny. The pitchers on the club, benefiting from such fielding as they did, were well aware of his value. Among men who know shortstops best, it may not be Billy Myers

282

two to one, but he was blessed with superlative natural ability.

The American League race went down to the wire with the Yankees gunning for their fifth straight flag, something never before accomplished. They found themselves engaged in a fight with the Cleveland Indians and Detroit Tigers. Finally, it was Detroit that won out by the margin of a single game, and the World Series was all set.

The Reds went into the series with Lombardi still limping badly on his swollen ankle, and Jimmy Wilson begged McKechnie to let him catch the classic games. The decision was postponed to the last possible moment. Lonnie Frey was also on the injured list, and Eddie Joost was sent to second base. What would have happened if Billy Myers had stayed in Columbus is not pleasant to think about.

3

It was Paul Derringer who was chosen to hold the Tigers in the first game of the 1940 World Series, played at Cincinnati on October 2. His opponent was the strutting, colorful Bobo Newsom, who had won 21 and lost only 5 in the American League during the regular season. The Tigers had the great Hank Greenberg, then in his prime, in left field. Charlie Gehringer, one of the best infield mechanics of all time, was at second base. The always dangerous Cherokee, Rudy York, was at first base; Pinky Higgins at third; and Barney McCosky, a brilliant rookie, in center field. The Michigan club had class!

And class was something that Paul Derringer lacked that autumn afternoon. In the second inning, the Tigers treated him rudely, scoring five times on as many hits, a base on balls, and an error by Bill Werber. The big hurler threw his glove to the side lines and dejectedly went to the dugout. Derringer had yet to win a game in World Series play, and brokenhearted fans, well aware of his skill, nevertheless felt that probably he never would. That inning was the ball game, and the fans went home dejectedly, after sitting it out while old Bobo strutted to a 7-to-2 victory.

But on the next afternoon Bucky Walters restored the Queen City's prestige when he beat the Bengals, 5 to 3, giving up only three hits. Two of the runs were scored in the first on two passes by Bucky, who was wild at the outset, and a timely single by Gehringer. But the Reds tied the score off Rowe in the second and moved ahead in the third when Jimmy Ripple hit a two-run homer into the right-field bleachers. When successive doubles by Walters and Werber gave the Reds their fifth run in the fourth, Rowe was removed and Johnny Gorsica substituted. But it was too late, and Walters merely toyed with Detroit after that.

The scene then shifted to Detroit, and the third game started as a duel between Jim Turner and Tommy Bridges. At the end of six innings, the score was 1 to 1. In the seventh the Tigers delighted the large home throng by blasting Turner as violently as they had Derringer two days before. Greenberg singled and York hit a terrific home run to left field. Bruce Campbell then singled, and Higgins hit the second two-run homer of the inning. That was all for Turner, and Whitey Moore finished the inning. In the eighth the Michigan team reached Beggs for two more runs, and won, 7 to 4, the Reds counting once in the eighth and twice in the ninth, after the cause was lost.

It was then up to Derringer to avenge his opening-day defeat and square the series at two victories apiece before the hostile crowd. Pitted against him was Dizzy Trout, one of Del Baker's young right-handers. In the third inning, singles by Goodman and Frank McCormick and a double by the ever helpful Ripple ended Trout's tenure. The Reds had previously scored twice in the first, and the three runs were enough for Derringer, who breezed to a 5-to-2 verdict, his first favorable nod in five World Series attempts.

Bobo Newsom took the center of the stage again in the fifth game. His father, who had come on to attend the struggle, had died of a heart attack early in the morning after the first game. It was a very subdued and determined Bobo who assumed the hill against Gene Thompson. Following the pattern of big innings, the Bengals reached Gene for three runs in the third and cannonaded him from the premises with a four-run outburst in the fourth. Newsom bore down all the way after that and yielded only three singles, Detroit winning, 8 to 0.

As the teams moved back to Cincinnati for the sixth game, it looked very much as if the Reds were on the run. But Bill McKechnie didn't think so.

"I think we've got 'em now," he told Warren Giles. "I've got Walters and Derringer to shoot at 'em. Don't give up yet."

Schoolboy Rowe squared off with Walters, the next afternoon, and had the misfortune to run into Bucky when he was at his best. Walters has pitched a lot of games of baseball in his career, but he was never better than in the all-important effort against Detroit. A double by Werber and singles by Goodman, Frank McCormick, and Ripple gave Bucky two runs and removed Rowe from the game, Gorsica coming on again. The Reds scored again in the sixth as Walters continued to mow down the Tigers in order, and then Bucky crowned his achievement by hitting a home run in his last time at bat in the eighth. The Reds won, 4 to 0, the Tigers making but five hits.

So the series went into a seventh and final game. Del Baker, faced with the task of coming up with a pitcher to match Derringer, selected Newsom, who took the slab with only one day's rest, gunning for his third triumph of the classic. Derringer, stouthearted as always, was primed to bring the National League its first series victory in six years.

Cincinnati's Crosley Field is small as ball parks go. Tickets for the final game had to be sold that morning, but a crowd of 26,854 swelled the attendance for the series to 281,927. It was a breathless throng that just sat back and hoped.

The Tigers scored the first run of the contest in the third on a single by Billy Sullivan, Newsom's sacrifice, and Werber's overthrow of first base on Gehringer's smash.

For six rounds the Reds were unable to do anything against Newsom. Then came their chance in the seventh. Frank McCormick, first up, smashed a line drive against the left-field fence and, representing the tying run, pulled up at second base. Then Jimmy Ripple hit a long fly ball to right center. Bruce Campbell raced over, but the ball just sailed over his outstretched arm. McCormick didn't know if the ball would be caught or not, and the fans thought he never would score. He rounded third and hesitated as Dick Bartell, the Tiger shortstop, handled the relay in short center field. Bartell had a play at the plate, but because of the noise of the crowd, he never heard the shouted instructions of his mates, and McCormick finally crossed safely with the tying run, and Ripple held up at second. Jimmy Wilson then neatly executed a sacrifice, Ripple taking third, and Big Lombardi, limping on his bad foot, was sent up to hit for Eddie Joost and was intentionally passed, with Lonny Frey going in to run for him. Billy Myers, hitting with a count of three balls and a strike, flied deep to McCosky in center, and Ripple scored after the catch, the run bringing the world's championship to Cincinnati.

Derringer was up to the task of retiring the Tigers in the eighth and ninth, and 2 to 1 was the final score.

It was typical of the Reds that they won the final series game by a single tally. Each team made seven hits, but the Reds had the edge. During the regular season, Cincinnati won forty-one games by one run, a record, and lost seventeen by a single marker. There was enough power in the line-up to back up the great pitching that the club received almost daily, but just enough to win the close ones.

As soon as the final out was made, Cincinnati went promptly berserk. The celebration was spontaneous and uninhibited, and in some quarters continued for several days. The downtown streets became an instant bedlam, and the police department blocked off the area and refused to permit automobiles to enter. But celebrants discovered unique methods of causing trouble on foot. Among other incidents of the night was the dismantling of a streetcar, which a riotous group of revelers simply pushed off the tracks and upset. Washington knew such a night when Bucky Harris brought the first championship to the city in 1924, and St. Louis experienced one two years later when Rogers Hornsby won

286

a seven-game struggle from the Yankees. Cincinnati, however, in 1940, produced the most riotous one of all.

Fandom, convalescing from the inevitable hangover, had the pleasant task of assessing the series to find a hero instead of a goat, as had been necessary the season before. And there were plenty of candidates. Besides Crosley and Giles and McKechnie, the obvious heroes, there was Paul Derringer, who finally throttled the American League's best. And there was Bill Werber, who hit .370 in the seven games; Jimmy Ripple, whose seventh-inning double supplied the spark; and Billy Myers, the much abused Captain Billy, who batted in the winning run of the deciding contest after almost electing to miss the games entirely.

But the real hero was Jimmy Wilson. Forty years of age and forced to play because of the suicide of Hershberger and the late-season injury to Big Lom, Wilson caught six of the seven games and hit .353, fielded perfectly, and stole the only base that was swiped when he made a successful larceny attempt in the final game. Each night he soaked his aching muscles in a solution of epsom salts, and by some heroic effort managed to take the field on each following afternoon. It was a real triumph of mind over matter.

Jimmy Wilson is dead now. He succumbed to a heart attack in Florida in the summer of 1947, when he was only forty-six. His performance in the 1940 World Series led to his being named manager of the Cubs, and after holding that job for three years, he returned to the Reds as a coach. His son, Bob, who worked out with the Reds as a prep-school student in 1940, preceded his father in death when his plane was shot down in India during World War II. There was a relationship between father and son that was touching, and when Bob died, something went out of Jimmy. Until then, there had never been a man who enjoyed life so much as Jimmy Wilson, and no one ever surpassed his enthusiasm for baseball. And in the World Series of 1940 he reached a pinnacle of skill and courage that is reserved for few.

⊖ 30 ⊖

THE PENDULUM SWINGS BACK

1

Of course, it's hardly a trade secret that the old order changeth, but the speed with which a world's champion ball club can disintegrate is nevertheless astonishing.

The Reds of 1941 had no more worlds to conquer, and that is the most dangerous stage in a club's history. Giles anticipated the situation, and tried to help the club where it needed help most. Shortstop Billy Myers was traded to the Cubs for outfielder Jim Gleason. It was felt that Eddie Joost could take care of the shortstop chores, and that Gleason would supply power in the outfield.

But just as the Durocher-Derringer swap of 1933 helped both teams involved, the Myers-Gleason exchange helped neither. Gleason proved to be a frost, and Myers in Chicago was a frightful shadow of his former self. The Reds neither gained nor lost by that transaction, which was important only in that it represented the first step in the dismantling of champions.

The Reds also acquired Monte Pearson, the Yankee pitcher more famous for his ailments than for his hurling, though with New York he always rose to the heights when the stakes were high. With the Reds he was utterly useless, winning but one game. For weeks he sat on the bench, and when finally given an opportunity to pitch, he replied that he had a sore arm.

Not that McKechnie had lost his skill with pitchers. On the contrary, the Reds came up with another one that soon had

288

the city buzzing with warm praise. His name was Elmer Riddle.

It was Bill McKechnie's custom to develop annually some unknown hurler. In his first year with the club, 1938, he carefully nurtured Johnny Vander Meer, with results that received nation-wide acclaim. The next season it was young Gene Thompson who stepped from nowhere to win 13 and lose 5, and pitch an important victory in the series with the Cardinals that assured the flag. Joe Beggs and Jim Turner were the surprises of 1940, the former becoming a relief ace and the latter a spot pitcher of remarkable talents. And now Riddle.

Elmer had come from the Indianapolis farm and broke into his first box score on the last day of the 1939 campaign. He spent the next full season on the bench before being given his chance in 1941.

Derringer, Vander Meer, and Walters were still on hand, and Riddle didn't receive credit for a decision until he beat the Braves in relief, on May 20. But after that he was unstoppable. He won three games as a fireman before getting a starting assignment, but after winning his spurs as a starter, he was the most dependable man on the staff. He had a record of eleven victories without defeat when he finally bowed to Leo Durocher's brawling Dodgers, 5 to 4, on July 23. And he ended the year with a mark of 19 victories and only 4 defeats.

Outside of Riddle, the fans had little to cheer them. It was apparent that the team would not repeat as champions, and the race developed into a struggle between the Cardinals and Dodgers, with the Reds a poor third.

Individual performances were not up to par. Frank McCormick, still playing daily at first base, fell off in the hitting department, and slumped below .300 for the first time since joining the club. Ival Goodman yielded to one injury after another and appeared to be at the end of the trail. Bill Werber was not himself, and Ernie Lombardi had the poorest batting season of his career.

It is a wonder, in the face of all these discouragements, that

Bill McKechnie was able to keep the team in the first division, but he did. The team won 88 times and lost 66, finishing third. Continued good pitching was largely responsible. Not a single member of the regular team hit .300, Mike McCormick leading the pack with a mediocre .287. Frank McCormick fell to .269, Lombardi to .264.

Giles and McKechnie knew that the champions were wearing out. But where to find replacements?

By the time the 1942 season approached, most fans had forgotten the careless days of the recent past to contemplate the grim task of winning the war. Pearl Harbor had brought an abrupt change in emphasis in people's thinking, and for Cincinnatians the affairs of the Reds were not seriously considered for the first time since the days of the Red Stockings. When Ernie Lombardi was sold to the Braves and Bill Werber to the Giants, there was little reaction.

Of course, they wanted the game to go on. Unlike the work-or-fight order of World War I, which made baseball curtail its schedule, the green light given by President Roosevelt at least assured the continuance of the game.

The major leagues in 1942 still retained most of the better players, though many of them by now had dates with draft boards. The supply of young players, though, was cut off entirely. Teams had to go ahead with what they had. Scouts stopped asking whether a player could run or throw and asked instead about his draft classification and whether he had three dependents or a punctured eardrum.

Bill McKechnie went about the task of putting another Red team on the field. Lombardi's old catching job was given to Ray Lamanno, a recruit from the farm chain. Bert Haas, an infielder purchased from Columbus, replaced Bill Werber at third.

Early in the season Giles swung a deal with St. Louis that brought Max Marshall, an outfielder, and Clyde Shoun, a southpaw pitcher, to the team. Marshall proved to be a player with all the physical requirements who never seemed to make use of them, and he was added to the long list of disappointments.

After playing 652 consecutive games at first base, Frank McCormick caught his spikes in the base while making a throw in practice and strained the ligaments in his back. As a consequence, he missed the May 25 game with Pittsburgh. Outfielder Gerald Walker, a veteran obtained after he had completed a long career in the American League, failed to bolster the club's attack, though his daring play on the bases delighted the customers.

Once more, McKechnie developed a good pitcher. This time it was Ray Starr, a veteran minor-leaguer who had had trials with the Cardinals, Giants, and Braves years before. Starr had a record of 12 victories and only 4 defeats at one stage of the season, but the attack of his mates was so apathetic that he had no chance of continuing at that clip, and wound up with 15 victories and 13 defeats.

The batting fell off to a whisper. By the end of the season the team had a collective mark of .231, the lowest recorded in the National League since Brooklyn hit .229 in 1910. McKechnie tried an even dozen players in the outfield, and only one, Max Marshall, hit over .250, and he hit .255.

The pennant race was between Brooklyn and St. Louis once more. The fiery Dodgers had won in 1941 and had fond hopes of repeating. And if the Reds didn't do anything else in 1942, they helped blight that Flatbush dream. On a Sunday afternoon, September 13, the weak-hitting Reds inflicted a double defeat on the Dodgers at Ebbets Field. That twin setback shoved the Bums out of first place, and they never regained it, the Cards rushing ahead of them to the pennant pole. Bucky Walters and Ray Starr were the pitchers responsible, the former beating Buck Newsom, 6 to 3, and the latter getting a 4-to-1 nod over Curt Davis.

But the Reds themselves were struggling to stay over the .500 mark. On the last day of the year they dropped two games to Pittsburgh and finished with 76 victories and 76 defeats. The champions of two seasons ago were now fourth.

By 1943 the war situation was beginning to be felt in all places. Ball teams were ordered to train north of the Ohio River and east of the Mississippi. Warren Giles, deprived of the proving grounds at Tampa, found an excellent substitute spot at Bloomington, Indiana, where the Reds were permitted to use the Indiana University field house on days when the weather did not permit outdoor work.

The atmosphere of the wartime training camps was nothing like the old days. Players would be in camp one day and on their way to a draft examination the next. The quality of big-league baseball quite naturally declined.

Even the baseball itself seemed to have become a war victim. The season started with a ball in use in the National League made of such inferior material that it would hardly co-operate when hit. When the Reds opened the season against St. Louis the two clubs managed to score only six runs in the four games. Johnny Vander Meer, back in form, beat Morton Cooper, 1 to 0, in eleven innings in the opener, and on the second day Ray Starr nosed out Ernie White by the same score in ten frames. Then the Cards retaliated with 2-to-1 and 1-to-0 triumphs.

The low scores continued until the magnates, led by Warren Giles, finally got action, and the manufacturers came up with a more lively ball. But the dismal games seemed to be in keeping with the low spirits of most of the fans, who by this time had members of their families scattered all over the globe.

Fans were more tolerant toward the game than at any previous time. They wanted it continued, but they didn't demand too much in the way of skill.

McKechnie did a remarkable job with the Reds in 1943. New faces continued to appear. Eric Tipton, an outfielder purchased from the Yankee chain, was sent to left field. Bert Haas moved from third base to first to center field and then into the Army, the hot-corner job going to Steve Mesner, an acquisition from the Pacific Coast League. Frank McCormick and Lonny Frey still held down jobs on the right side of the infield.

The most important addition to the club was Eddie Miller, a shortstop of rare talents. Miller had originally belonged to the Reds when Larry MacPhail ran the organization, but had been shipped to the Yankee chain in the deal for Willard Hershberger prior to the 1938 season. Meanwhile, he had developed into a star and had graduated to the Boston Braves. In order to secure him from Boston, Giles parted with a large amount of money and the contract of Eddie Joost. Though not a formidable hitter, Miller socked a long ball on occasion. And his work at the short field made the fans gasp in admiration.

Another importation was Ray Mueller, a catcher, with previous experience at Boston and Pittsburgh, but who came to the Reds from Sacramento. When Lamanno entered the Navy, Mueller stepped into his job and filled it most acceptably.

With Miller and Mueller added and with other teams losing stars to the armed forces right and left, the Reds braced in 1943 and fought their way to a second-place finish, with 87 wins and 67 defeats. Though the Cardinals were out in front all season long, the Reds were the most entertaining of the other seven teams.

But by 1944 the manpower situation was getting worse. In his search for players of any description, Warren Giles was induced to sign players who would have been given no consideration under normal conditions. One was Jesus (Chucho) Ramos, an outfielder from Venezuela, who was recommended by letter and who arrived without having been scouted. Ramos was something of a freak in that he batted right-handed and threw left-handed. This was a style adopted by Hal Chase and Rube Bressler. But any similarity to Chase and Bressler ended there. Chucho could not fill the bill, and was shipped to Syracuse.

Selective service was now calling all players between the ages of eighteen and thirty-eight. Somehow, players were obtained who were under and over those limits. A pitcher from Hamilton, Ohio, named Joe Nuxhall actually appeared in a championship National League game for the Reds before his sixteenth birthday. A left-hander, Nuxhall was introduced to the majors on June 10 and finished a game that the Reds lost to the Cardinals, 18 to 0.

Regular players who were not yet drafted were called upon for almost superhuman efforts. It is customary, for instance, to rest a catcher. But Ray Mueller appeared behind the bat in all of the 155 games the Reds played in 1944, after catching the final 62 in 1943.

Other clubs were up against the same thing. Bill McKechnie made the most of what he had, played for one run, stressed defense, and got the most out of his pitching. He piloted the team to third, with 89 victories and 65 defeats, finishing in the first division for the seventh straight year.

Fans who by this time were overseas must have wondered who some of the players were whose names were now appearing in the line-ups. Players reached the big leagues in 1944 who had been considered washed up five years previously. Others, kids, attained the top two seasons before they were ready. It was a strange collection of flotsam washed up on the major-league shore.

Not only players, but umpires, groundkeepers, and others had gone to war. Gabe Paul, the handsome young assistant of Warren Giles, found himself a hardened infantryman more accustomed to bivouacs than beefsteaks.

Interest in baseball slackened, and attendance dwindled. But the teams carried on, and the public wanted it that way. There were still exciting games. Clyde Shoun, the left-hander obtained from St. Louis, dropped another no-hit game into the Redleg records when he let down Boston without a blow, winning 1 to 0, and defeating Jim Tobin, a pitcher who himself had tossed a no-hitter a few weeks previously. Shoun walked only one man and the Reds played errorless ball. It was the closest to a perfect game that any Cincinnati pitcher had ever come.

⊗ **31** ⊗

JUST BEFORE THE DAWN

1

The quality of major-league baseball reached its all-time low during the season of 1945, just before the close of the war. It was not the end of an era but a hiatus between eras that awaited only the return of stellar players to launch a brighter chapter in the game's long and exciting story.

When the Reds were about to depart for Bloomington for the third successive spring, the personnel problem was acute. So hard up was Warren Giles for pitchers that on the eve of the camp's opening he let himself be cheered by the signing of three egregious has-beens, Horace Lisenbee, Guy Bush, and Walter (Boom Boom) Beck. Lisenbee had shown promise in the American League eighteen years before, but was now forty-four years old. Beck, called Boom Boom because of the resounding way that batters greeted his delivery, had started with the St. Louis Browns in 1924. Bush had been a top-notch pitcher for the Chicago Cubs, but hadn't pitched an inning in the majors for seven years. Yet these men were names, and on the blackboard in Warren's office they represented pitchers.

Of the 1940 champions who still belonged to the team, Mike McCormick, Lonny Frey, Johnny Vander Meer, Gene Thompson, and Joe Beggs were all in service. Paul Derringer, Bill Werber, Ival Goodman, Harry Craft, Billy Myers, and Jimmy Ripple had all passed on to other clubs.

Frank McCormick was still around to play first base, and Eddie Miller was a fixture at short. They were about the only two "name players," exclusive of pitchers, on the club. Second base was manned by Woody Williams, obtained from the minors, and third by Steve Mesner. Mueller had been drafted, and the catching duties fell upon Al Lakeman, a native Cincinnatian.

Among the newcomers to the outfield were Al Libke, a towering Giant from the Pacific Coast League, who hit a very long ball on occasion but who was extremely awkward in the field, and Dick Sipek, a deaf-mute from the farm chain.

Bucky Walters started the opening game against the Pirates, but ancient Horace Lisenbee was used as a relief pitcher, and when the Reds won out, 7 to 6, in eleven innings, Horace was the winning pitcher. It was the only game he was to win all season. Outfielder Dain Clay, a speedster who came up in 1943, was by now the regular center fielder, and his contribution to the victory was a home run with the bases loaded. It was to be his only round-tripper of the year.

McKechnie's ingenuity was taxed by the events of that campaign. His ability with pitchers was put to the supreme test. Outside of Walters, the Reds relied on a hodgepodge of hurlers such as Ed Heusser, a much-traveled veteran; southpaw Arnold Carter, a farm product; Frank Dasso, a castoff of the Red Sox system; and Howard Fox, a young man with great possibilities who was not ready for the majors. In addition, there was Melvin Bosser, who said he was a pitcher and who was found by Bill McKechnie in the lobby of the team's Bloomington hotel as the Deacon was returning from church on Easter. Bosser had so little on the ball that opposing batters found him hard to hit because of the novelty of his delivery.

As the season progressed, other castoffs were picked up, including Joe Bowman and Vern Kennedy, both veterans of many clubs.

But the Reds soon made it apparent that they had relinquished all claim to a first-division berth. Not since Chuck Dressen's 1937 club had a Cincinnati team put up such a poor performance.

Somehow the Reds staggered through that season, and in the knowledge that help would not be long in coming, Warren Giles bided his time. The Reds eventually finished seventh, only the Phils trailing them.

But by the spring of 1946, things were beginning to return to normal. Once more the Redlegs made their headquarters at Tampa. Such players as Joe Beggs and Johnny Vander Meer, Ray Mueller and Lonny Frey, had returned from the armed forces. It was a time to start building.

Frank McCormick, after eight seasons as a regular, was sold to Philadelphia, opening the way for Bert Haas to take over the first-base job. Among the new players, the most exciting prospect was Grady Hatton, a third baseman who had never played professionally but who had attracted all sorts of attention while playing in the service. He was a left-handed hitter and a good one, and made good without the necessity of any apprenticeship in the minors.

Of the new pitchers, the most celebrated was Ewell Blackwell, a giant right-hander with a snake whip for an arm, who was discharged from the Army as the Reds were completing their spring training.

The club was better than in 1945, but so was the league, and the team found the going rough. Bucky Walters, though still a capable moundsman on occasion, was no longer able to pitch with his accustomed regularity, and Joe Beggs was moved from the bull pen to a starting job. Blackwell showed flashes of brilliance, but was not a regular winner.

Some of the players who had been to war showed signs of wear and tear. Lonny Frey, for instance, was no longer able to cavort around second base in his prewar manner, and he split the work there with a pair of recruits, Bobby Adams and Benny Zientara. Eddie Miller played short with his usual skill during the season's first half, then fell victim to a lame arm and yielded the post to Claude Corbitt, an inconsistent performer.

McKechnie had his usual outfield headache. Al Libke, the slugger from the Coast, failed to improve much afield, and was in and out of the line-up. Dain Clay did most of the work in center, and two rookies, Eddie Lukon and Bob Usher, saw service in left. McKechnie even experimented with Lonny

Frey and Grady Hatton in the outfield, in an attempt to come up with a formidable trio of gardeners.

The team played one memorable game. On September 11, at Ebbets Field, they battled the Dodgers for nineteen innings in a scoreless deadlock. Johnny Vander Meer went fifteen rounds, struck out fourteen, walked only two, and yielded only seven safeties. Harry Gumbert finished, pitching four scoreless heats before darkness ended play. Brooklyn used four pitchers, who limited the Reds to ten blows. The game was the longest double shutout in the history of the majors, surpassing an eighteen-inning affair between the Tigers and Senators played in 1909.

On the evening of September 22, Bill McKechnie announced that he would not return to the club in 1947. That day the Reds won a double-header at Pittsburgh and took a firm hold on sixth place, one notch higher than they had finished in 1945, and in the clubhouse after the game coach Hank Gowdy read Bill's retirement statement to the players.

McKechnie was the most successful manager the Cincinnati ball club ever had, winning 743 games and losing 630 in nine seasons of play. During his last years at Crosley Field he operated virtually without a farm system, and few players of worth were added to the club.

Of course, he had his critics. All managers do. Some felt that he played the game too close to his vest, overworked the bunt, and stressed defensive play. He was a percentage manager, and seldom took daring strategic chances. But he certainly got the most out of his clubs that was possible, and finished in the first division in 7 of the 9 campaigns.

2

Warren Giles did not wait long in finding a successor. When the Reds were playing their last series of the season, Giles got in touch with Johnny Neun, who was finishing the campaign as temporary pilot of the New York Yankees, met him in Lexington, Kentucky, and offered him the job. Neun accepted, and the announcement was made during the World Series.

The selection of Neun was a complete surprise. An American Leaguer during most of his career, Johnny was not well known by the fans of Cincinnati, but the more they studied Warren Giles's choice, the more they liked it.

He had started as a first baseman with Martinsburg of the Blue Ridge League in 1920, and his trail led to Birmingham and St. Paul before he reached the majors with Detroit. He played under Ty Cobb with the Bengals, lasted with the team four seasons, and then put in two years with the Boston Braves.

Neun became a manager with the Yankee organization in 1935 at Akron, and he later advanced to Norfolk, Newark, and Kansas City. In nine seasons he won 772 games and lost 554, copped four pennants and a Junior World Series, and finished out of the first division only once. He was made a coach on the Yankees in 1944, serving under Joe McCarthy, who recommended him strongly to Giles. When Larry MacPhail dismissed Bill Dickey late in 1946, Neun finished the season as manager of the Bombers, winning 8 and losing 6 contests.

An extremely versatile chap, Neun was a basketball official of note and the soccer editor of the *Baltimore Evening Sun,* work he pursued all through his career.

One distinction that Neun has is that of making the last unassisted triple play in the major leagues. He performed the stunt against Cleveland on May 31, 1927, Detroit winning, 1 to 0. The triple killing came in the ninth inning. With two men on base, Homer Summa hit a wicked line drive that Neun caught for the first out, and he tagged Charlie Jamieson, who had wandered off first for the second out. Then he saw that he could run to second base with the ball before the runner could return to that bag.

"Throw the ball, John," one of his mates called.

"Throw it, heck," Neun yelled. "I'm running with it right into the Hall of Fame."

It was only the eighth unassisted triple play in major-league history, and the only one that closed a game.

Giles felt that Neun's long association with the Yankee

organization would make him stress offensive play and use tactics designed to play for the big inning.

Other changes were made in the executive setup of the team. Powel Crosley announced that Warren Giles had been named president as a reward for his fine work, and Crosley stepped into the job of chairman of the board. Gabe Paul was named assistant to the president, though no new duties for him were announced. Work was begun to expand the farm system under the direction of Fred Fleig.

Neun's first training camp contained a host of new men, most of them war veterans whose careers had just begun to develop. The only winter deal of consequence saw the veteran hurler Ed Heusser traded to Brooklyn for outfielder Augie Galan, and that transaction was a ten-strike.

All during the winter months Eddie Miller, shortstop and key man on the club, announced that he would not play, and the club issued a statement saying that Miller did not fit into its plans. But at the last minute he reported and assumed his old job. In the infield with Miller were Bert Haas at first, Bobby Adams and Benny Zientara at second, and Grady Hatton at third.

Frankie Baumholtz, a product of the farm chain and a veteran of Navy service, won the right-field job, and Augie Galan was sent to left. Center field proved to be a constant problem. Clyde Vollmer, a native Cincinnatian, had all the defensive skill the job required, but could not hit consistently. Finally, in midseason, Giles and Neun traded Joe Beggs for Babe Young, a slugging first baseman who was so much excess baggage on the Giants with Johnny Mize on the job. That deal enabled Bert Haas to move from the initial sack to center field.

The league in 1947 was still below prewar quality, but silver linings were beginning to streak through the sky. Great prospects were in the stage of developing.

As far as the Reds were concerned, the player of the year was Ewell Blackwell. He defeated the Cardinals, 3 to 1, on opening day, limiting the Cardinals to three hits, and the fans felt that they had seen a new star in the making. Blackwell did not wait long to prove how right they were.

Starting on May 10, when he defeated the Cubs 5 to 1, Blackie become the hottest pitcher in the circuit. He won sixteen games in a row, more than any pitcher in the league had put together since Rube Marquard copped nineteen straight for the 1912 Giants.

During the course of the streak, he pitched a no-hit game against Boston on June 18, and four days later he almost emulated Johnny Vander Meer's 1938 achievement of successive no-hit games. Starting against Brooklyn, Blackwell pitched eight hitless innings, and then, with one out in the ninth, yielded a single to Eddie Stanky that went between the gangling hurler's feet. Jackie Robinson added another safety, but Blackie had come within two outs of immortality. In his no-hitter against the Braves, Blackie walked four and fanned three.

Blackwell was the talk of the circuit, and was given the honor of starting the All-Star game against the American League. He contributed three scoreless innings to that classic game, though the American Leaguers eventually won out.

Ewell was discovered by Pat Patterson, an old catcher and an unusually astute Cincinnati scout. Patterson spied him pitching on the sand lots of California, and bagged him for the Reds. He wasn't given a large bonus, but was given a chance to make the grade in the majors, and trained with the Reds at Tampa in 1942. Bill McKechnie knew full well that he had a star in the making, and Blackie was sent to Syracuse for experience that year. He was an instant hit in the International League, winning 15 and losing 10 and pitching 4 shutouts. Then he entered the Army, not returning to the team until 1946, when as a freshman he won 9 and lost 13.

Blackwell was tabbed as one of the greatest pitching prospects to come along in years. He stands six feet five in height and has extremely long arms. One batter described his puzzling delivery by saying that he looked as if he were falling out of a tree when he whipped the ball up to the plate.

Excited by Blackwell, who ended the year with 22 victories

301

and 8 defeats, and pleased by the dashing style of play that Neun employed, Cincinnati fans poured through the turnstiles in great numbers, indicating a great revival of interest as the game began to approach its prewar eminence.

The pitching department, outside of Blackwell, bogged down. Two other youngsters, Ed Erautt and Kent Peterson, were disappointing, though both are still classified as excellent prospects. Bucky Walters managed to win eight games and lose as many, creeping to within two victories of the two-hundred mark, a total reached by few hurlers. Harry Gumbert developed into an excellent relief artist.

Under Johnny Neun the Reds were definitely a team of the future. Warren Giles, aided by Fred Fleig, had rebuilt the farm empire that was just starting to produce when World War II came. In 1946 the Reds had clubs at Syracuse, New York; Columbia, South Carolina; Providence, Rhode Island; Tyler, Texas; Ogden, Utah; Muncie, Indiana; and Lockport, New York. After the season, Giles announced the purchase of the Tulsa franchise of the Texas League.

Today on the diamonds of the lesser minor leagues are players destined for glory in the uniform of the Cincinnati Reds, but their names are not yet known. Those are the Reds of the future, central characters of a story that is not yet written.

INDEX

by William F. Hugo of the Society of American Baseball Research

303

305

Herman, Floyd "Babe," 215–17, 229, 239, 241

Herrmann, August "Garry," 73, 125, 175, 181, 197–98; deals made, 111, 113, 115, 168–69, 171, 177–79; and managers, 84–85, 87–91; and Moran, 130, 154–59, 161; as president, 74–78, 93–99, 101–8, 163–64, 193; and White Sox World Series scandal, 140, 143, 151

Hershberger, Willard, 266, 278–80, 287, 293

Herzog, Buck (playing manager), 105–7, 109–12, 114–15, 117–18, 133, 162–63

Heusser, Ed, 296, 300

Heydler, John (league president), 99, 125–26, 143–44, 146, 163, 165, 176

Higgins, Pinky, 283–84

High, Andy, 187–88, 218, 220

Hildebrand, Oral, 274

Hill, Bill, 62–63

Hoblitzell, Dick, 89, 92–93, 107

Hoernchemeyer, Leopold, 123–25, 131, 139

Hoffer, Bill, 57

Hofman, Artie, 85

Holke, Walter, 131, 177–78

Holliday, Bub, 37, 47, 55–56

Hollingsworth, Al, 237–38, 259

Hopp, Johnny, 269

Hornsby, Rogers, 139, 170–71; as manager, 230, 286–87; as playing manager, 181, 189, 200

Hornung, Joe, 174

Hotaling, Pete, 19

Howley, "Howling Dan," 206–11, 216–17

Hoy, William "Dummy," 50–51, 55–56. 59, 62, 175

Hoyt, Waite, 203, 238, 243

Hubbell, Carl, 219

Huggins, Miller, 79, 82

Hulbert, William A. (league president), 14

Hulswitt, Rudy, 89

Humphries, Bert, 103

Hunter, Eddie, 220

Huntzinger, Walter, 174

Hurley, Richard, 4, 6

Irwin, Charlie, 57, 67, 70

Jackson, "Shoeless" Joe, 141–42, 144, 147–51

James, Bill, 110, 145

Jamieson, Charlie, 299

Jeffries, Irvine, 224

Jennings, Hughie, 57, 84, 207

Johnson, Byron Bancroft, 51, 242; as league president, 52–53, 72, 91, 143–44, 146, 149–50

Johnson, George Murphy "Chief," 104, 106

Johnson, Silas, 201, 216, 228, 232, 238

Johnson, Sylvester, 224, 228

Johnson, Walter, 80, 106, 141, 191

Jones, Charlie, 10, 12, 14, 17, 22, 34

Jones, Charles L. "Bumpus," 49–50, 63

Jones, David C. (club director), 222

Joost, Eddie, 283, 286, 288, 293

Jordan, Baxter, 250–51

Josephs, Joseph. See Borden, Joseph

Jude, Frank, 86

Kampouris, Alex, 231, 238, 244, 251, 258, 266

Kane, Johnny, 89

Karger, Ed, 92

Karst, Gene (club publicity director), 241

Kauff, Benny, 132–33

Keating, Ray, 104

Keck, Frank "Cactus," 164

Keck, Josiah L. (club president), 9, 12–15

Keefe, Tim, 28, 31

Keeler, Willie, 24, 57, 84

Keenan, Jim, 31, 37

Keller, Charlie, 272–75

Kelley, Joe, 57, 72, 77–82, 84, 89–90

Kellogg, Bill, 107

Kellum, Win, 80

Kelly, George, 193–95, 202–3, 208–9, 212, 253